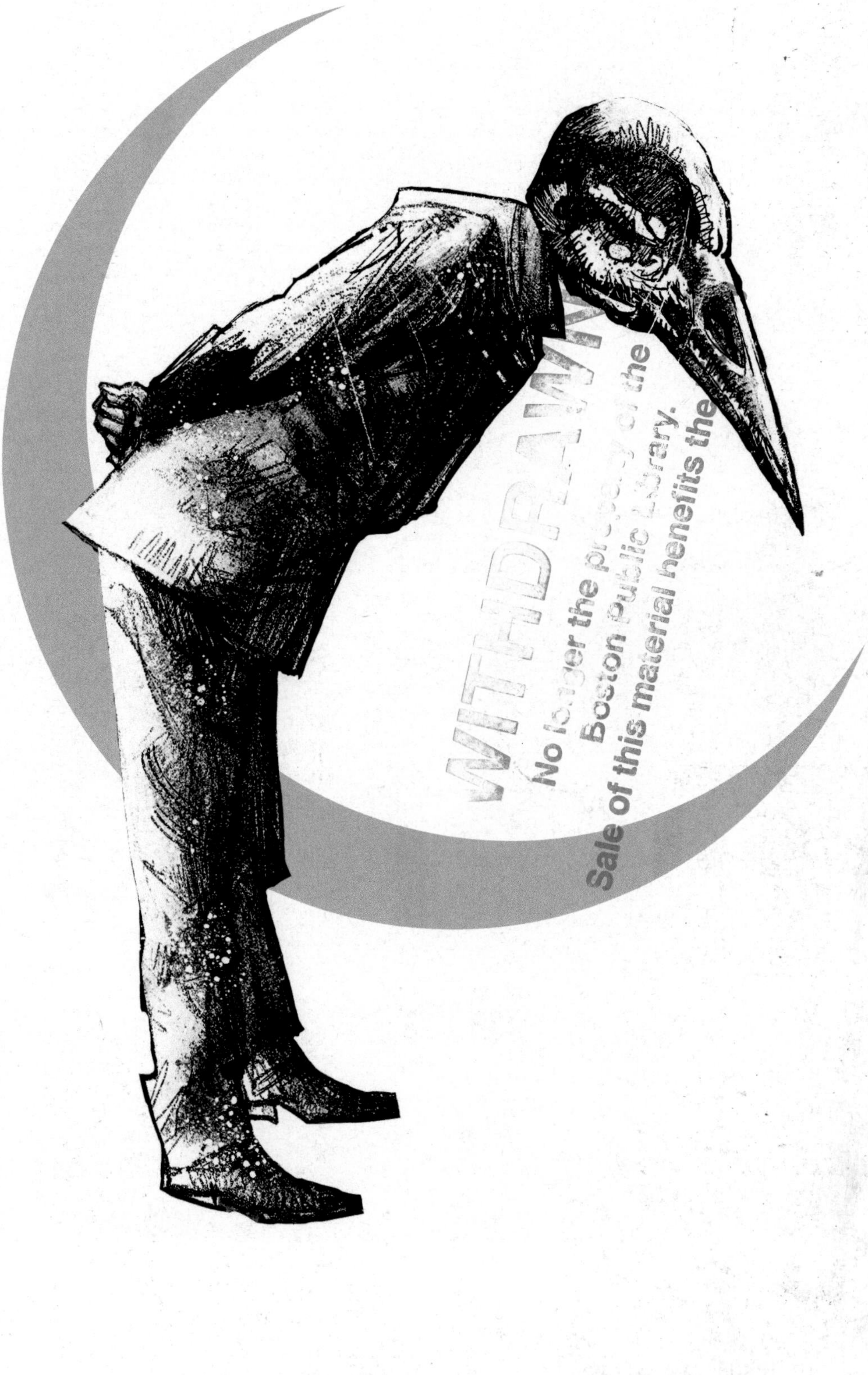

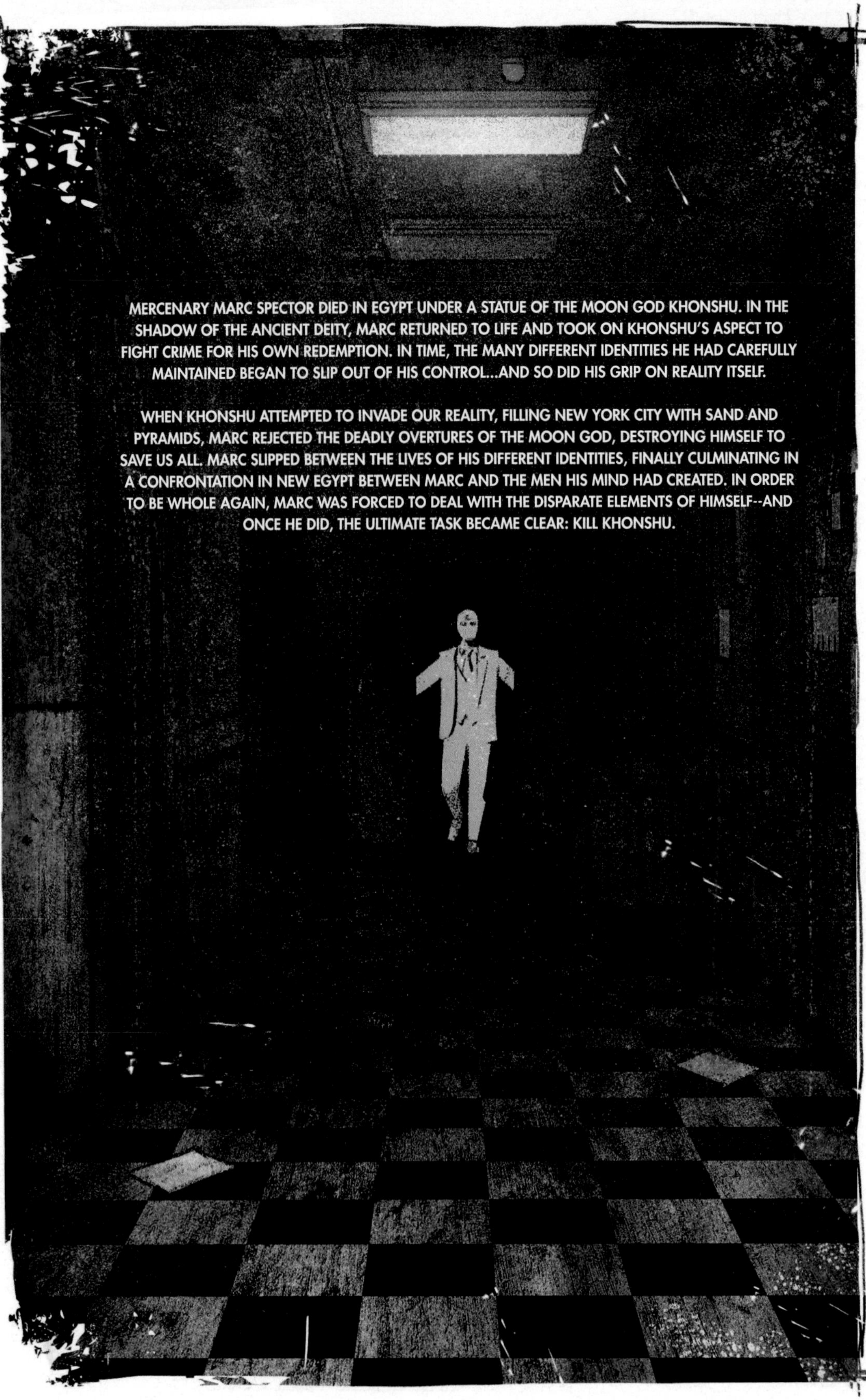
MERCENARY MARC SPECTOR DIED IN EGYPT UNDER A STATUE OF THE MOON GOD KHONSHU. IN THE SHADOW OF THE ANCIENT DEITY, MARC RETURNED TO LIFE AND TOOK ON KHONSHU'S ASPECT TO FIGHT CRIME FOR HIS OWN REDEMPTION. IN TIME, THE MANY DIFFERENT IDENTITIES HE HAD CAREFULLY MAINTAINED BEGAN TO SLIP OUT OF HIS CONTROL...AND SO DID HIS GRIP ON REALITY ITSELF.
WHEN KHONSHU ATTEMPTED TO INVADE OUR REALITY, FILLING NEW YORK CITY WITH SAND AND PYRAMIDS, MARC REJECTED THE DEADLY OVERTURES OF THE MOON GOD, DESTROYING HIMSELF TO SAVE US ALL. MARC SLIPPED BETWEEN THE LIVES OF HIS DIFFERENT IDENTITIES, FINALLY CULMINATING IN A CONFRONTATION IN NEW EGYPT BETWEEN MARC AND THE MEN HIS MIND HAD CREATED. IN ORDER TO BE WHOLE AGAIN, MARC WAS FORCED TO DEAL WITH THE DISPARATE ELEMENTS OF HIMSELF--AND ONCE HE DID, THE ULTIMATE TASK BECAME CLEAR: KILL KHONSHU.

MOON KNIGHT:
BIRTH AND DEATH

WRITER
JEFF LEMIRE

ARTIST
GREG SMALLWOOD

COLOR ARTIST
JORDIE BELLAIRE

LETTERER
VC's CORY PETIT

COVER ART
GREG SMALLWOOD

ASSISTANT EDITOR
KATHLEEN WISNESKI

EDITOR
JAKE THOMAS

COLLECTION EDITOR: JENNIFER GRÜNWALD
ASSISTANT EDITOR: CAITLIN O'CONNELL
ASSOCIATE MANAGING EDITOR: KATERI WOODY
EDITOR, SPECIAL PROJECTS: MARK D. BEAZLEY
VP PRODUCTION & SPECIAL PROJECTS: JEFF YOUNGQUIST
SVP PRINT, SALES & MARKETING: DAVID GABRIEL
BOOK DESIGN: JAY BOWEN

EDITOR IN CHIEF: AXEL ALONSO
CHIEF CREATIVE OFFICER: JOE QUESADA
PRESIDENT: DAN BUCKLEY
EXECUTIVE PRODUCER: ALAN FINE

MOON KNIGHT VOL. 3: BIRTH AND DEATH. Contains material originally published in magazine form as MOON KNIGHT #10-14. First printing 2017. ISBN# 978-1-302-90288-9. Published by MARVEL WORLDWIDE, INC., a subsidiary of MARVEL ENTERTAINMENT, LLC. OFFICE OF PUBLICATION: 135 West 50th Street, New York, NY 10020. Copyright © 2017 MARVEL No similarity between any of the names, characters, persons, and/or institutions in this magazine with those of any living or dead person or institution is intended, and any such similarity which may exist is purely coincidental. **Printed in the U.S.A.** DAN BUCKLEY, President, Marvel Entertainment; JOE QUESADA, Chief Creative Officer; TOM BREVOORT, SVP of Publishing; DAVID BOGART, SVP of Business Affairs & Operations, Publishing & Partnership; C.B. CEBULSKI, VP of Brand Management & Development, Asia; DAVID GABRIEL, SVP of Sales & Marketing, Publishing; JEFF YOUNGQUIST, VP of Production & Special Projects; DAN CARR, Executive Director of Publishing Technology; ALEX MORALES, Director of Publishing Operations; SUSAN CRESPI, Production Manager; STAN LEE, Chairman Emeritus. For information regarding advertising in Marvel Comics or on Marvel.com, please contact Vit DeBellis, Integrated Sales Manager, at vdebellis@marvel.com. For Marvel subscription inquiries, please call 888-511-5480. **Manufactured between 7/28/2017 and 8/28/2017 by QUAD/GRAPHICS WASECA, WASECA, MN, USA.**

10 9 8 7 6 5 4 3 2 1

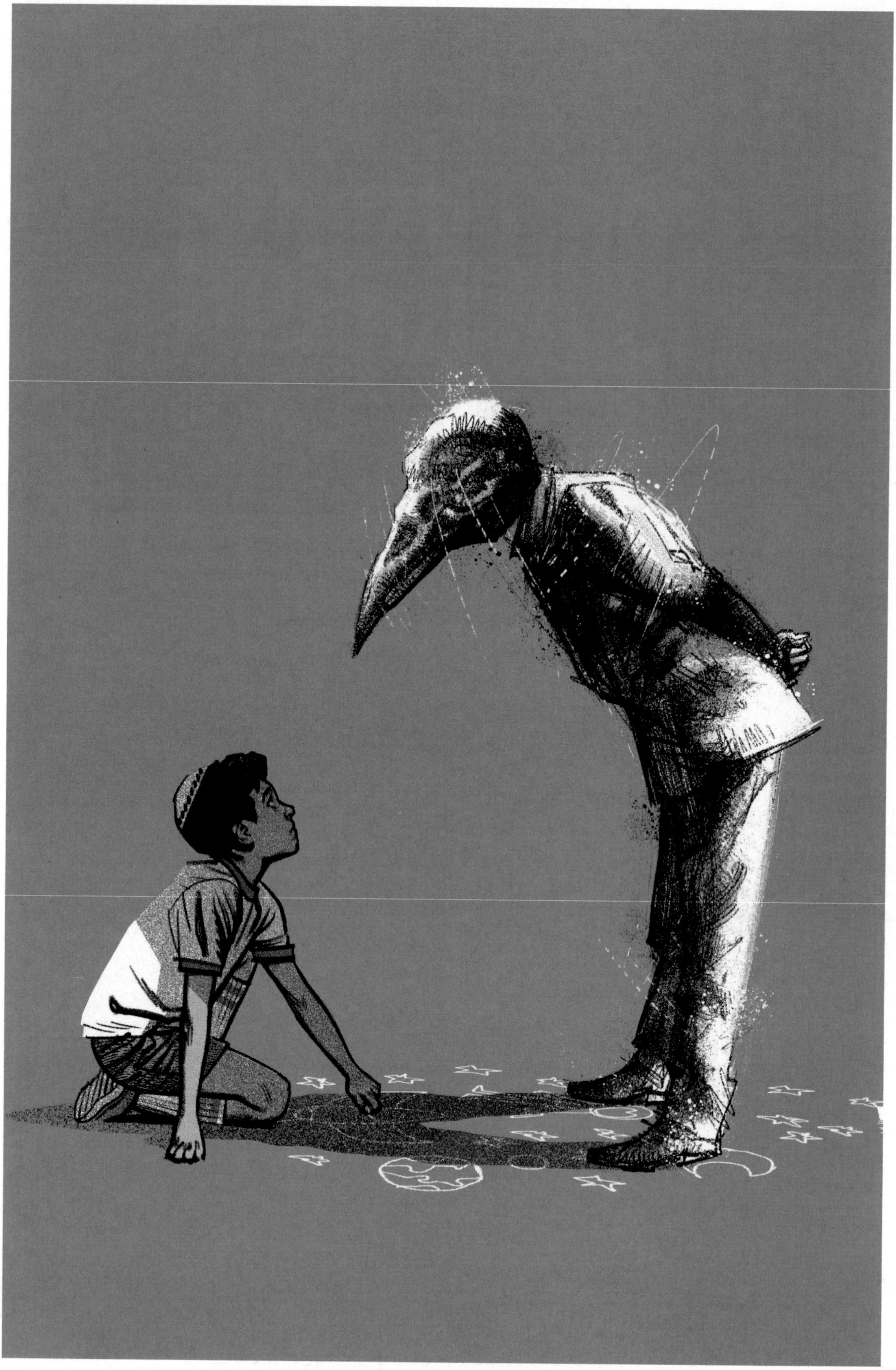

BIRTH AND DEATH
PART ONE

10

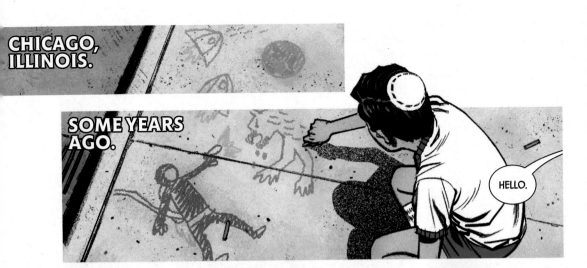

CHICAGO, ILLINOIS.

SOME YEARS AGO.

HELLO.

HUH? OH, HI.

WHAT ARE YOU DOING?

JUST DRAWING.

CAN I DRAW, TOO?

UM, SURE.

MY NAME IS MARC SPECTOR. I LIVE THERE, IN THAT APARTMENT BUILDING.

I KNOW.

YOU DO?

YEAH, I'VE SEEN YOU AROUND. I LIVE THERE, TOO.

OH. WHAT'S YOUR NAME?

MY NAME IS STEVEN. STEVEN GRANT.

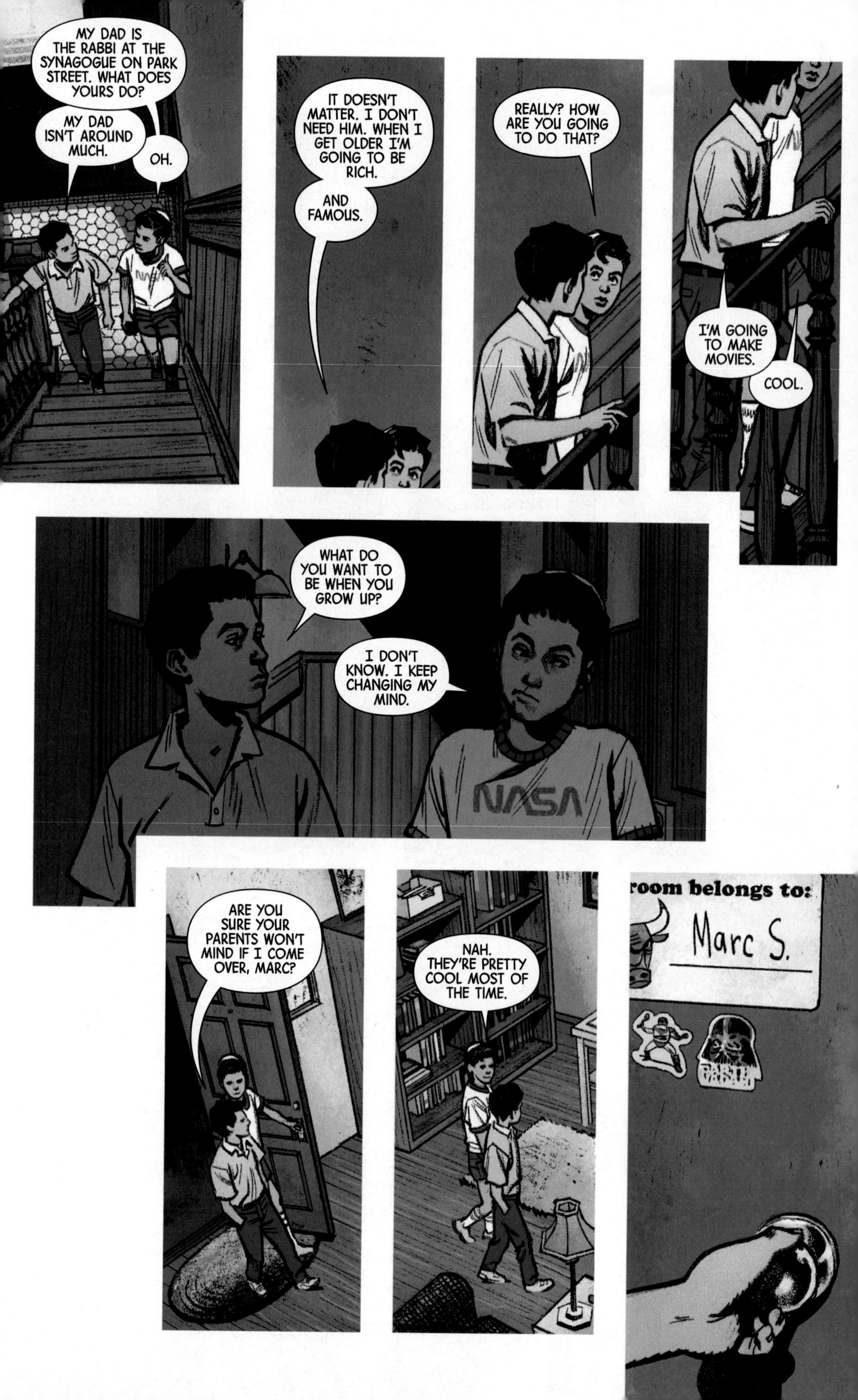
MY DAD IS THE RABBI AT THE SYNAGOGUE ON PARK STREET. WHAT DOES YOURS DO?
MY DAD ISN'T AROUND MUCH.
OH.
IT DOESN'T MATTER. I DON'T NEED HIM. WHEN I GET OLDER I'M GOING TO BE RICH.
AND FAMOUS.
REALLY? HOW ARE YOU GOING TO DO THAT?
I'M GOING TO MAKE MOVIES.
COOL.
WHAT DO YOU WANT TO BE WHEN YOU GROW UP?
I DON'T KNOW. I KEEP CHANGING MY MIND.
NASA
ARE YOU SURE YOUR PARENTS WON'T MIND IF I COME OVER, MARC?
NAH. THEY'RE PRETTY COOL MOST OF THE TIME.
room belongs to:
Marc S.

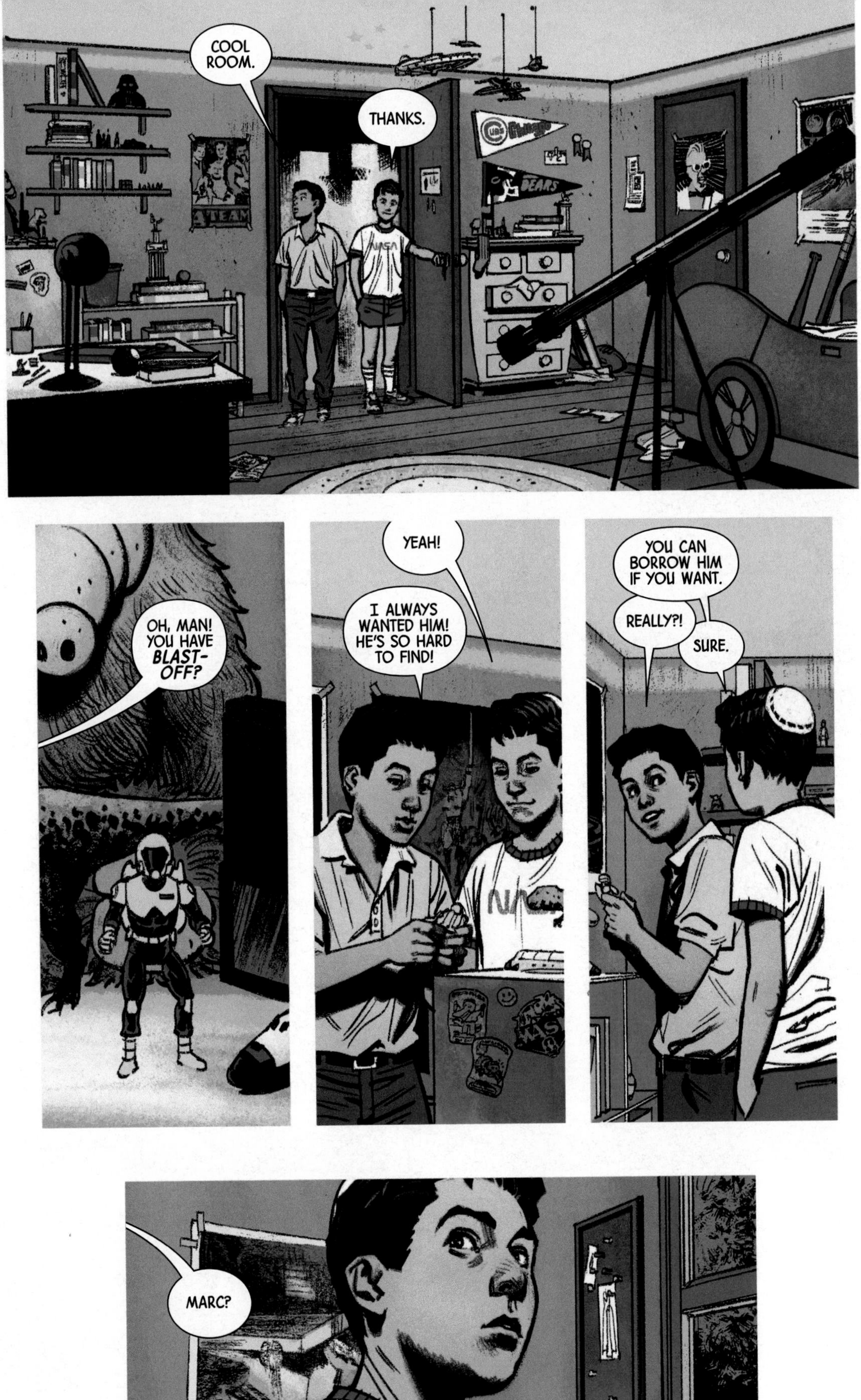
COOL ROOM.
THANKS.
OH, MAN! YOU HAVE *BLAST-OFF?*
YEAH!
I ALWAYS WANTED HIM! HE'S SO HARD TO FIND!
YOU CAN BORROW HIM IF YOU WANT.
REALLY?!
SURE.
MARC?

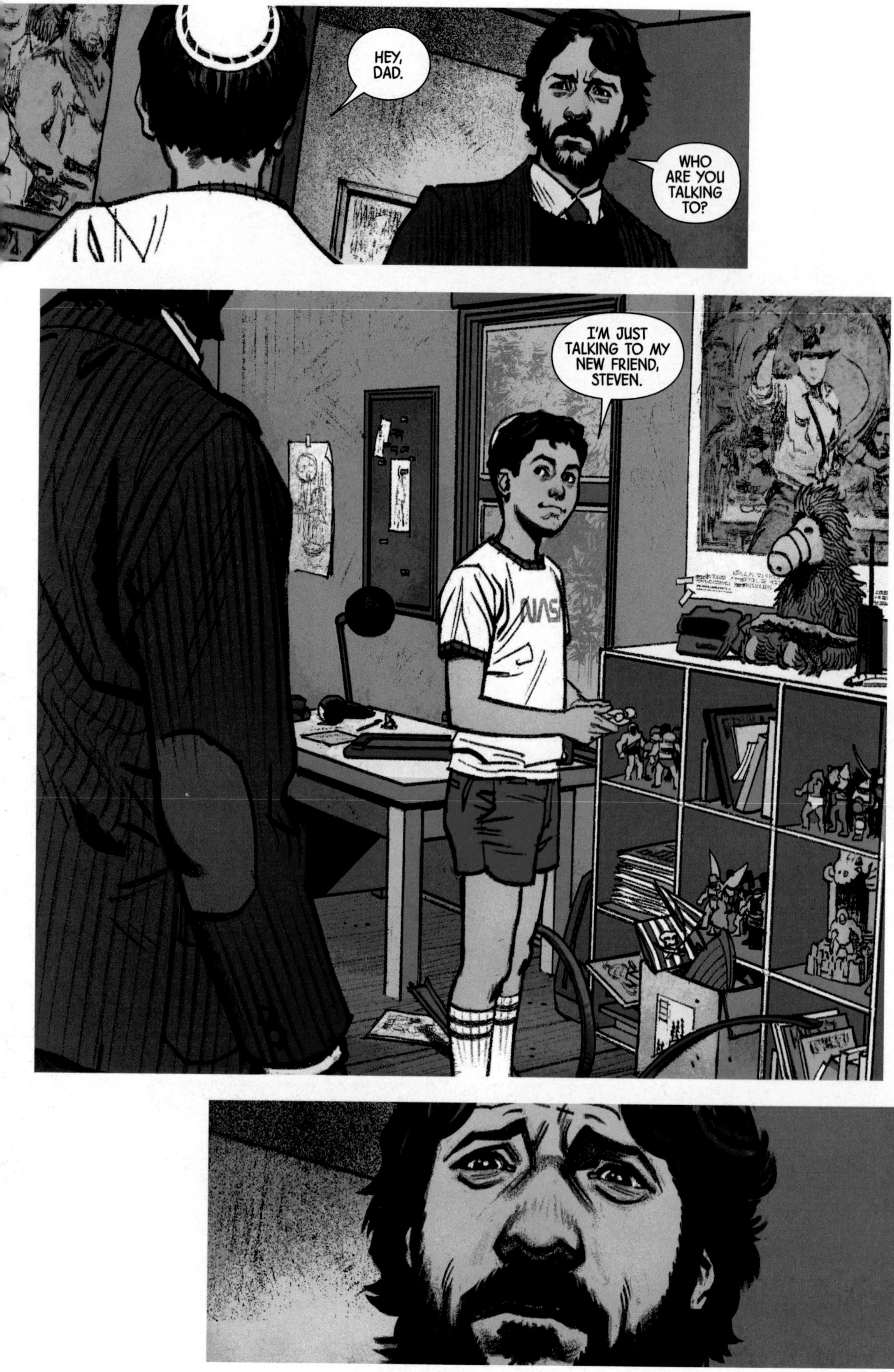
HEY, DAD.
WHO ARE YOU TALKING TO?
I'M JUST TALKING TO MY NEW FRIEND, STEVEN.

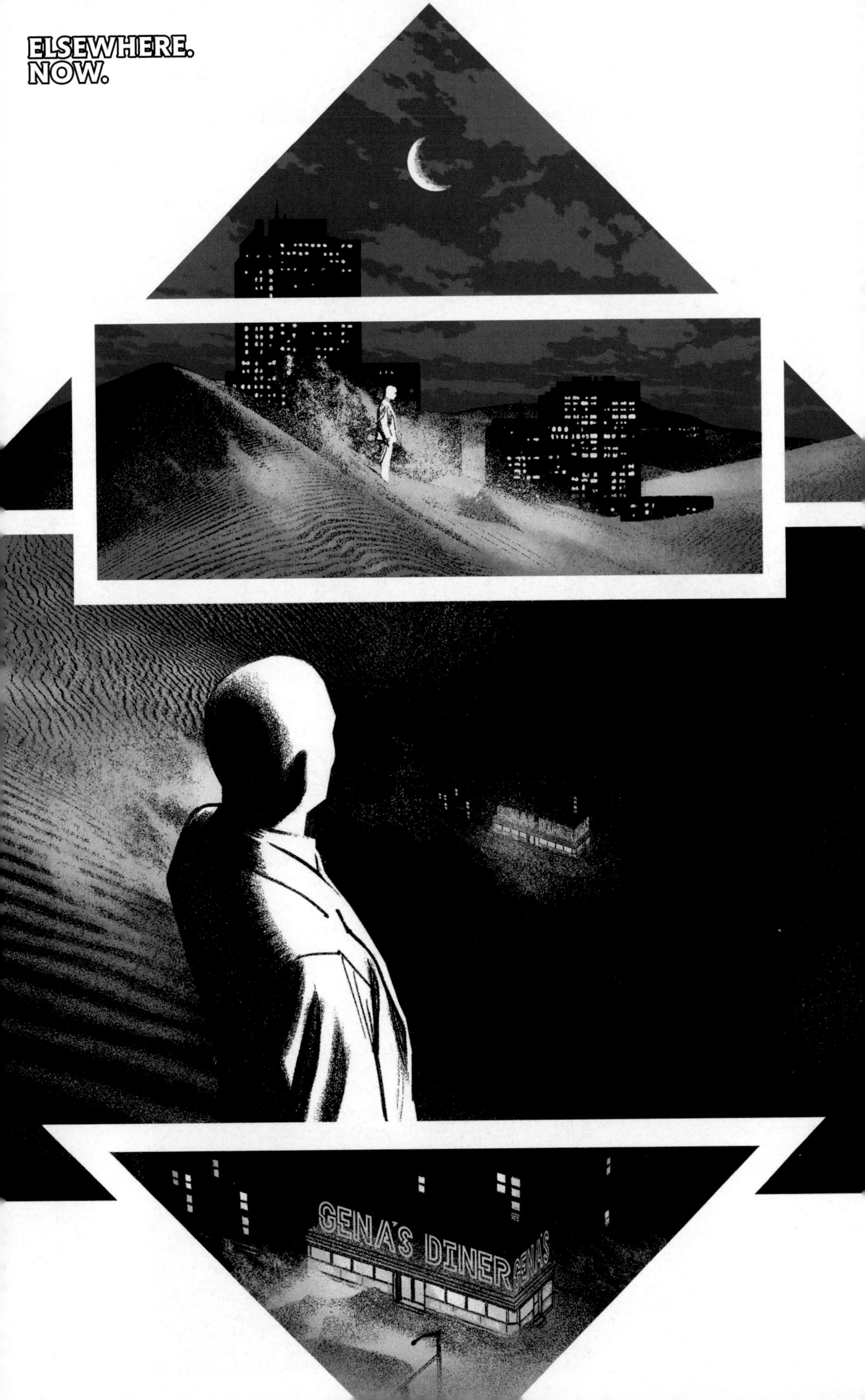
ELSEWHERE.
NOW.
GENA'S DINER
GENA'S

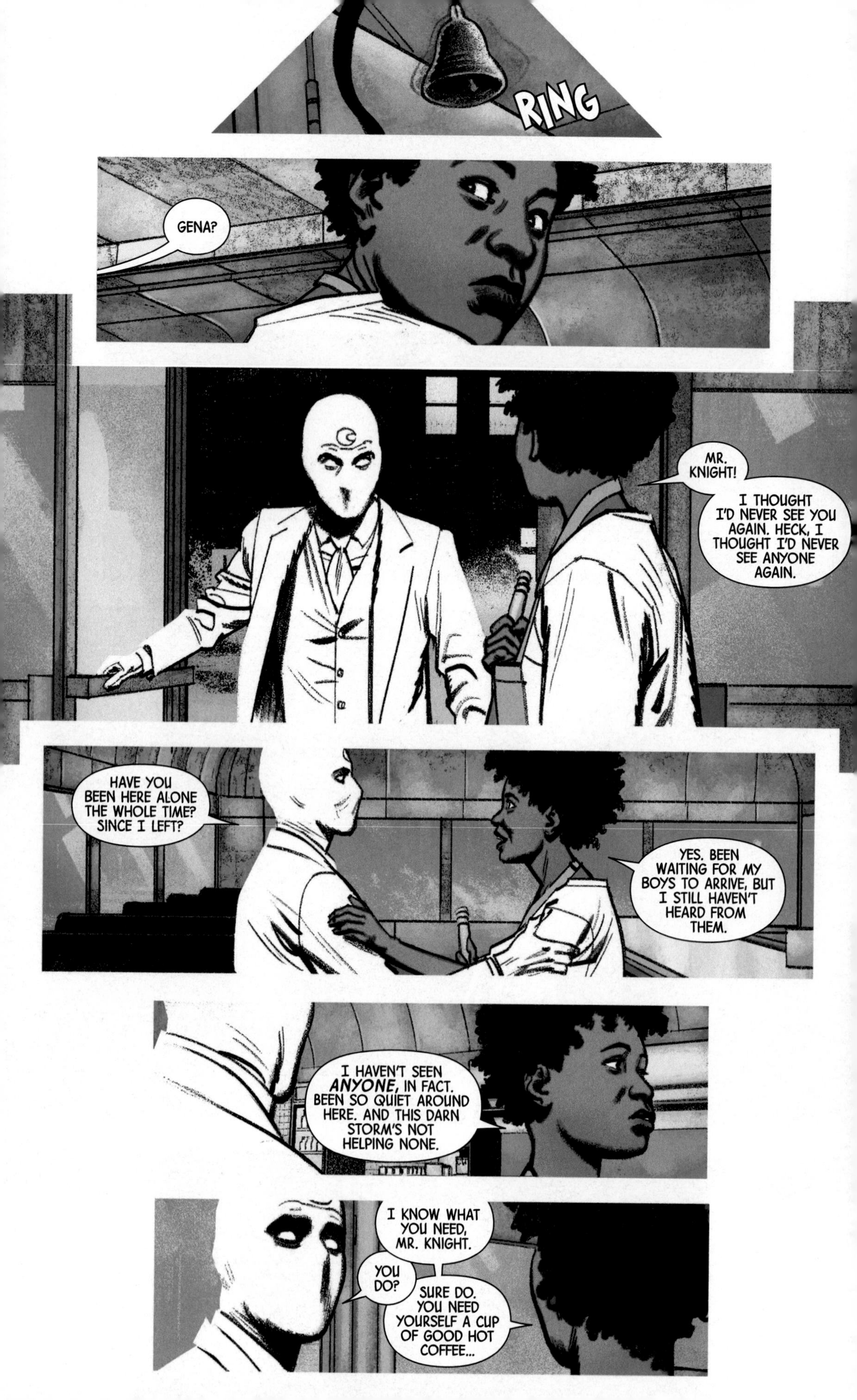
RING
GENA?
MR. KNIGHT!
I THOUGHT I'D NEVER SEE YOU AGAIN. HECK, I THOUGHT I'D NEVER SEE ANYONE AGAIN.
HAVE YOU BEEN HERE ALONE THE WHOLE TIME? SINCE I LEFT?
YES. BEEN WAITING FOR MY BOYS TO ARRIVE, BUT I STILL HAVEN'T HEARD FROM THEM.
I HAVEN'T SEEN ANYONE, IN FACT. BEEN SO QUIET AROUND HERE. AND THIS DARN STORM'S NOT HELPING NONE.
I KNOW WHAT YOU NEED, MR. KNIGHT.
YOU DO?
SURE DO. YOU NEED YOURSELF A CUP OF GOOD HOT COFFEE...

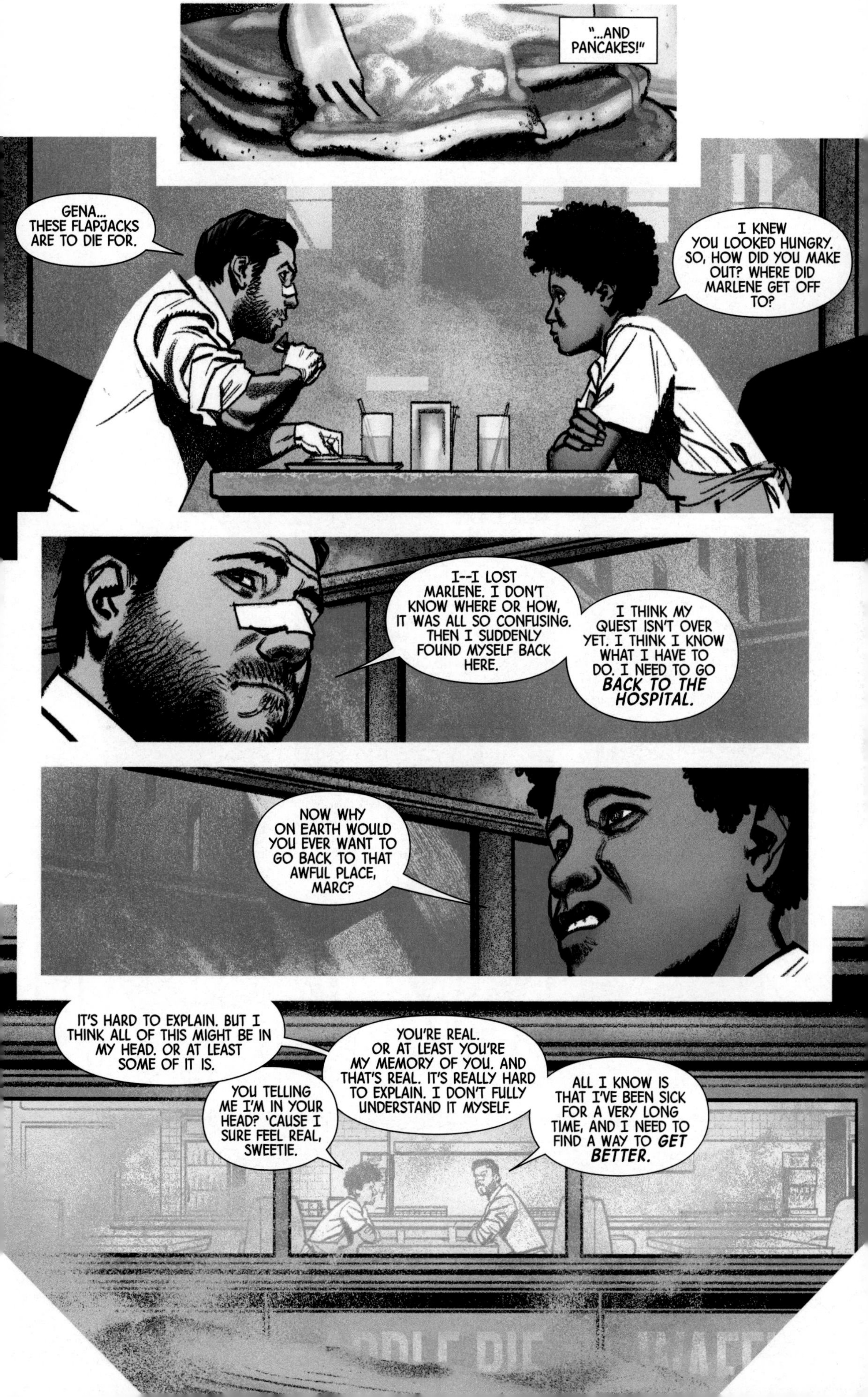
"...AND PANCAKES!"
GENA... THESE FLAPJACKS ARE TO DIE FOR.
I KNEW YOU LOOKED HUNGRY. SO, HOW DID YOU MAKE OUT? WHERE DID MARLENE GET OFF TO?
I--I LOST MARLENE. I DON'T KNOW WHERE OR HOW, IT WAS ALL SO CONFUSING. THEN I SUDDENLY FOUND MYSELF BACK HERE.
I THINK MY QUEST ISN'T OVER YET. I THINK I KNOW WHAT I HAVE TO DO. I NEED TO GO *BACK TO THE HOSPITAL.*
NOW WHY ON EARTH WOULD YOU EVER WANT TO GO BACK TO THAT AWFUL PLACE, MARC?
IT'S HARD TO EXPLAIN. BUT I THINK ALL OF THIS MIGHT BE IN MY HEAD. OR AT LEAST SOME OF IT IS.
YOU TELLING ME I'M IN YOUR HEAD? 'CAUSE I SURE FEEL REAL, SWEETIE.
YOU'RE REAL. OR AT LEAST YOU'RE MY MEMORY OF YOU. AND THAT'S REAL. IT'S REALLY HARD TO EXPLAIN. I DON'T FULLY UNDERSTAND IT MYSELF.
ALL I KNOW IS THAT I'VE BEEN SICK FOR A VERY LONG TIME, AND I NEED TO FIND A WAY TO *GET BETTER.*

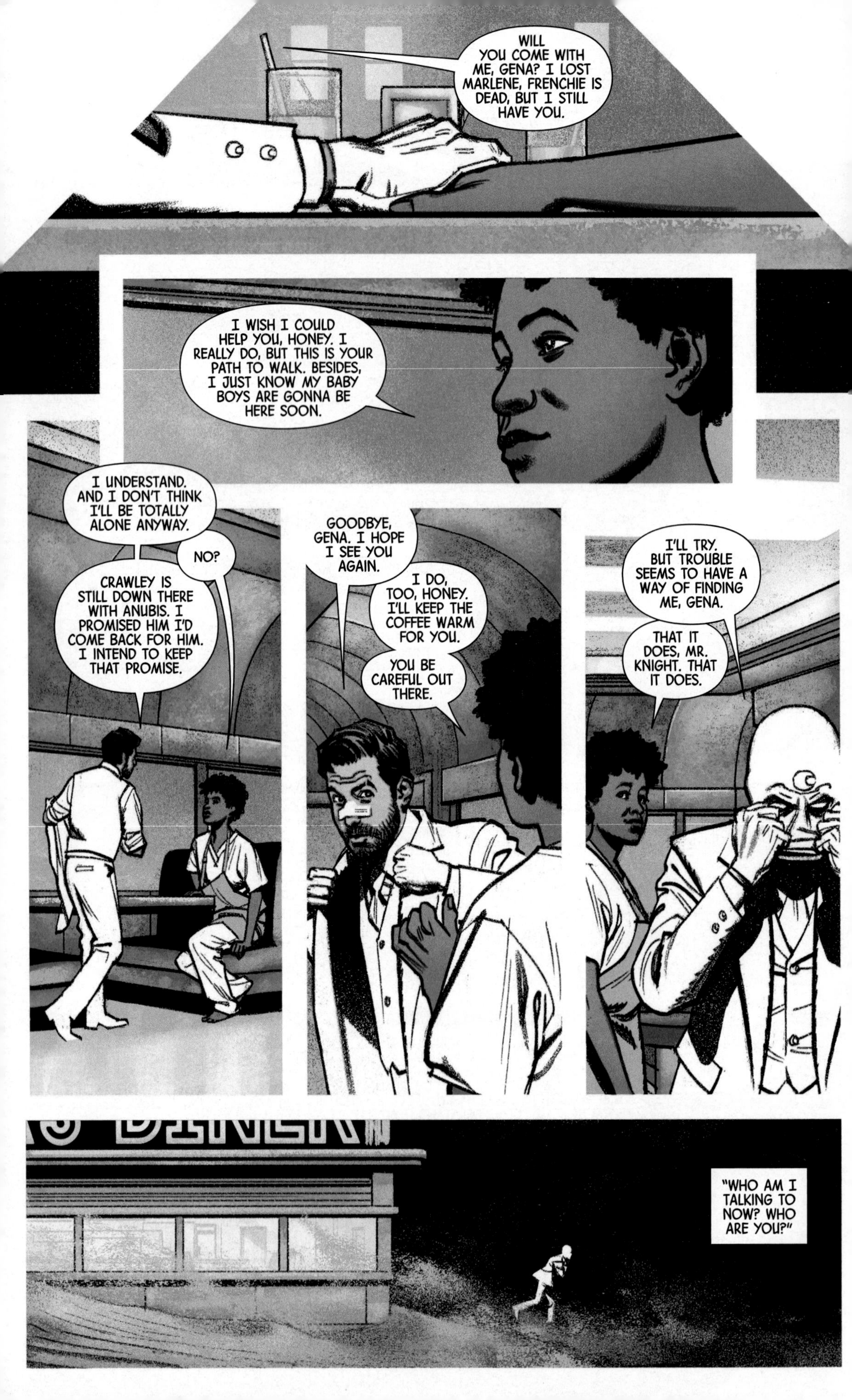
WILL YOU COME WITH ME, GENA? I LOST MARLENE, FRENCHIE IS DEAD, BUT I STILL HAVE YOU.
I WISH I COULD HELP YOU, HONEY. I REALLY DO, BUT THIS IS YOUR PATH TO WALK. BESIDES, I JUST KNOW MY BABY BOYS ARE GONNA BE HERE SOON.
I UNDERSTAND. AND I DON'T THINK I'LL BE TOTALLY ALONE ANYWAY.
NO?
CRAWLEY IS STILL DOWN THERE WITH ANUBIS. I PROMISED HIM I'D COME BACK FOR HIM. I INTEND TO KEEP THAT PROMISE.
GOODBYE, GENA. I HOPE I SEE YOU AGAIN.
I DO, TOO, HONEY. I'LL KEEP THE COFFEE WARM FOR YOU.
YOU BE CAREFUL OUT THERE.
I'LL TRY. BUT TROUBLE SEEMS TO HAVE A WAY OF FINDING ME, GENA.
THAT IT DOES, MR. KNIGHT. THAT IT DOES.
DINER
"WHO AM I TALKING TO NOW? WHO ARE YOU?"

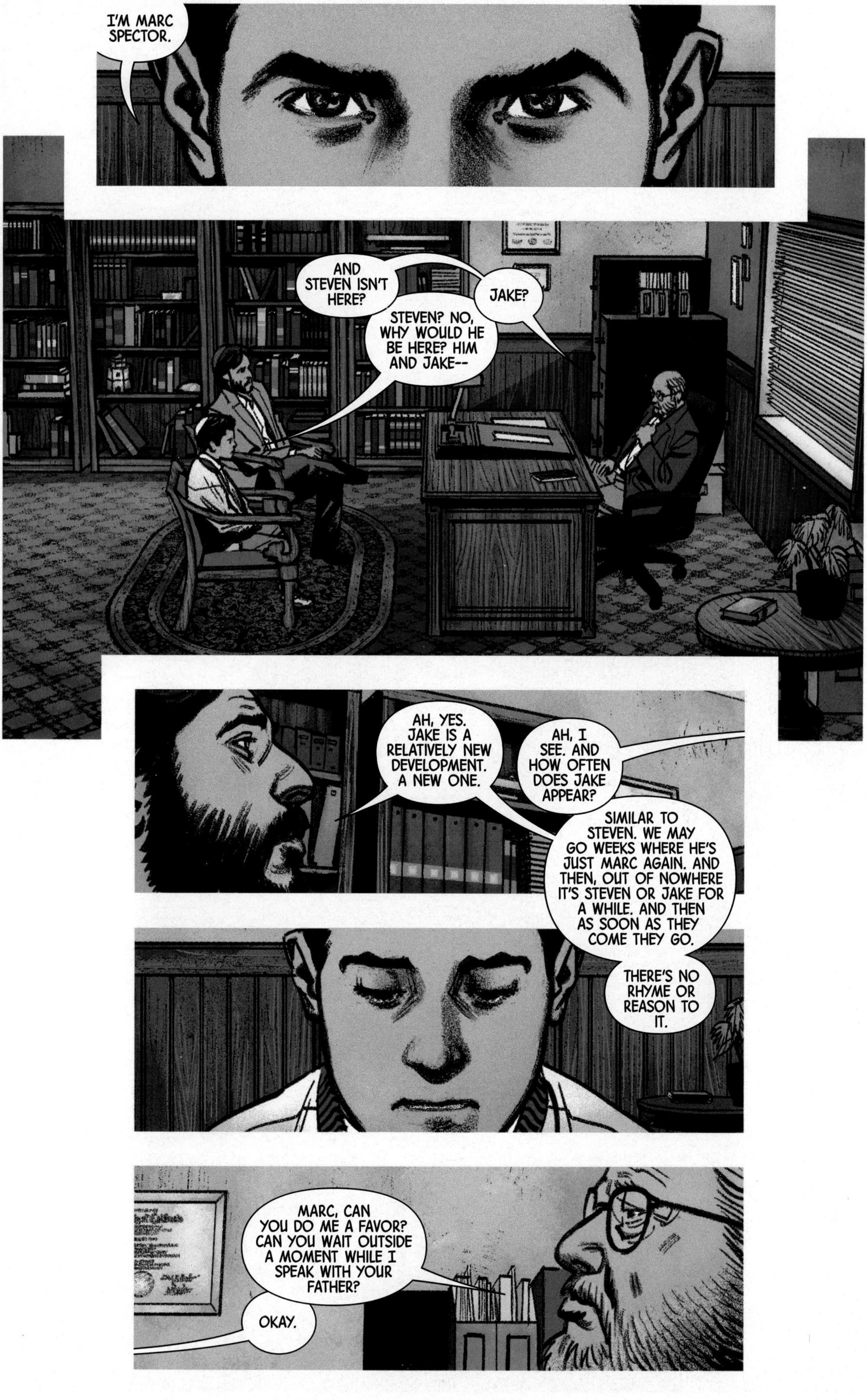
I'M MARC SPECTOR.
AND STEVEN ISN'T HERE?
JAKE?
STEVEN? NO, WHY WOULD HE BE HERE? HIM AND JAKE--
AH, YES. JAKE IS A RELATIVELY NEW DEVELOPMENT. A NEW ONE.
AH, I SEE. AND HOW OFTEN DOES JAKE APPEAR?
SIMILAR TO STEVEN. WE MAY GO WEEKS WHERE HE'S JUST MARC AGAIN. AND THEN, OUT OF NOWHERE IT'S STEVEN OR JAKE FOR A WHILE. AND THEN AS SOON AS THEY COME THEY GO.
THERE'S NO RHYME OR REASON TO IT.
MARC, CAN YOU DO ME A FAVOR? CAN YOU WAIT OUTSIDE A MOMENT WHILE I SPEAK WITH YOUR FATHER?
OKAY.

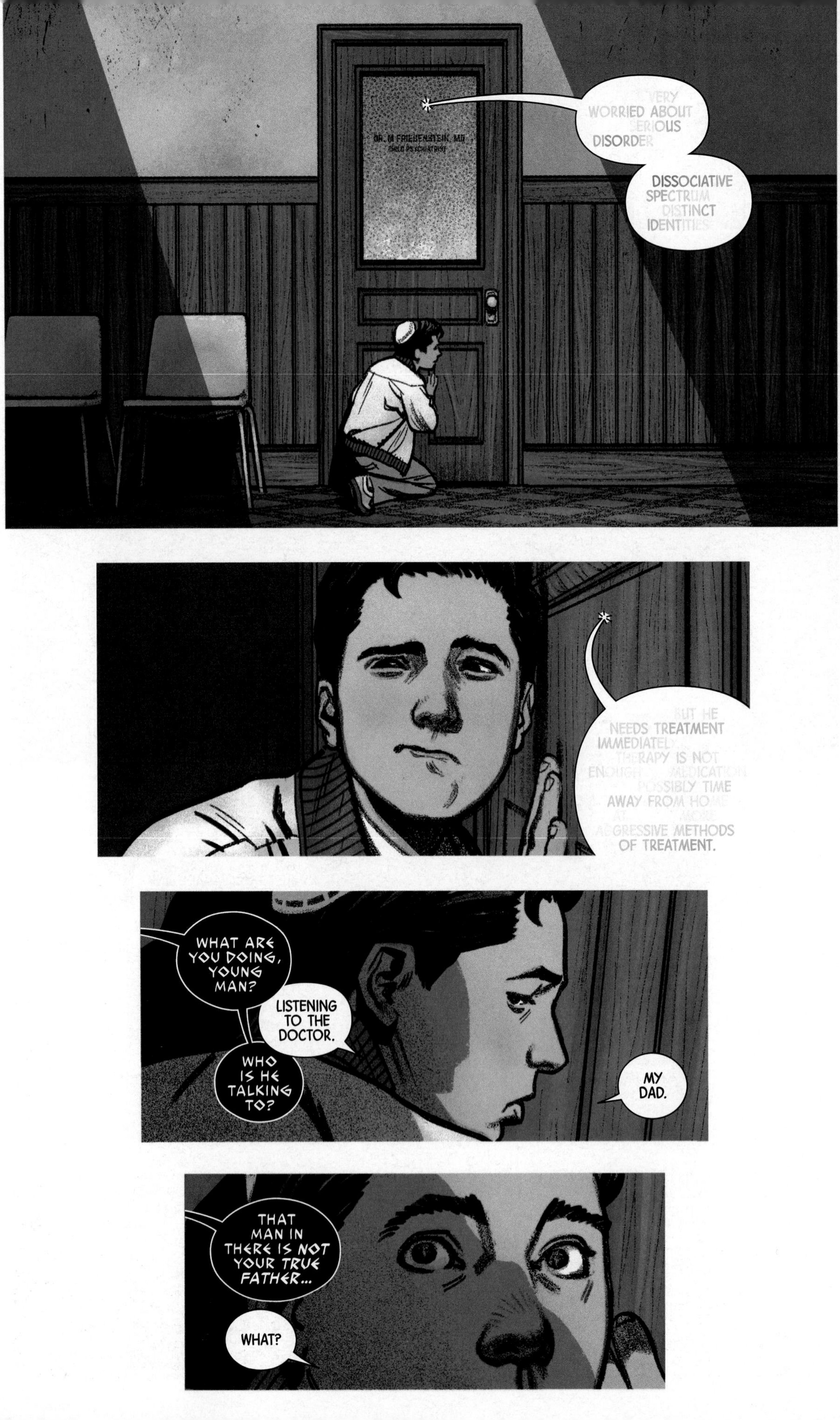
DR. M FRIEBENSTEIN, MD
CHILD PSYCHIATRIST
VERY WORRIED ABOUT SERIOUS DISORDER
DISSOCIATIVE SPECTRUM DISTINCT IDENTITIES
BUT HE NEEDS TREATMENT IMMEDIATELY THERAPY IS NOT ENOUGH MEDICATION POSSIBLY TIME AWAY FROM HOME AT MORE AGGRESSIVE METHODS OF TREATMENT.
WHAT ARE YOU DOING, YOUNG MAN?
LISTENING TO THE DOCTOR.
WHO IS HE TALKING TO?
MY DAD.
THAT MAN IN THERE IS NOT YOUR TRUE FATHER...
WHAT?

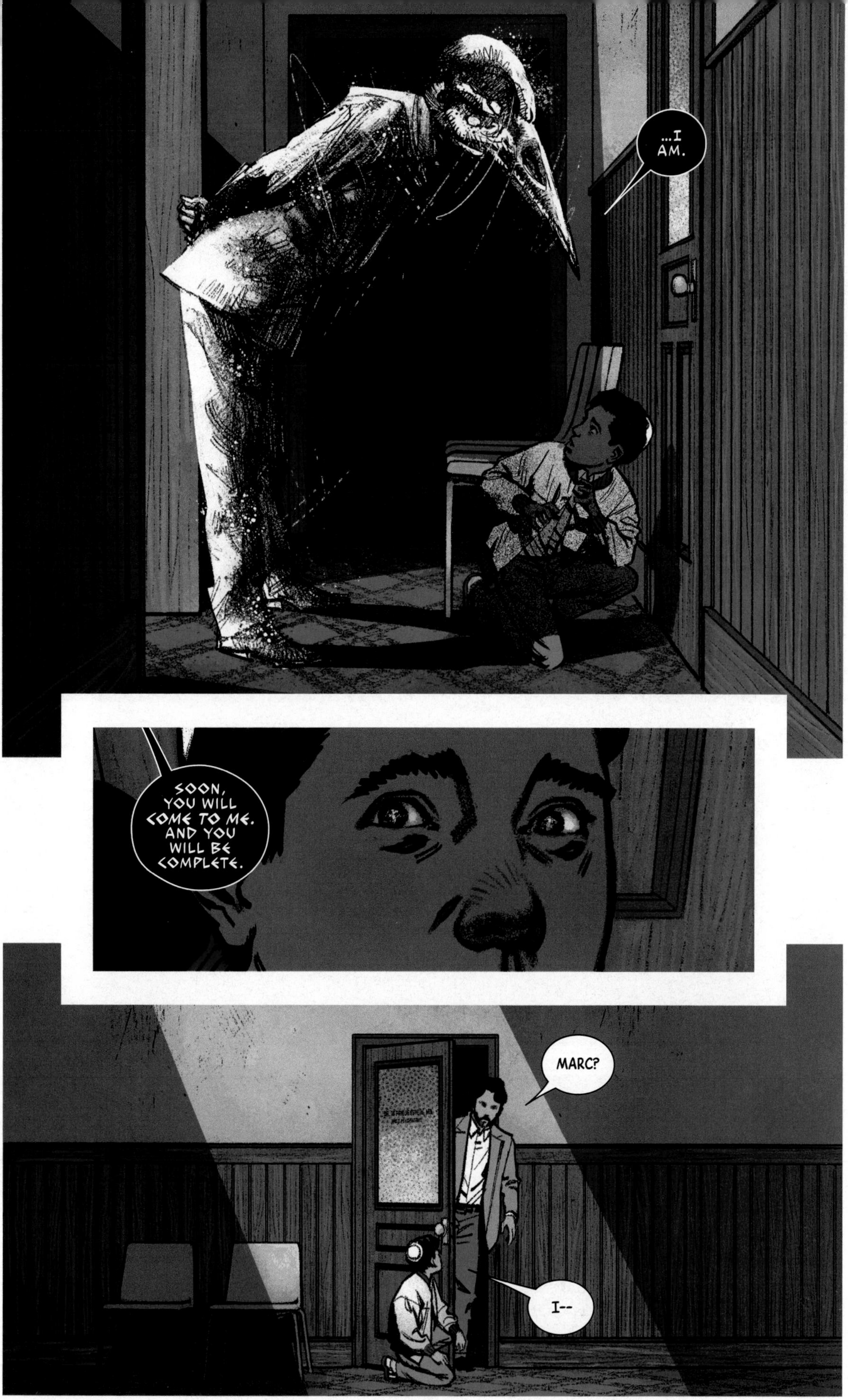
...I AM.
SOON, YOU WILL COME TO ME. AND YOU WILL BE COMPLETE.
MARC?
I--

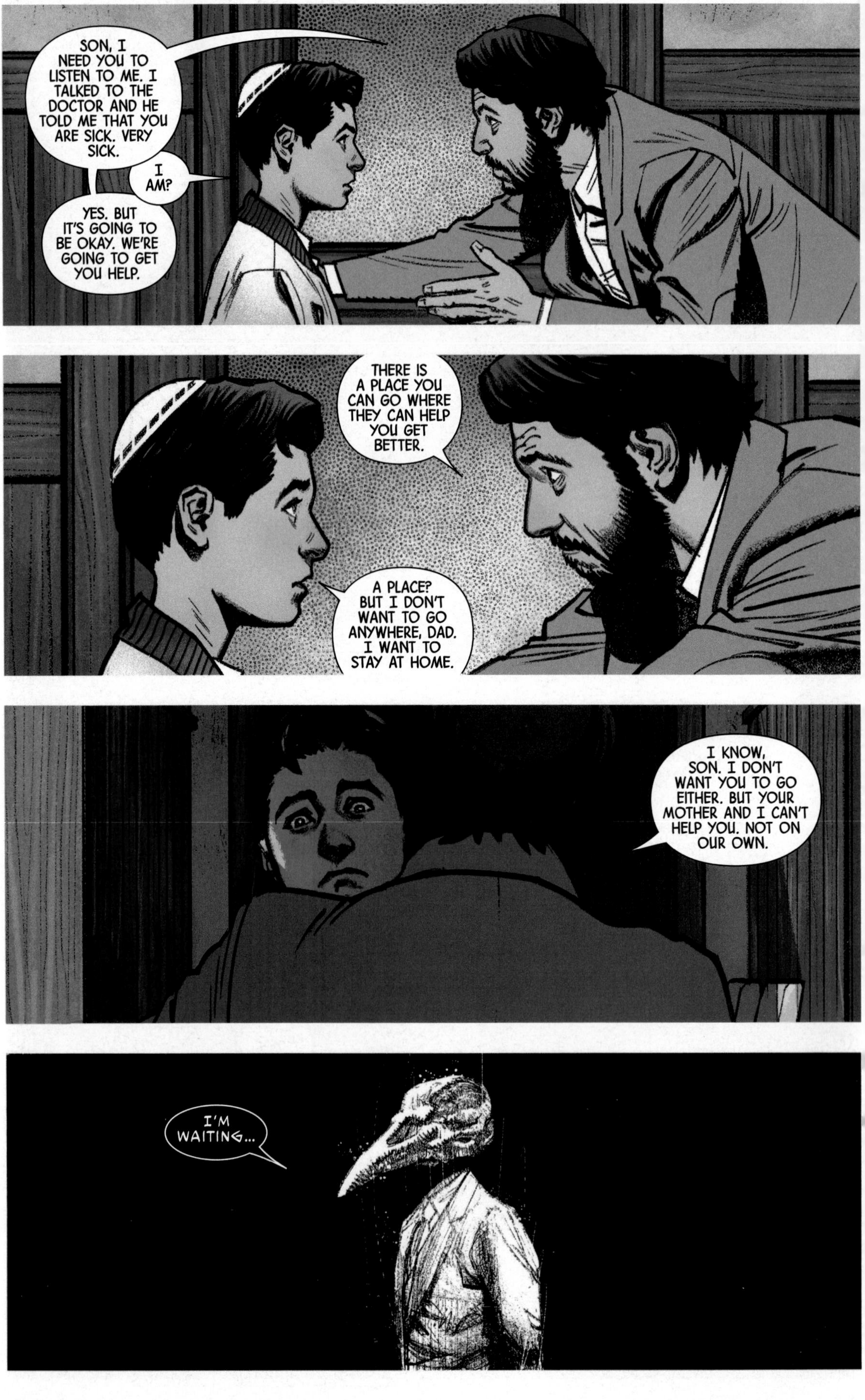
SON, I NEED YOU TO LISTEN TO ME. I TALKED TO THE DOCTOR AND HE TOLD ME THAT YOU ARE SICK. VERY SICK.
I AM?
YES. BUT IT'S GOING TO BE OKAY. WE'RE GOING TO GET YOU HELP.
THERE IS A PLACE YOU CAN GO WHERE THEY CAN HELP YOU GET BETTER.
A PLACE? BUT I DON'T WANT TO GO ANYWHERE, DAD. I WANT TO STAY AT HOME.
I KNOW, SON. I DON'T WANT YOU TO GO EITHER. BUT YOUR MOTHER AND I CAN'T HELP YOU. NOT ON OUR OWN.
I'M WAITING...

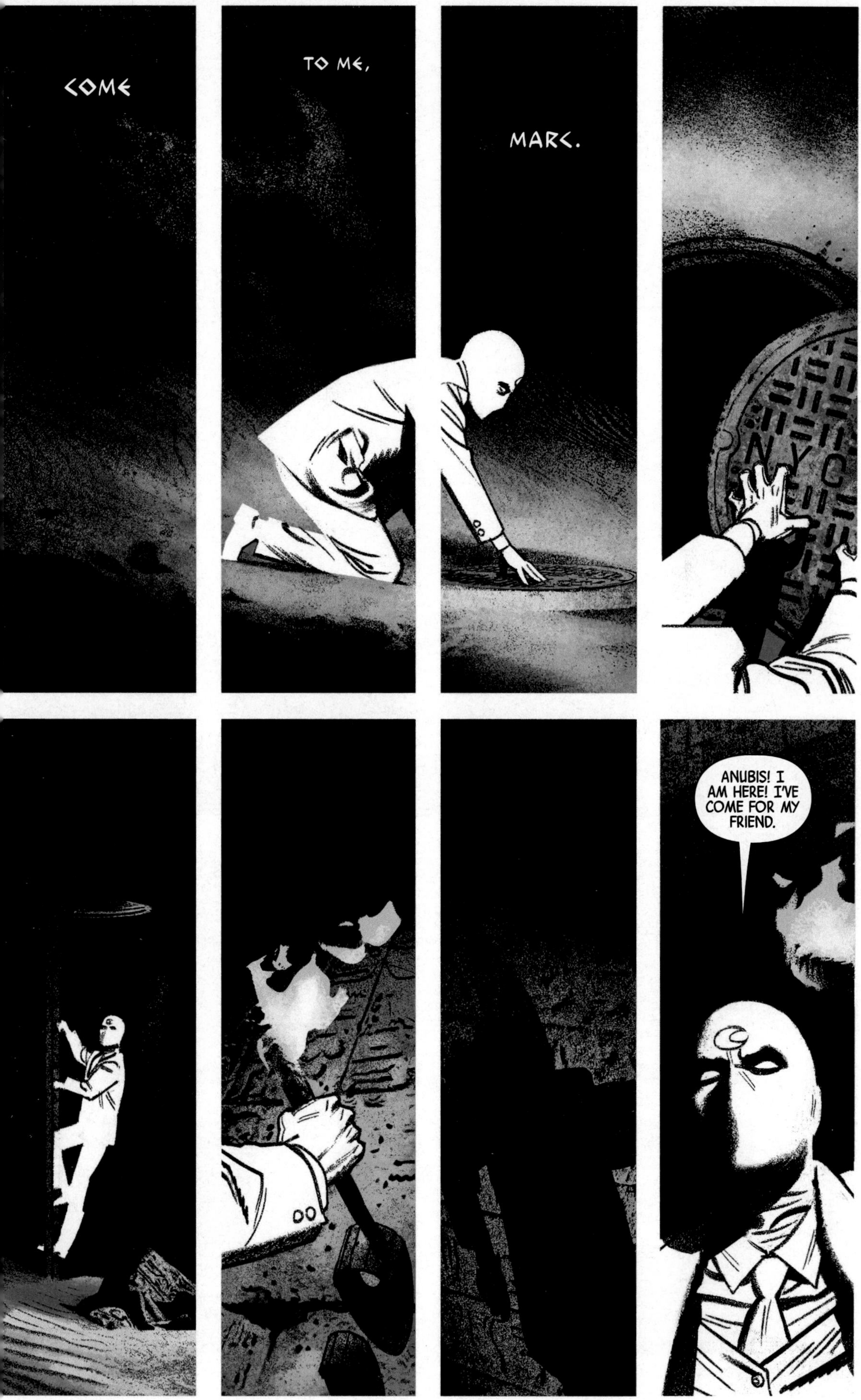
COME
TO ME,
MARC.
ANUBIS! I AM HERE! I'VE COME FOR MY FRIEND.

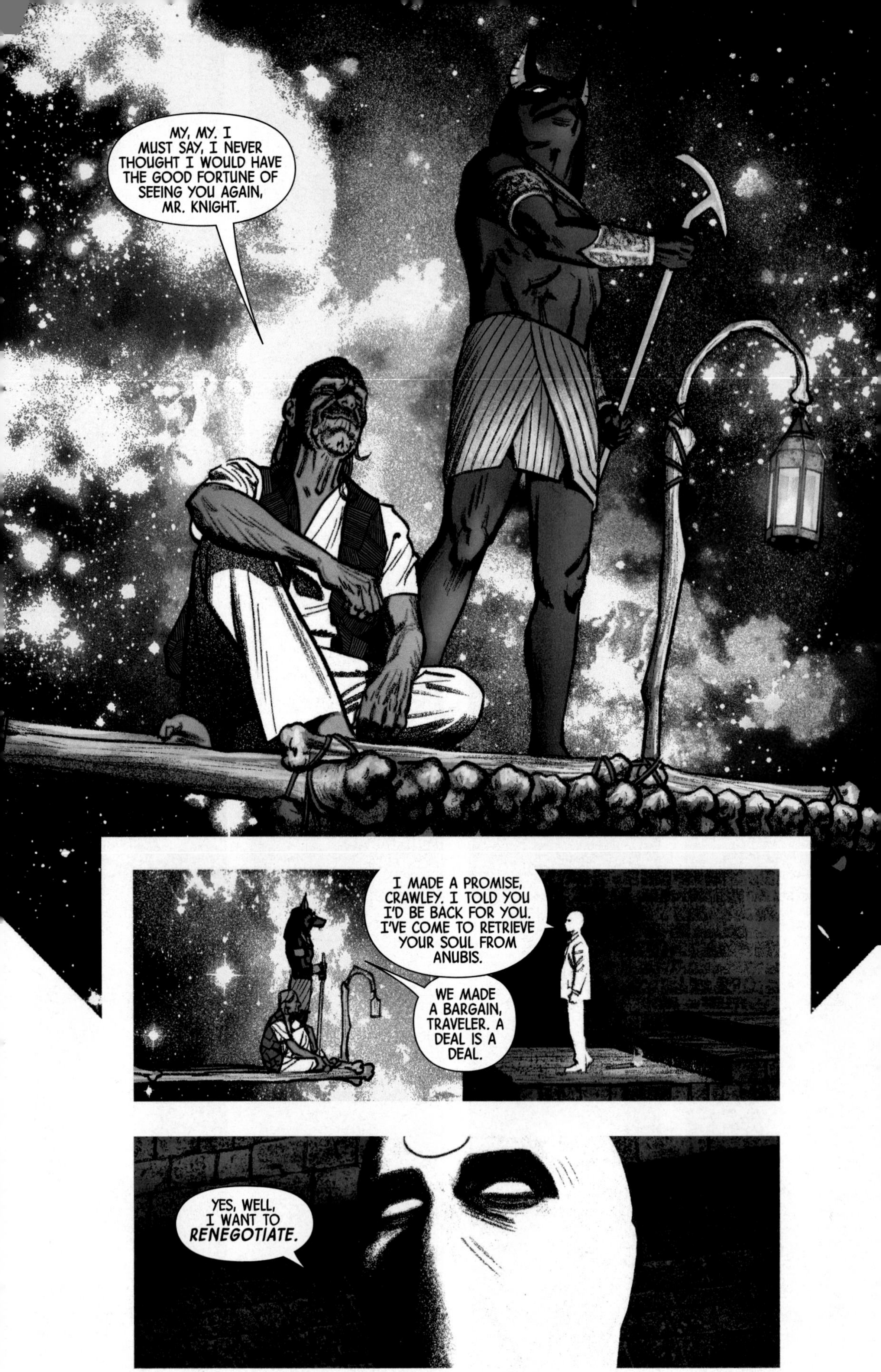
MY, MY. I MUST SAY, I NEVER THOUGHT I WOULD HAVE THE GOOD FORTUNE OF SEEING YOU AGAIN, MR. KNIGHT.
I MADE A PROMISE, CRAWLEY. I TOLD YOU I'D BE BACK FOR YOU. I'VE COME TO RETRIEVE YOUR SOUL FROM ANUBIS.
WE MADE A BARGAIN, TRAVELER. A DEAL IS A DEAL.
YES, WELL, I WANT TO *RENEGOTIATE.*

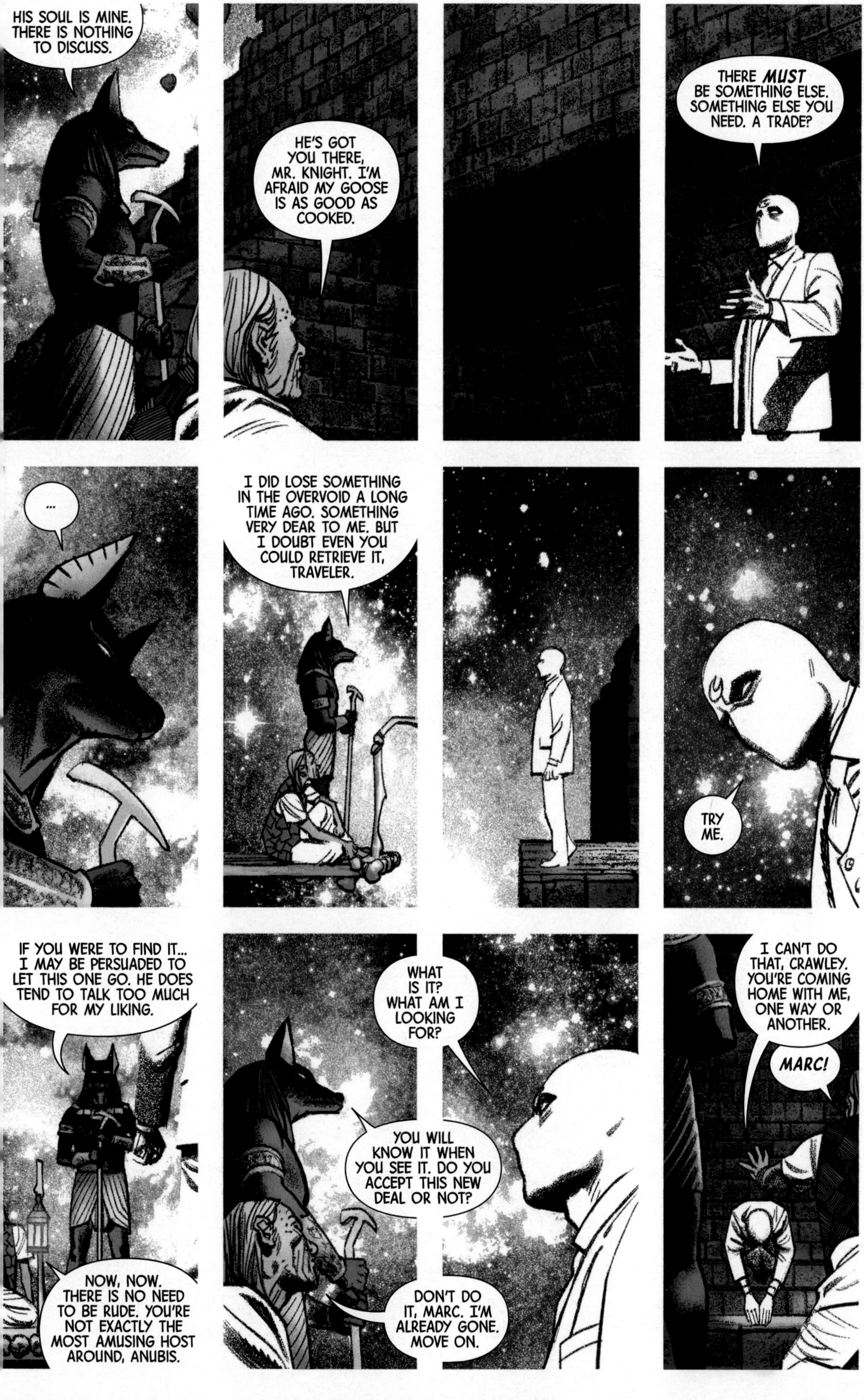
HIS SOUL IS MINE. THERE IS NOTHING TO DISCUSS.
HE'S GOT YOU THERE, MR. KNIGHT. I'M AFRAID MY GOOSE IS AS GOOD AS COOKED.
THERE MUST BE SOMETHING ELSE. SOMETHING ELSE YOU NEED. A TRADE?
...
I DID LOSE SOMETHING IN THE OVERVOID A LONG TIME AGO. SOMETHING VERY DEAR TO ME. BUT I DOUBT EVEN YOU COULD RETRIEVE IT, TRAVELER.
TRY ME.
IF YOU WERE TO FIND IT... I MAY BE PERSUADED TO LET THIS ONE GO. HE DOES TEND TO TALK TOO MUCH FOR MY LIKING.
NOW, NOW. THERE IS NO NEED TO BE RUDE. YOU'RE NOT EXACTLY THE MOST AMUSING HOST AROUND, ANUBIS.
WHAT IS IT? WHAT AM I LOOKING FOR?
YOU WILL KNOW IT WHEN YOU SEE IT. DO YOU ACCEPT THIS NEW DEAL OR NOT?
DON'T DO IT, MARC. I'M ALREADY GONE. MOVE ON.
I CAN'T DO THAT, CRAWLEY. YOU'RE COMING HOME WITH ME, ONE WAY OR ANOTHER.
MARC!

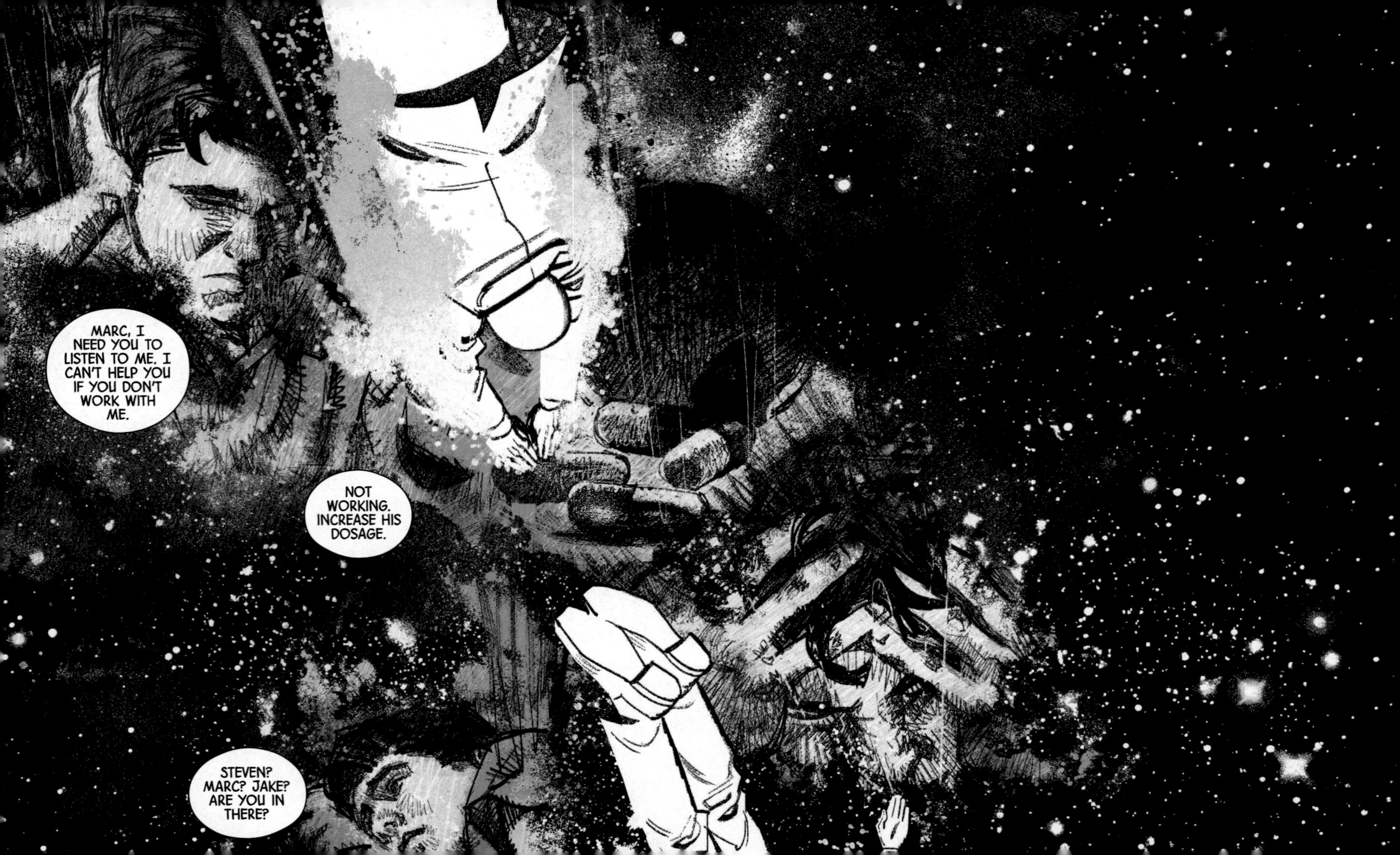
MARC, I NEED YOU TO LISTEN TO ME. I CAN'T HELP YOU IF YOU DON'T WORK WITH ME.
NOT WORKING. INCREASE HIS DOSAGE.
STEVEN? MARC? JAKE? ARE YOU IN THERE?

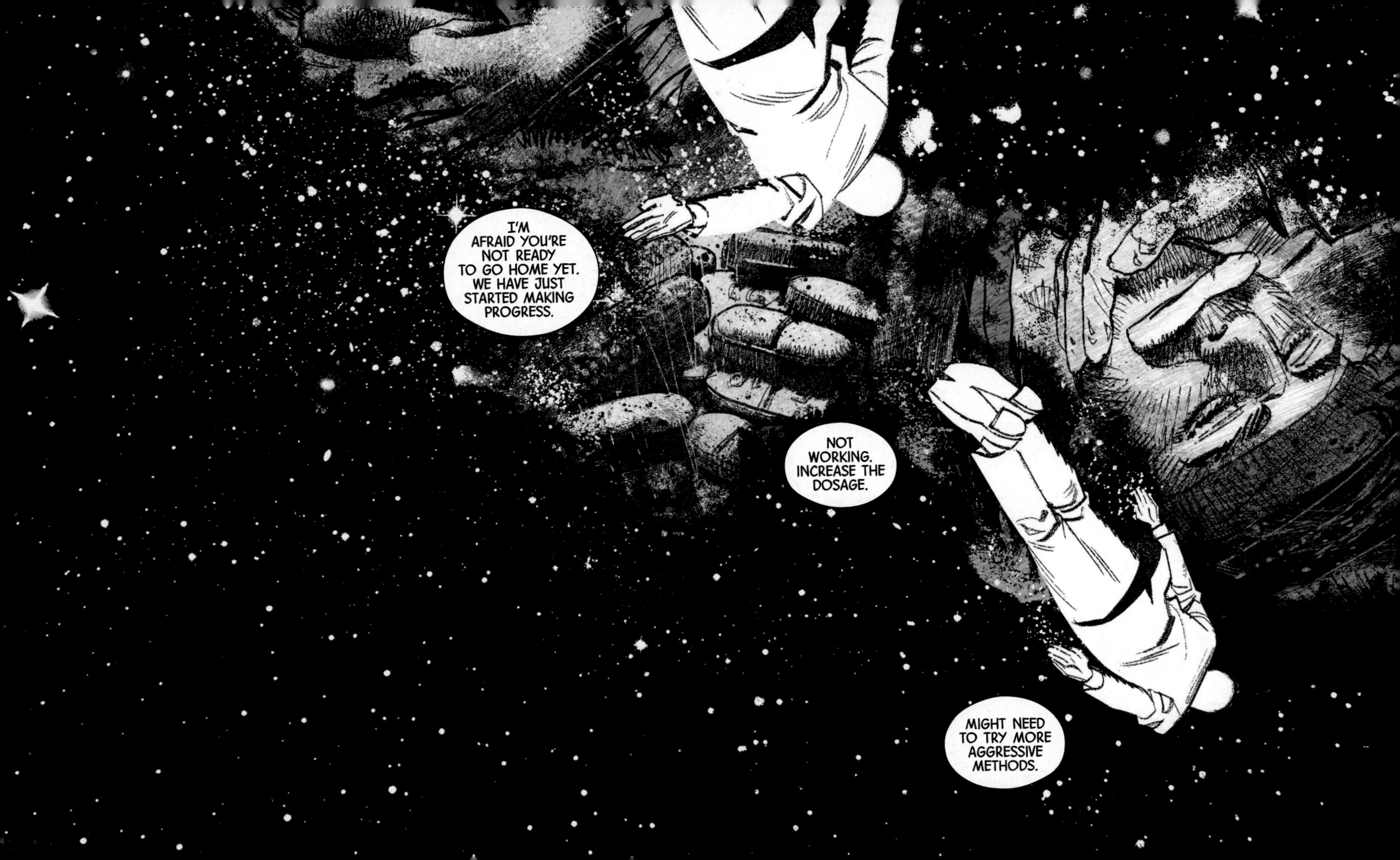

I'M AFRAID YOU'RE NOT READY TO GO HOME YET. WE HAVE JUST STARTED MAKING PROGRESS.
NOT WORKING. INCREASE THE DOSAGE.
MIGHT NEED TO TRY MORE AGGRESSIVE METHODS.

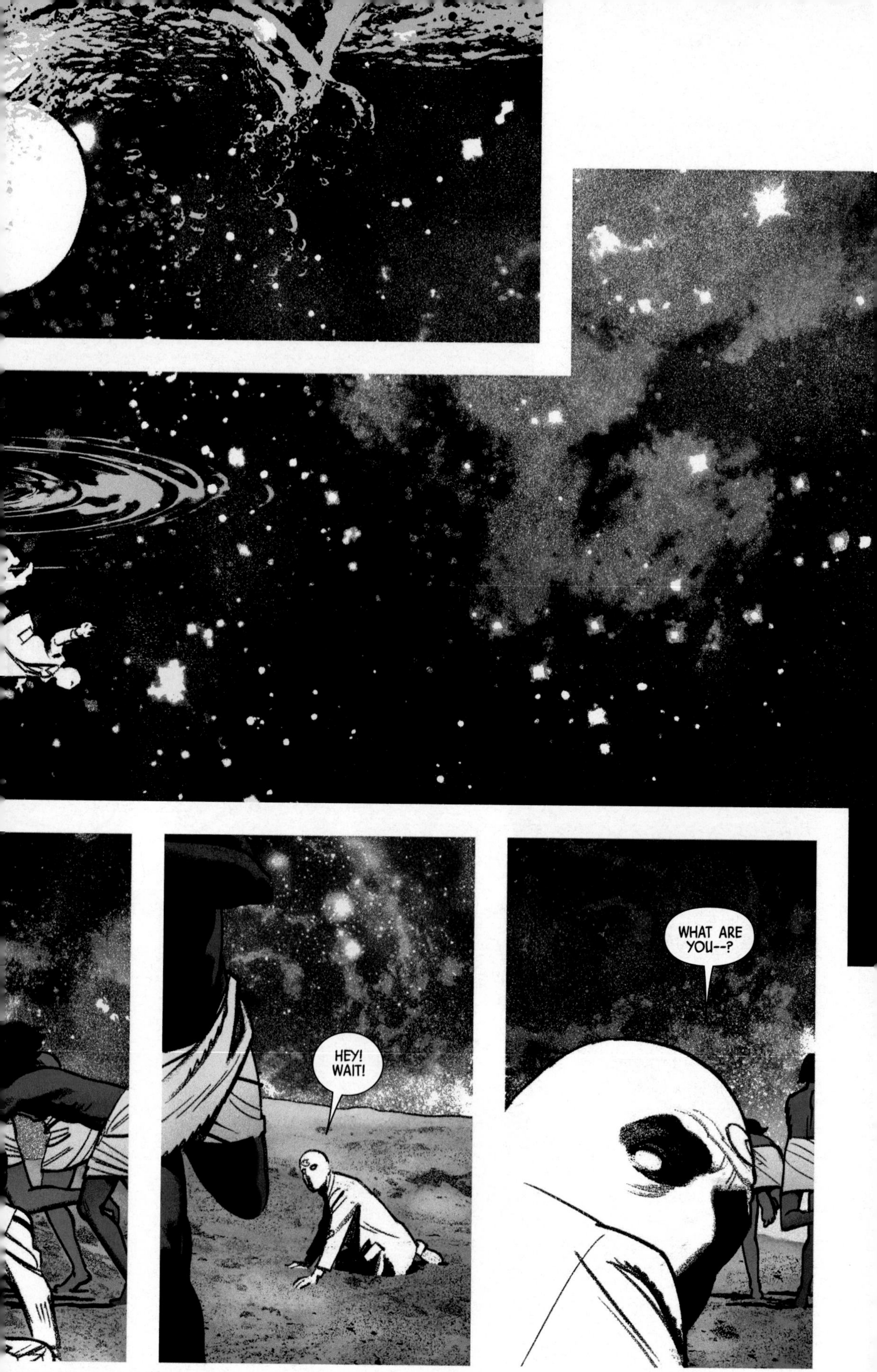
HEY! WAIT!
WHAT ARE YOU--?

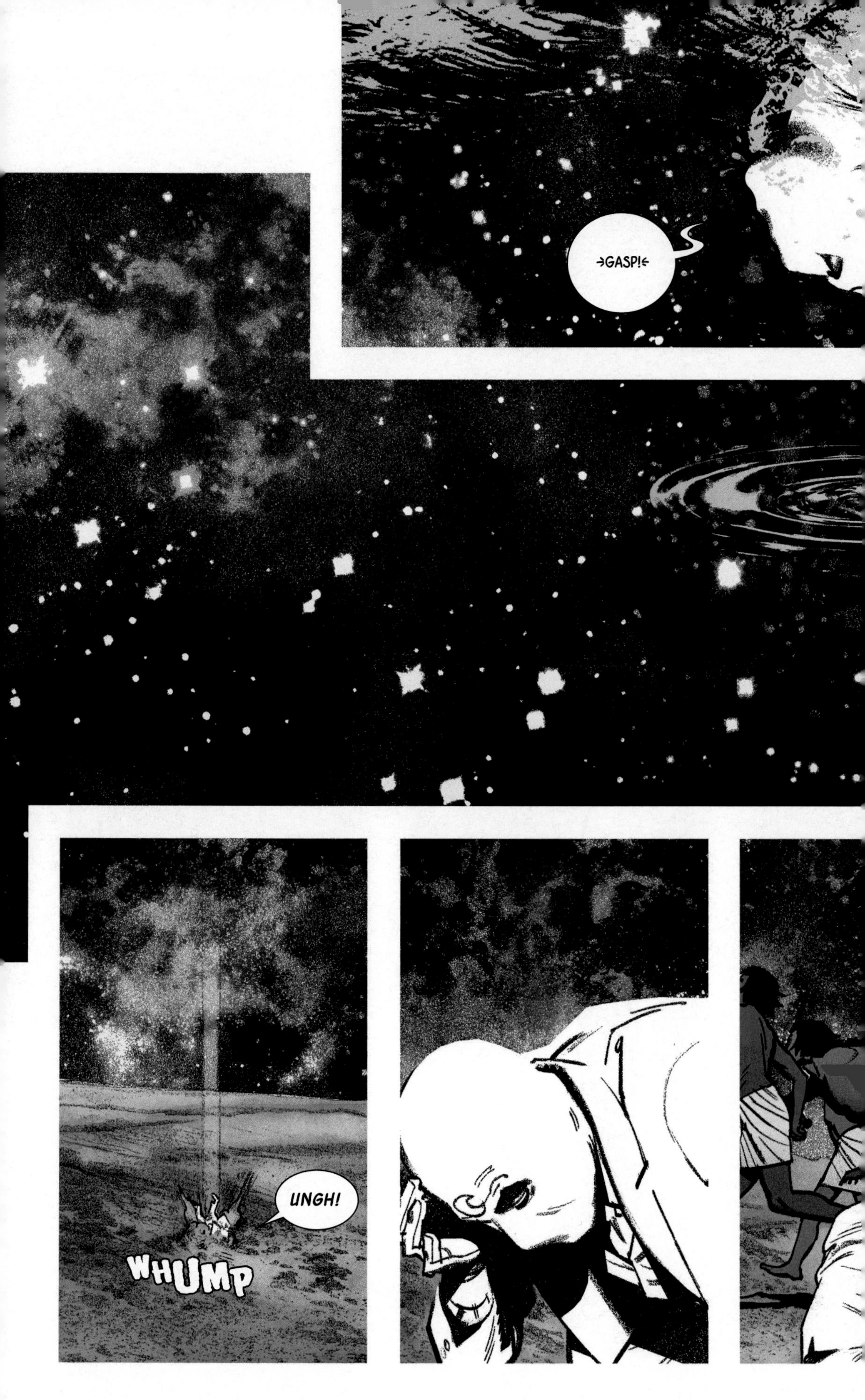

GASP!
UNGH!
WHUMP

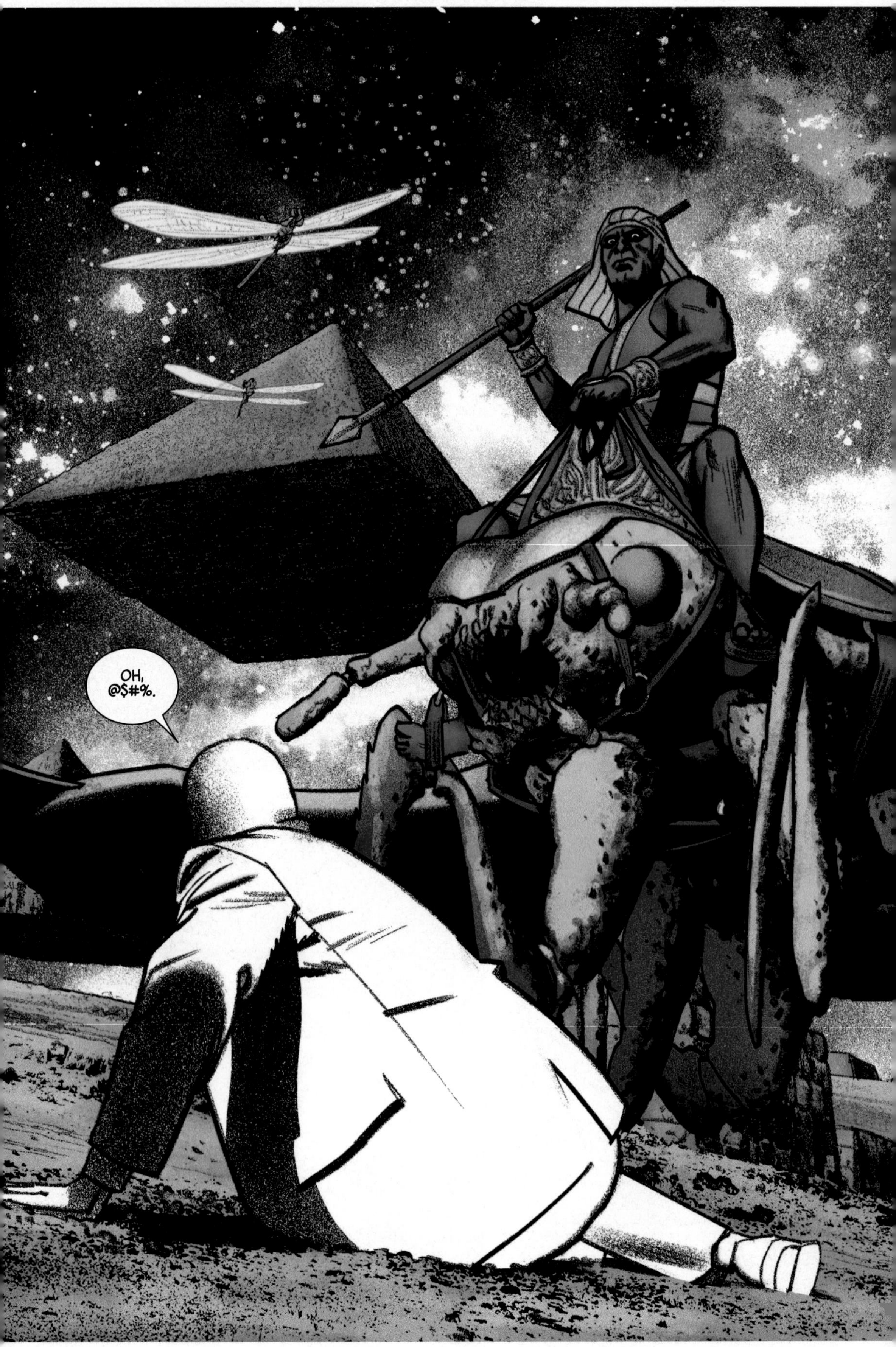
OH, @$#%.

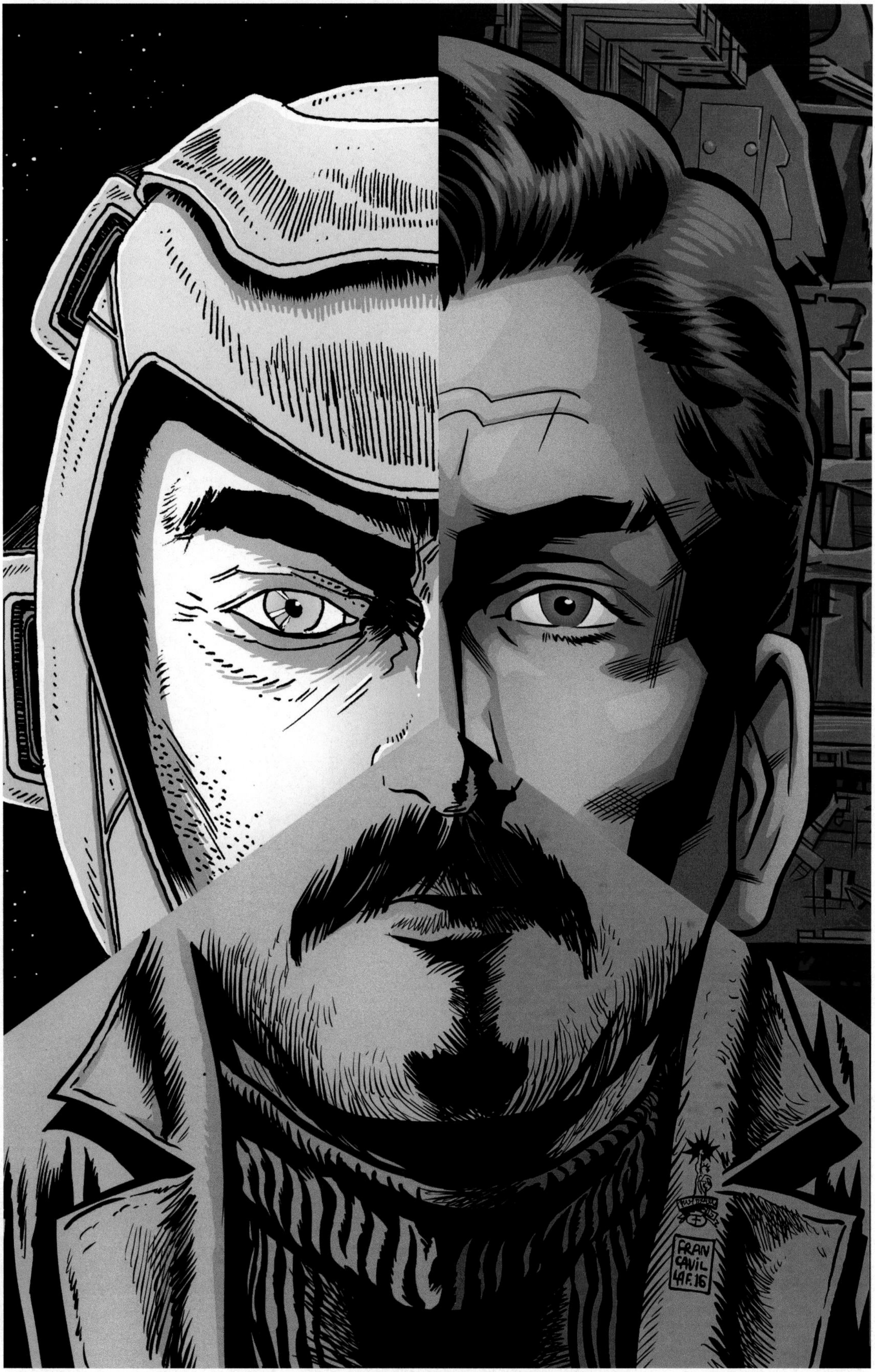
FRAN CAVIL LA F. 16

#10 STORY THUS FAR VARIANT BY FRANCESCO FRANCAVILLA, JAMES STOKOE, WILFREDO TORRES & MICHAEL GARLAND

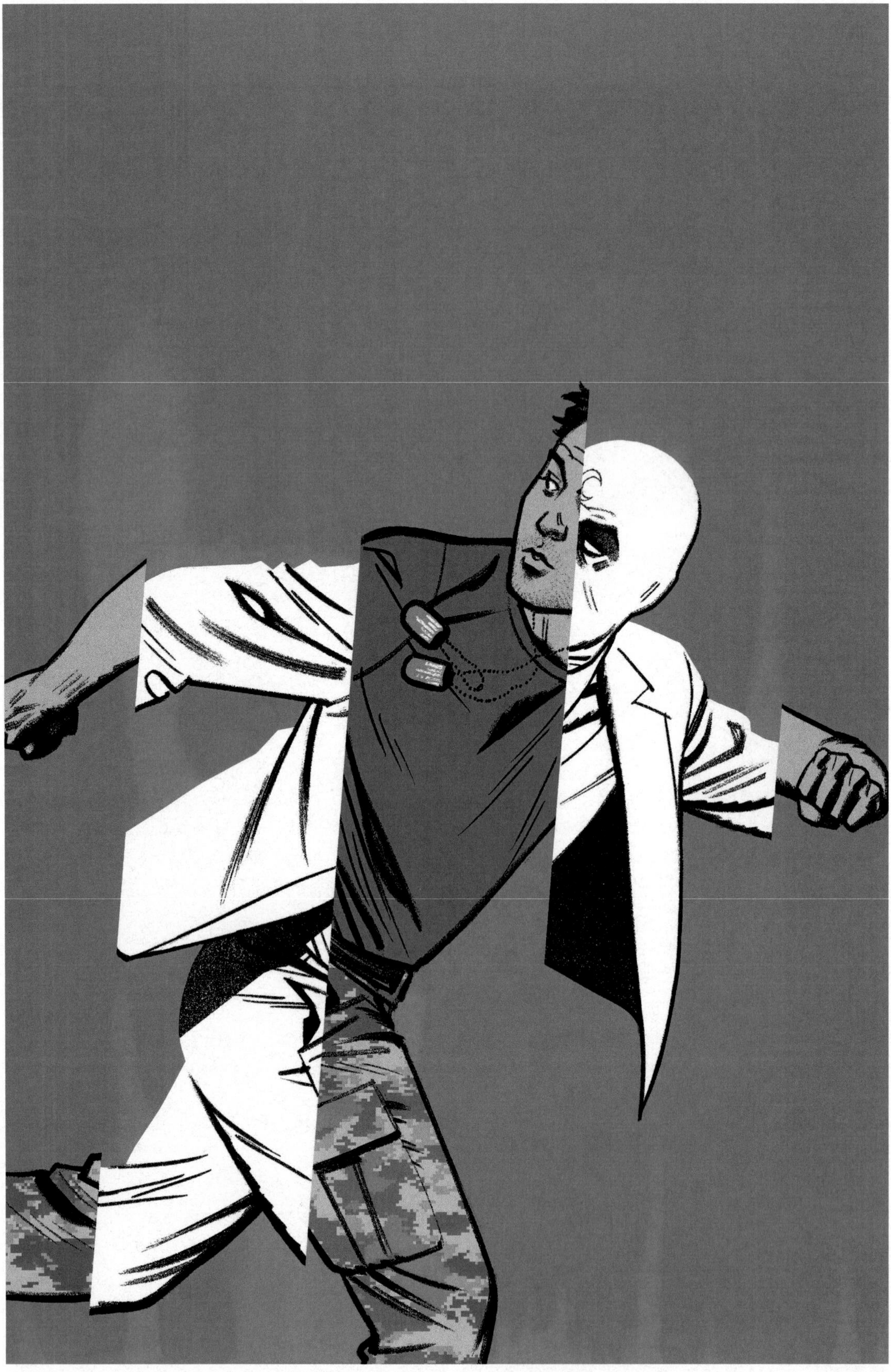

BIRTH AND DEATH
PART TWO

11

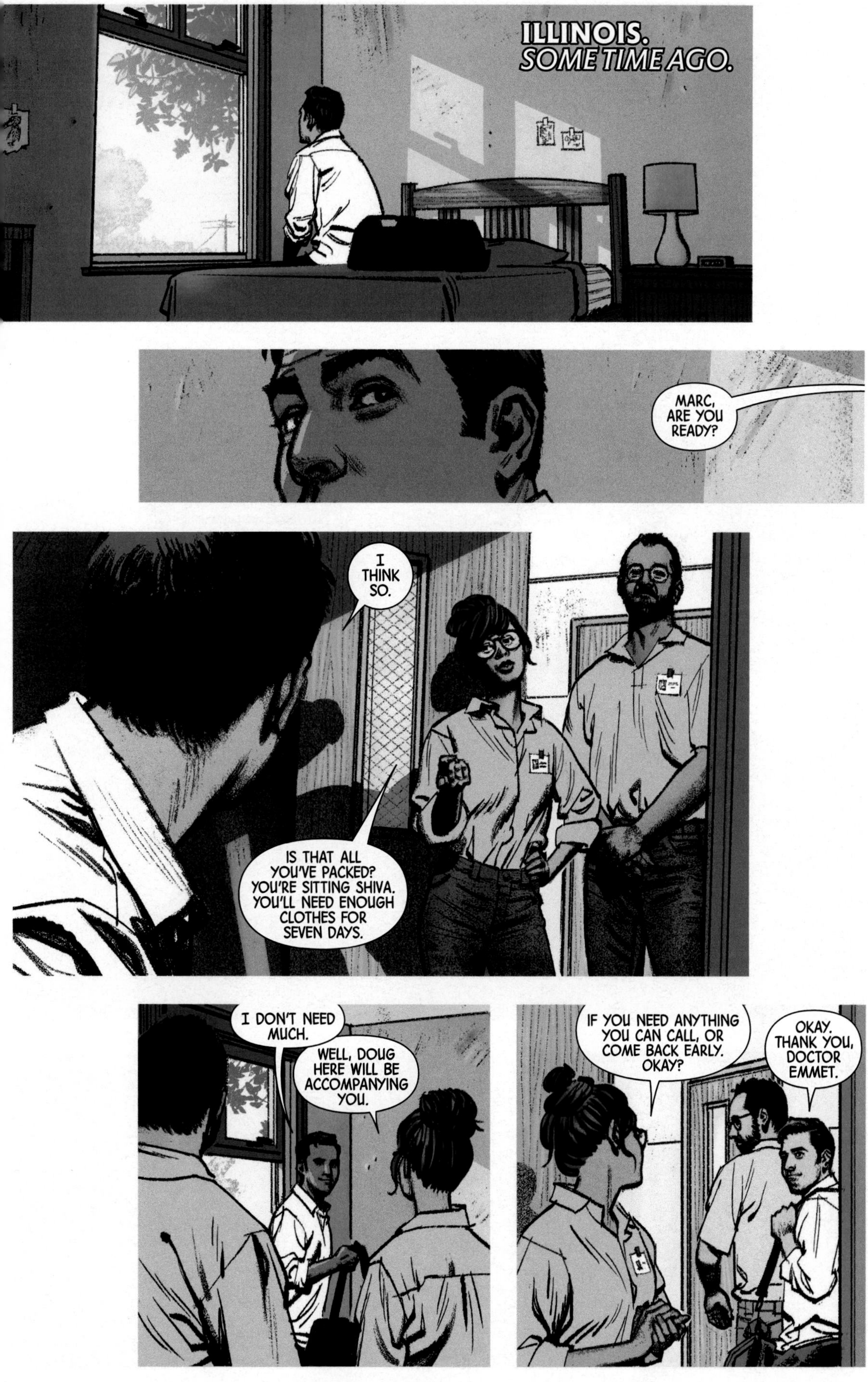
ILLINOIS.
SOME TIME AGO.
MARC, ARE YOU READY?
I THINK SO.
IS THAT ALL YOU'VE PACKED? YOU'RE SITTING SHIVA. YOU'LL NEED ENOUGH CLOTHES FOR SEVEN DAYS.
I DON'T NEED MUCH.
WELL, DOUG HERE WILL BE ACCOMPANYING YOU.
IF YOU NEED ANYTHING YOU CAN CALL, OR COME BACK EARLY. OKAY?
OKAY. THANK YOU, DOCTOR EMMET.

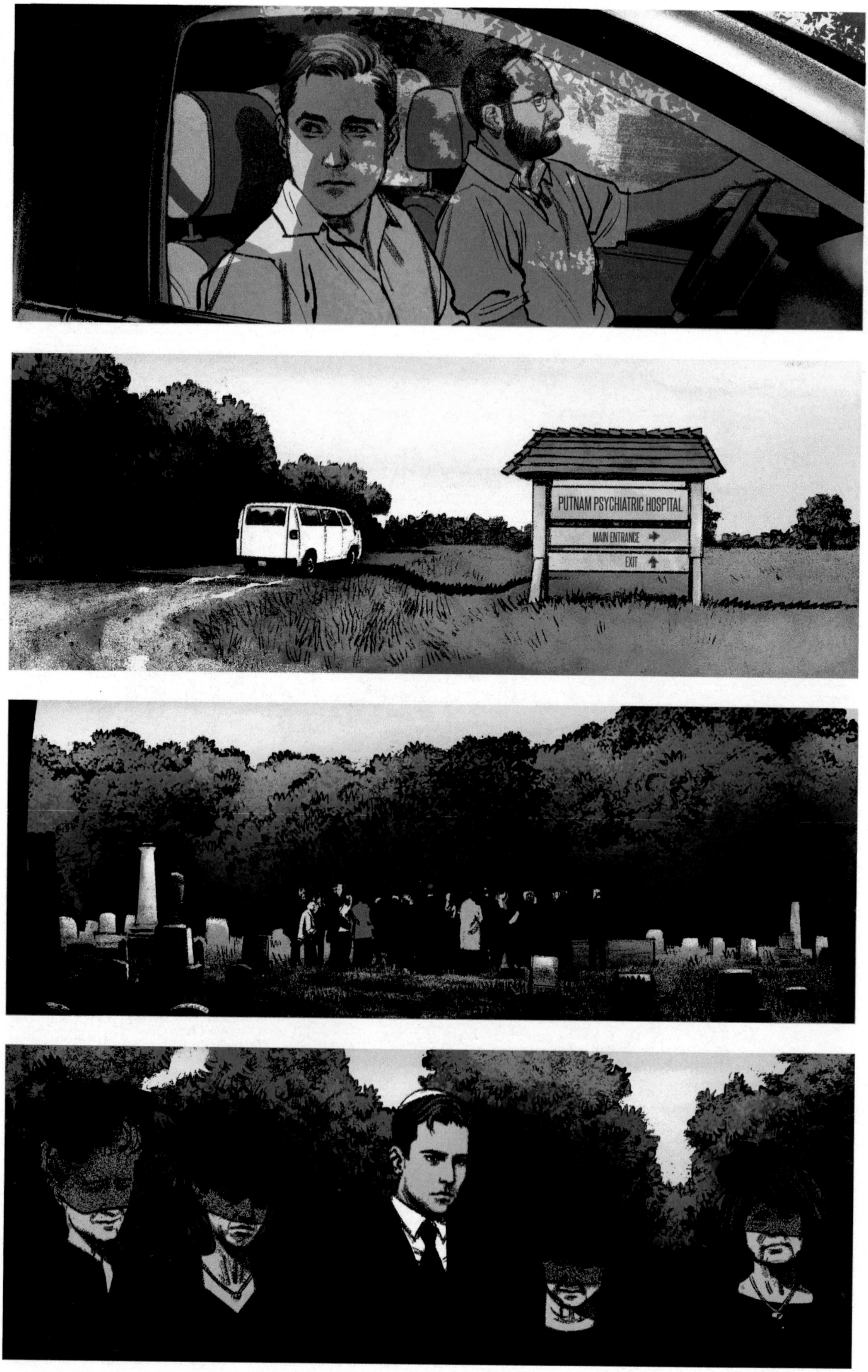
PUTNAM PSYCHIATRIC HOSPITAL
MAIN ENTRANCE
EXIT

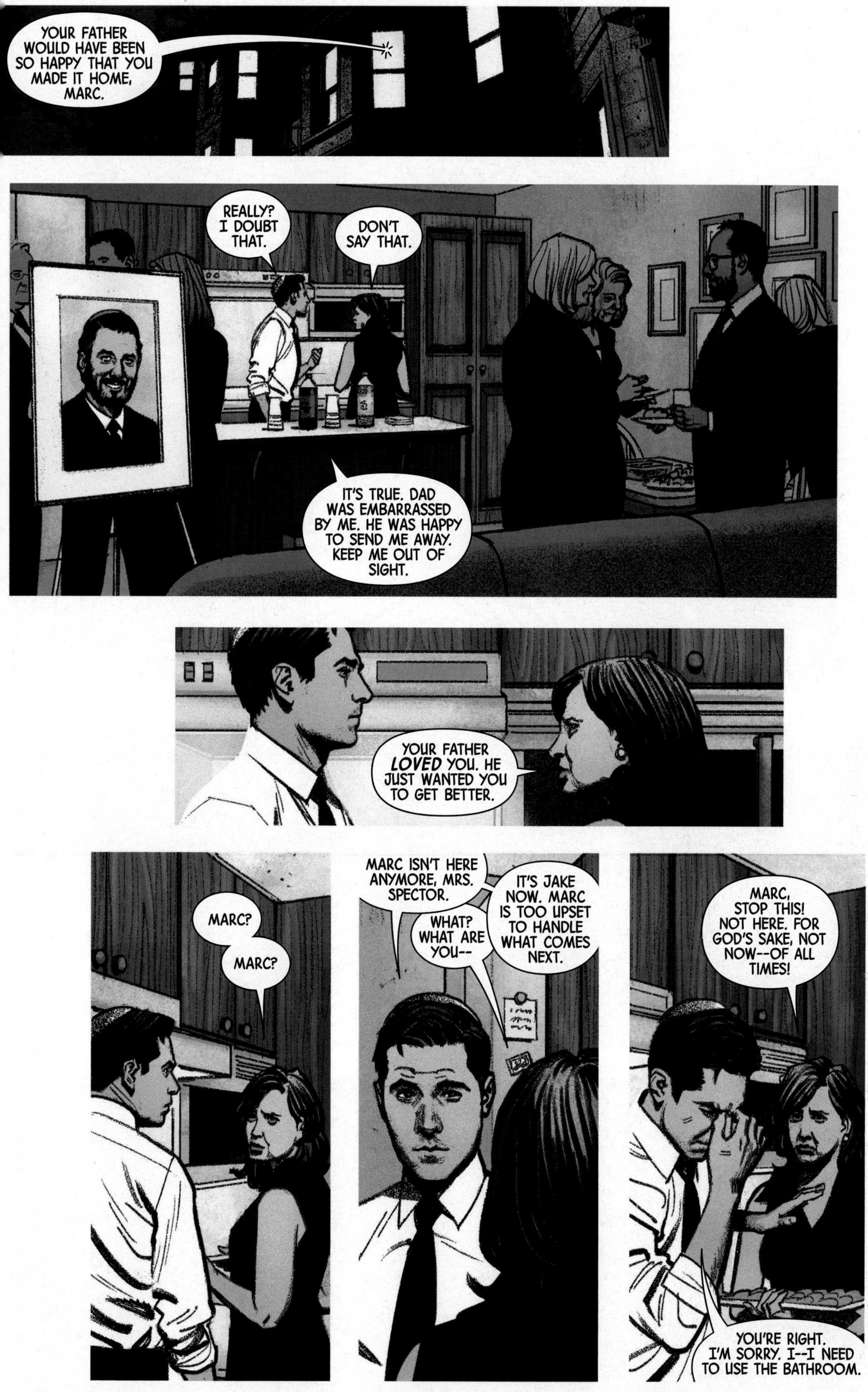
YOUR FATHER WOULD HAVE BEEN SO HAPPY THAT YOU MADE IT HOME, MARC.
REALLY? I DOUBT THAT.
DON'T SAY THAT.
IT'S TRUE. DAD WAS EMBARRASSED BY ME. HE WAS HAPPY TO SEND ME AWAY. KEEP ME OUT OF SIGHT.
YOUR FATHER LOVED YOU. HE JUST WANTED YOU TO GET BETTER.
MARC?
MARC?
MARC ISN'T HERE ANYMORE, MRS. SPECTOR.
WHAT? WHAT ARE YOU--
IT'S JAKE NOW. MARC IS TOO UPSET TO HANDLE WHAT COMES NEXT.
MARC, STOP THIS! NOT HERE. FOR GOD'S SAKE, NOT NOW--OF ALL TIMES!
YOU'RE RIGHT. I'M SORRY. I--I NEED TO USE THE BATHROOM.

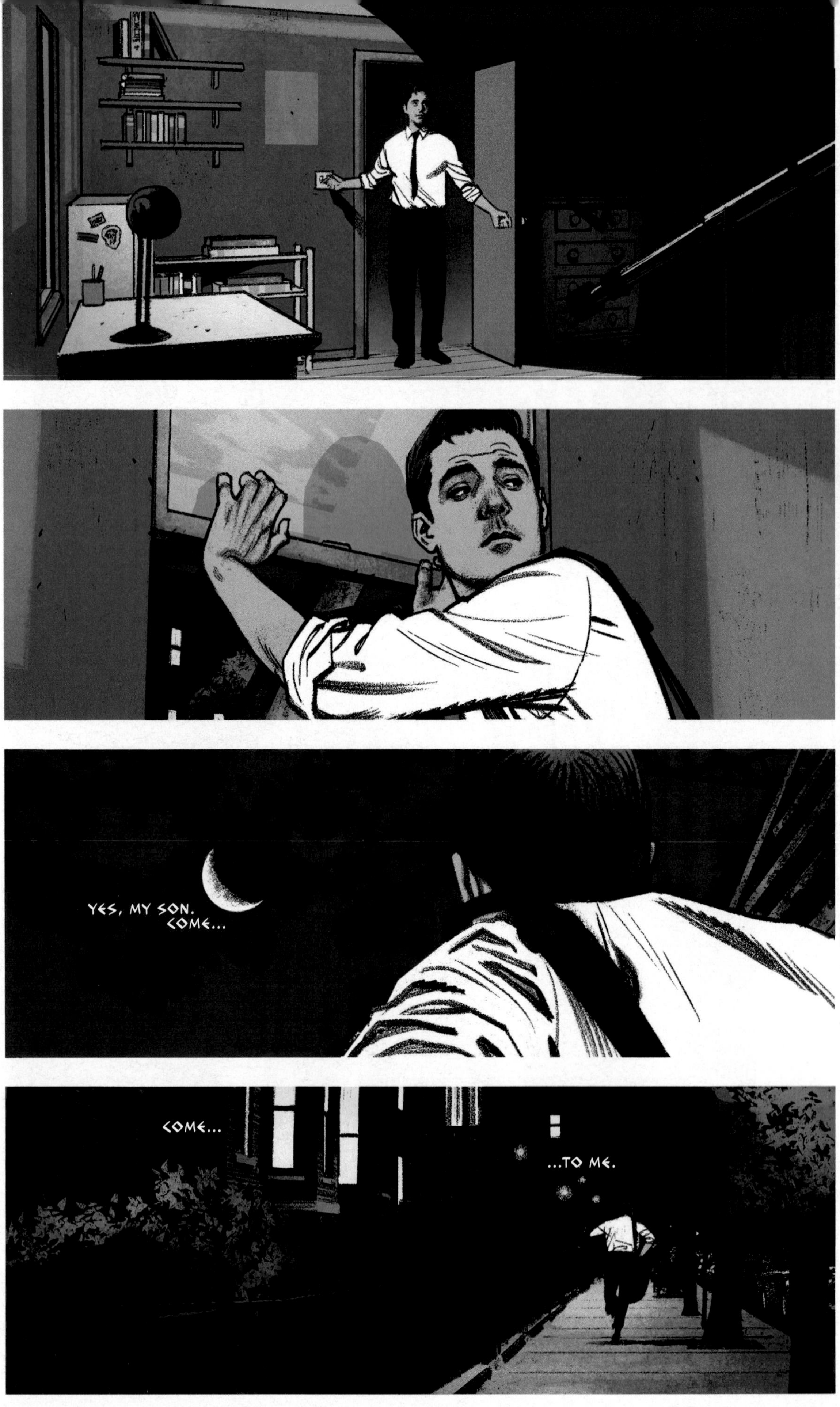
YES, MY SON.
COME...
COME...
...TO ME.

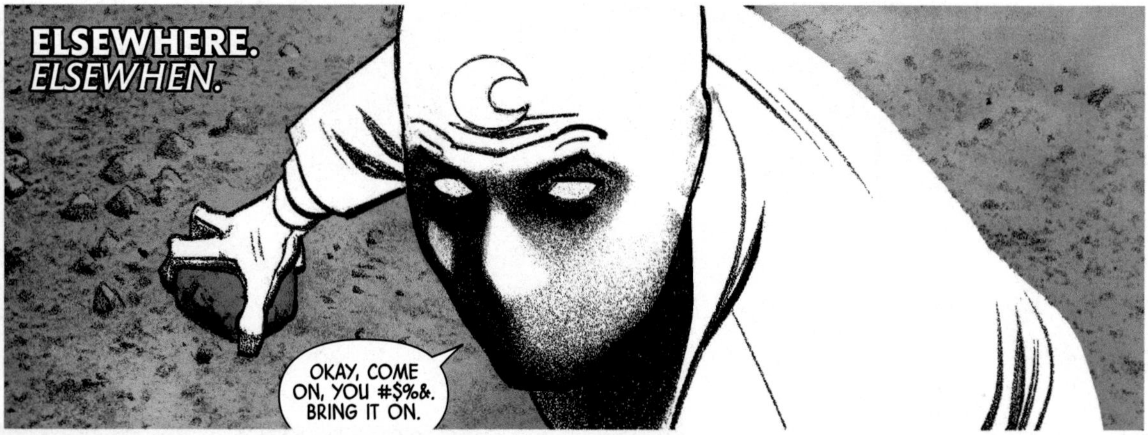
ELSEWHERE.
ELSEWHEN.
OKAY, COME ON, YOU #$%&. BRING IT ON.

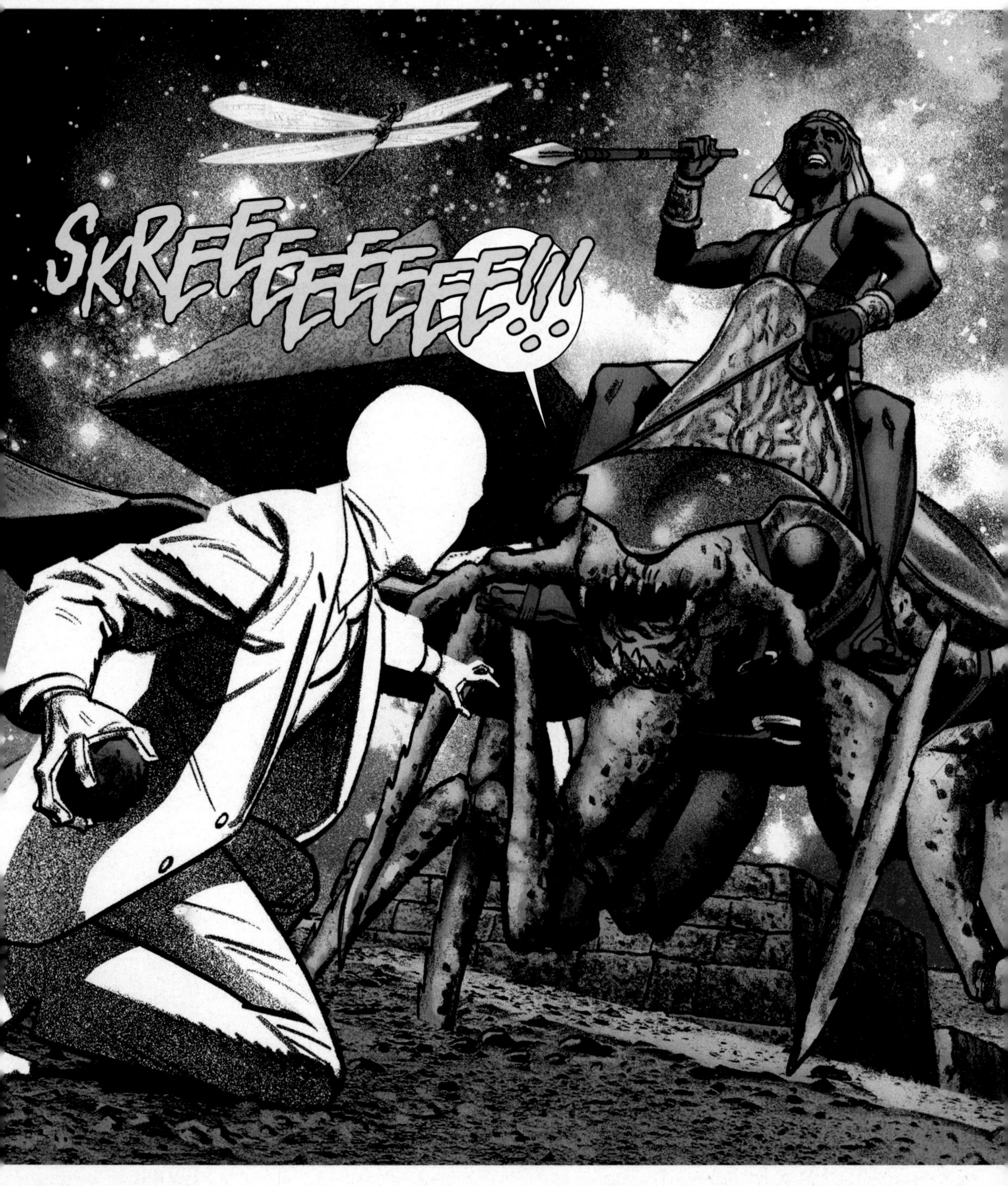
SKREEEEEEEEEE!!!

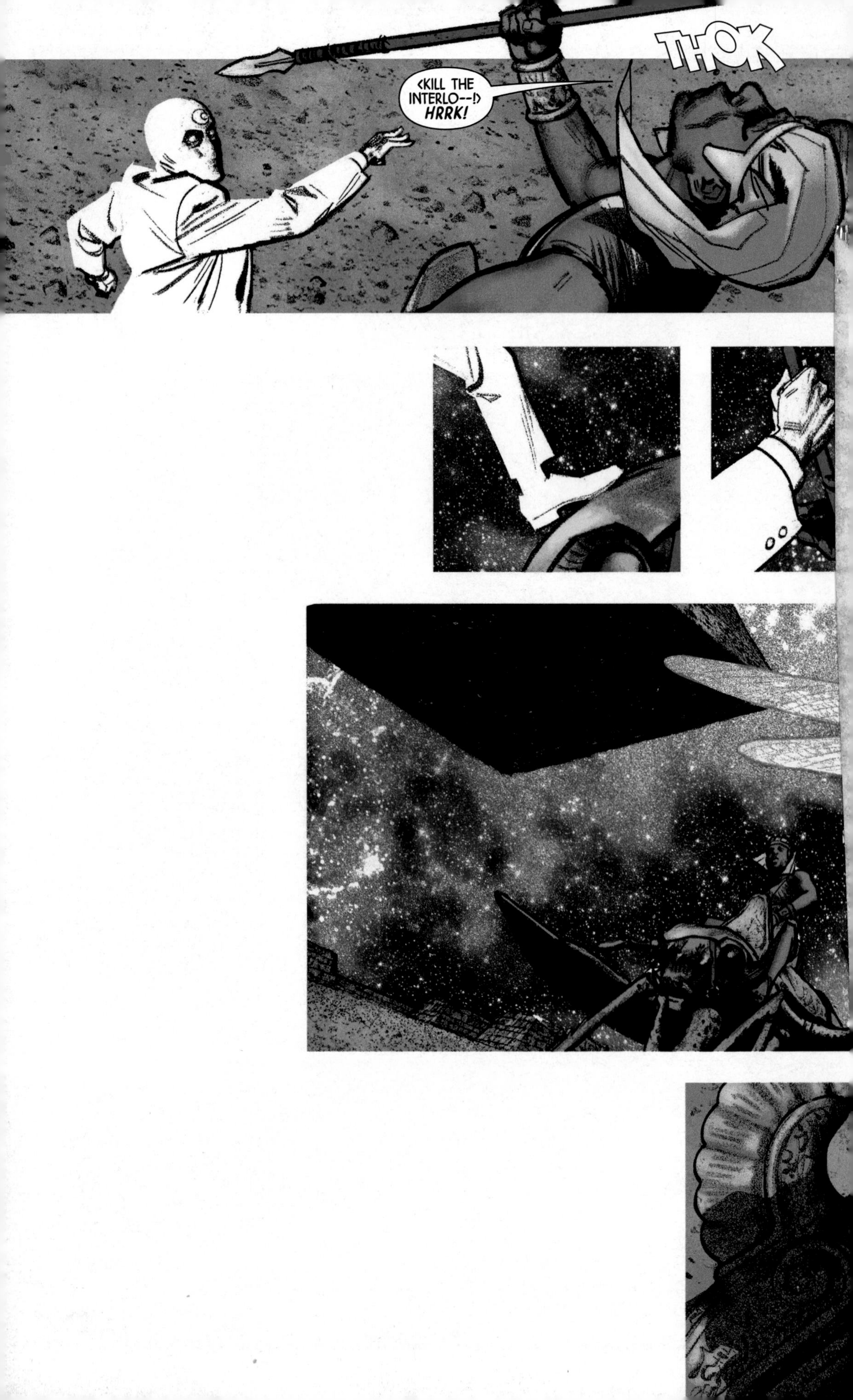
<KILL THE INTERLO--!> HRRK!
THOK

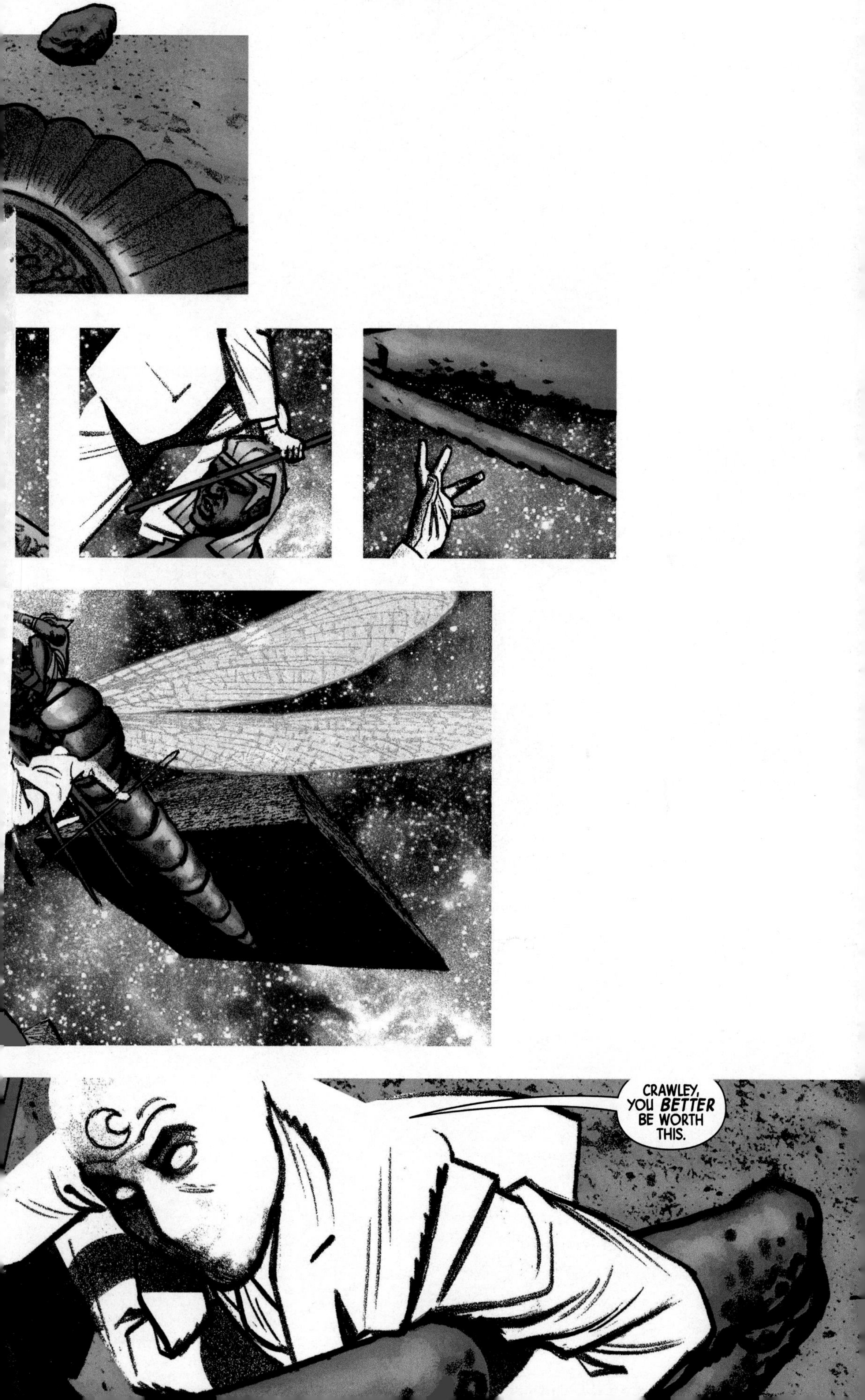
CRAWLEY, YOU BETTER BE WORTH THIS.

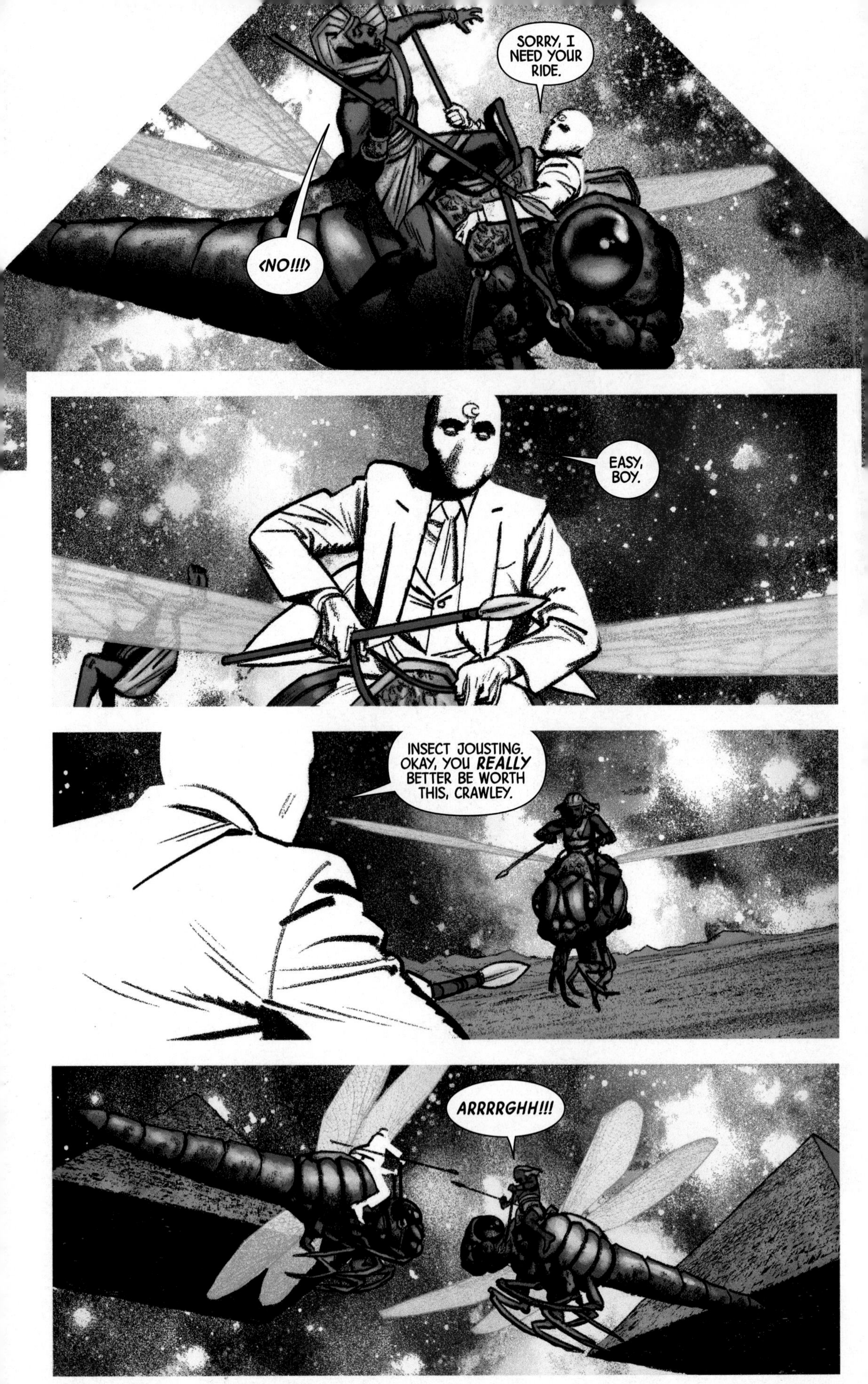
SORRY, I NEED YOUR RIDE.
<NO!!!>
EASY, BOY.
INSECT JOUSTING. OKAY, YOU *REALLY* BETTER BE WORTH THIS, CRAWLEY.
ARRRRGHH!!!

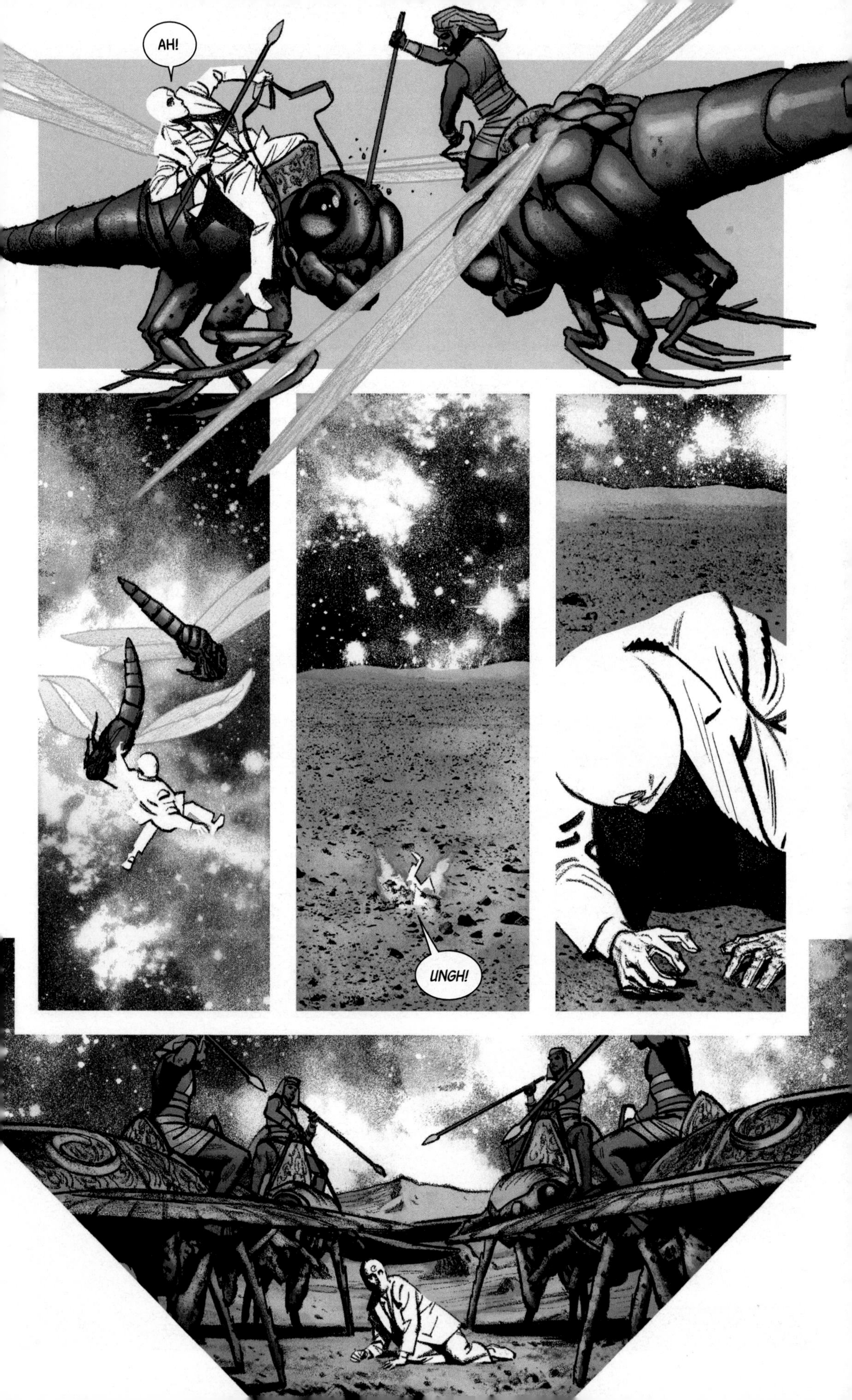
AH!
UNGH!

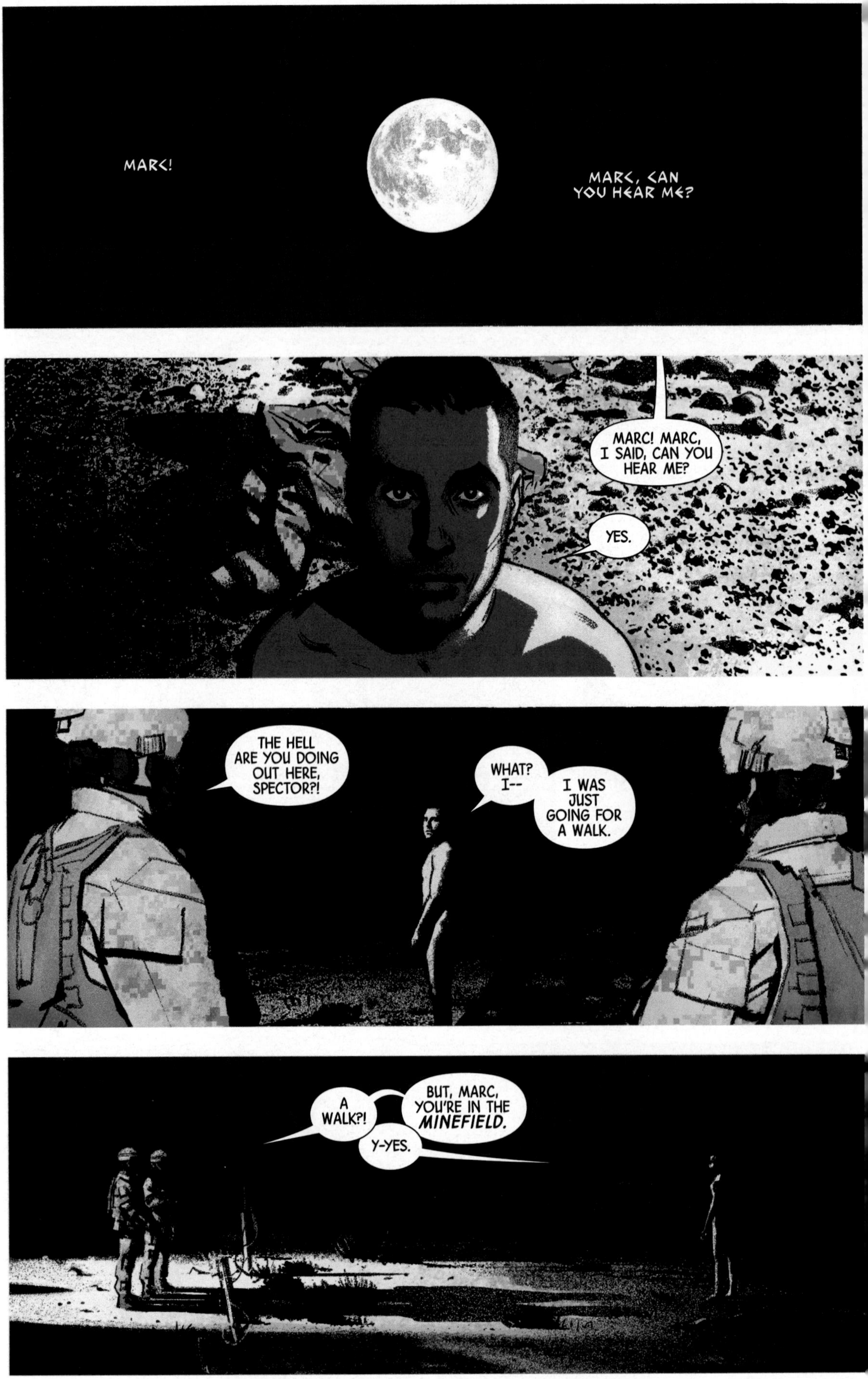
MARC!
MARC, CAN YOU HEAR ME?
MARC! MARC, I SAID, CAN YOU HEAR ME?
YES.
THE HELL ARE YOU DOING OUT HERE, SPECTOR?!
WHAT? I--
I WAS JUST GOING FOR A WALK.
A WALK?!
BUT, MARC, YOU'RE IN THE *MINEFIELD.*
Y-YES.

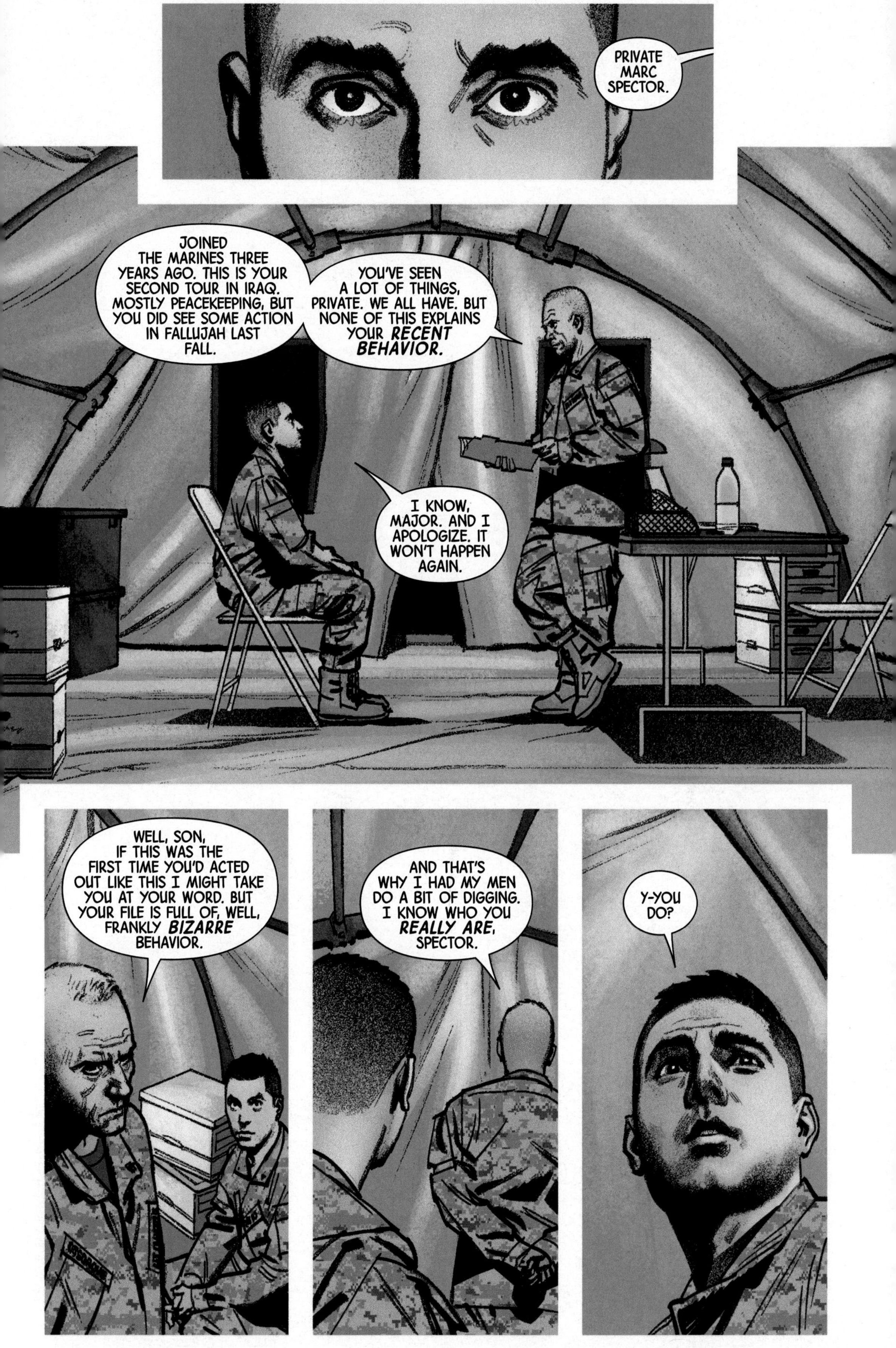
PRIVATE MARC SPECTOR.
JOINED THE MARINES THREE YEARS AGO. THIS IS YOUR SECOND TOUR IN IRAQ. MOSTLY PEACEKEEPING, BUT YOU DID SEE SOME ACTION IN FALLUJAH LAST FALL.
YOU'VE SEEN A LOT OF THINGS, PRIVATE. WE ALL HAVE. BUT NONE OF THIS EXPLAINS YOUR RECENT BEHAVIOR.
I KNOW, MAJOR. AND I APOLOGIZE. IT WON'T HAPPEN AGAIN.
WELL, SON, IF THIS WAS THE FIRST TIME YOU'D ACTED OUT LIKE THIS I MIGHT TAKE YOU AT YOUR WORD. BUT YOUR FILE IS FULL OF, WELL, FRANKLY BIZARRE BEHAVIOR.
AND THAT'S WHY I HAD MY MEN DO A BIT OF DIGGING. I KNOW WHO YOU REALLY ARE, SPECTOR.
Y-YOU DO?

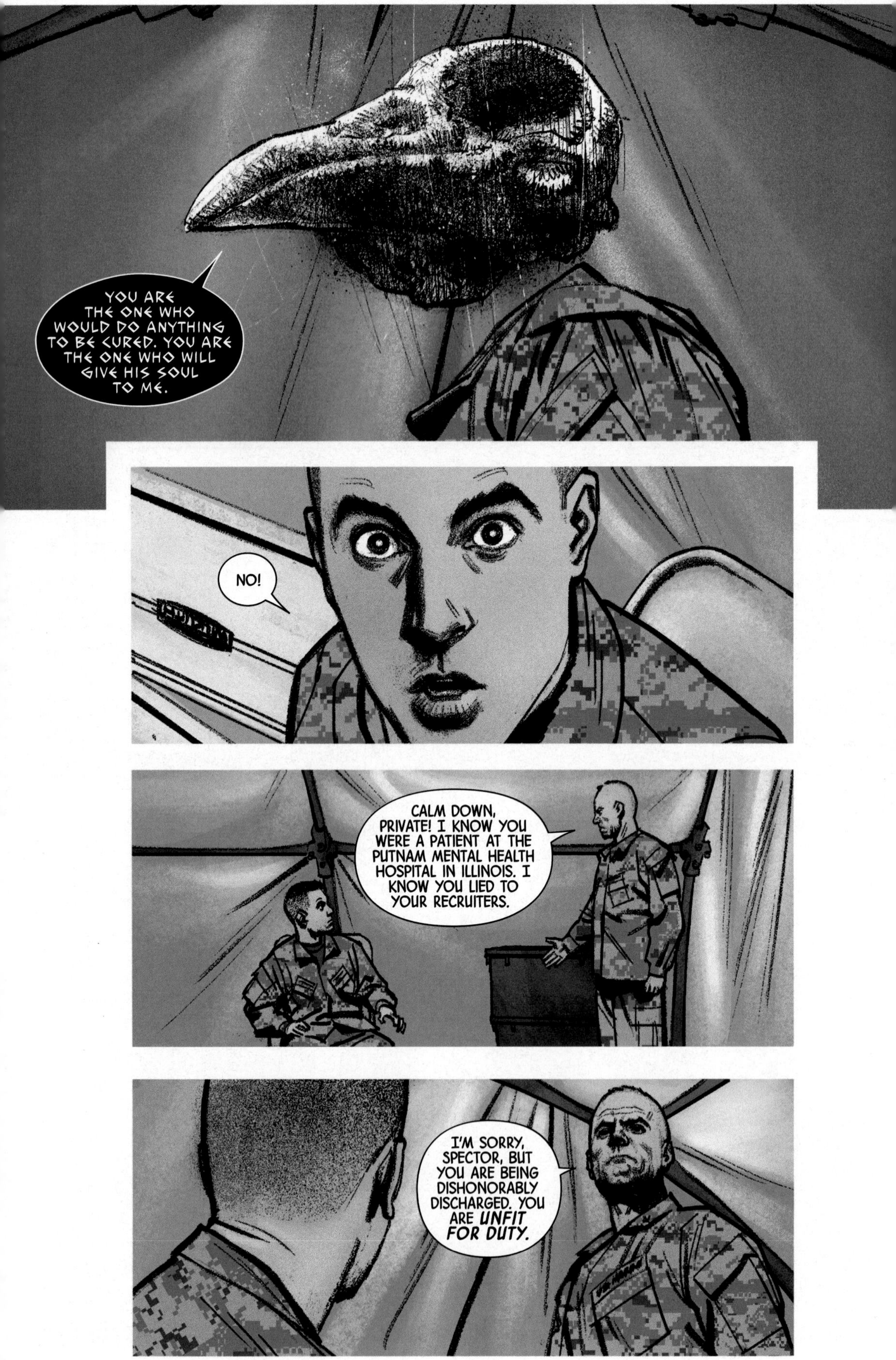
YOU ARE THE ONE WHO WOULD DO ANYTHING TO BE CURED. YOU ARE THE ONE WHO WILL GIVE HIS SOUL TO ME.
NO!
CALM DOWN, PRIVATE! I KNOW YOU WERE A PATIENT AT THE PUTNAM MENTAL HEALTH HOSPITAL IN ILLINOIS. I KNOW YOU LIED TO YOUR RECRUITERS.
I'M SORRY, SPECTOR, BUT YOU ARE BEING DISHONORABLY DISCHARGED. YOU ARE *UNFIT FOR DUTY.*

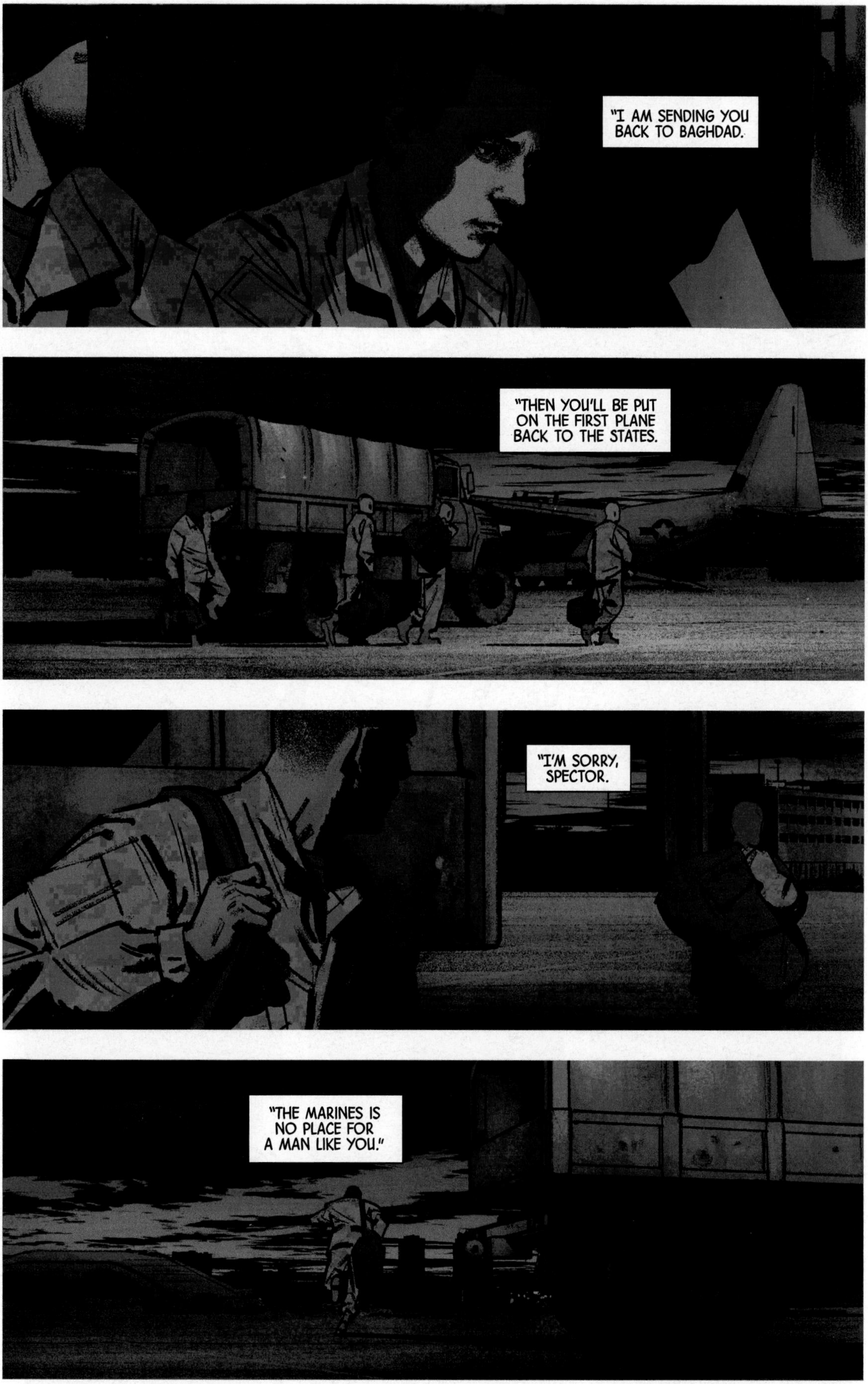
"I AM SENDING YOU BACK TO BAGHDAD.
"THEN YOU'LL BE PUT ON THE FIRST PLANE BACK TO THE STATES.
"I'M SORRY, SPECTOR.
"THE MARINES IS NO PLACE FOR A MAN LIKE YOU."

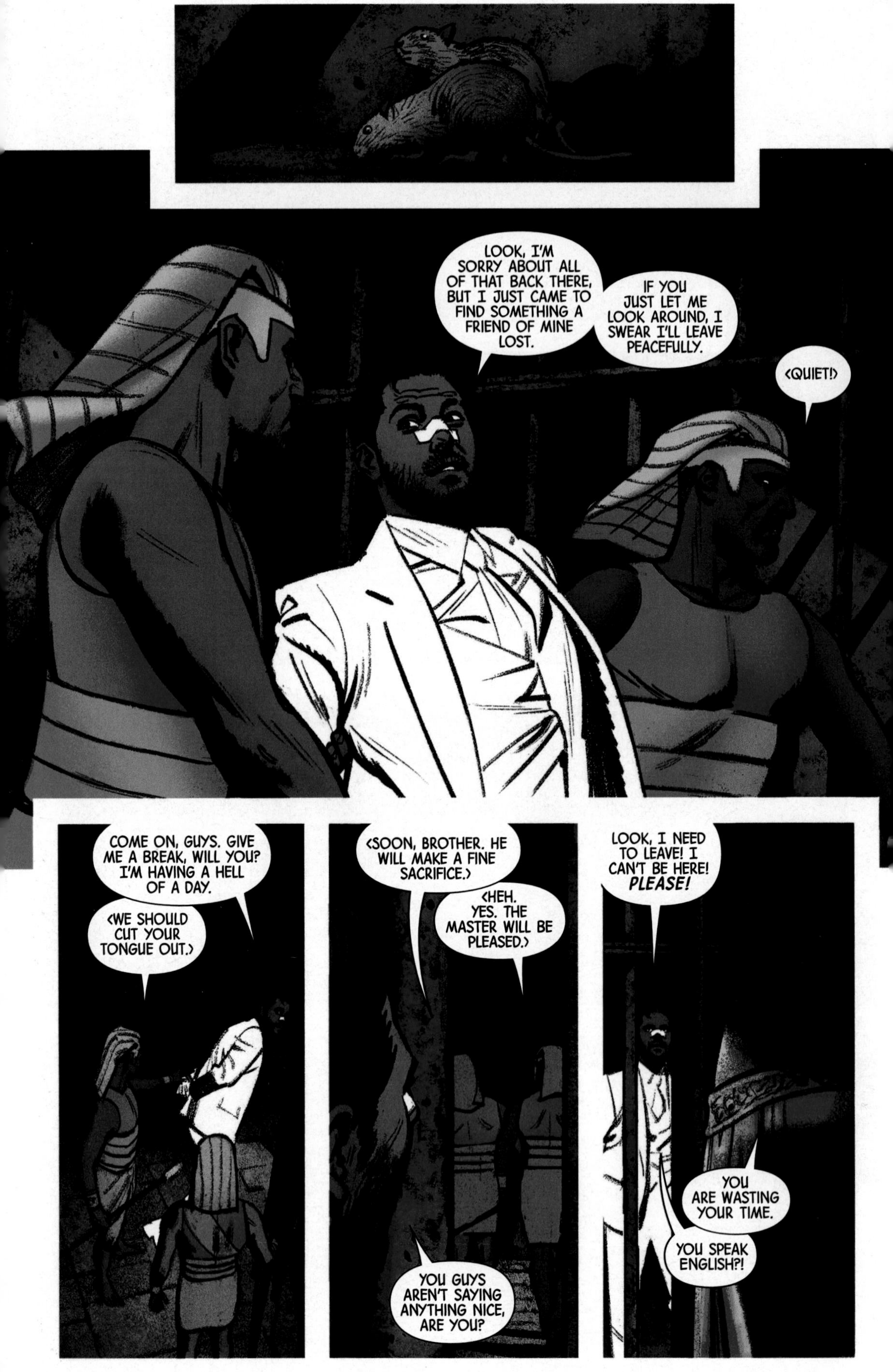
LOOK, I'M SORRY ABOUT ALL OF THAT BACK THERE, BUT I JUST CAME TO FIND SOMETHING A FRIEND OF MINE LOST.
IF YOU JUST LET ME LOOK AROUND, I SWEAR I'LL LEAVE PEACEFULLY.
<QUIET!>
COME ON, GUYS. GIVE ME A BREAK, WILL YOU? I'M HAVING A HELL OF A DAY.
<WE SHOULD CUT YOUR TONGUE OUT.>
<SOON, BROTHER. HE WILL MAKE A FINE SACRIFICE.>
<HEH. YES. THE MASTER WILL BE PLEASED.>
YOU GUYS AREN'T SAYING ANYTHING NICE, ARE YOU?
LOOK, I NEED TO LEAVE! I CAN'T BE HERE! *PLEASE!*
YOU ARE WASTING YOUR TIME.
YOU SPEAK ENGLISH?!

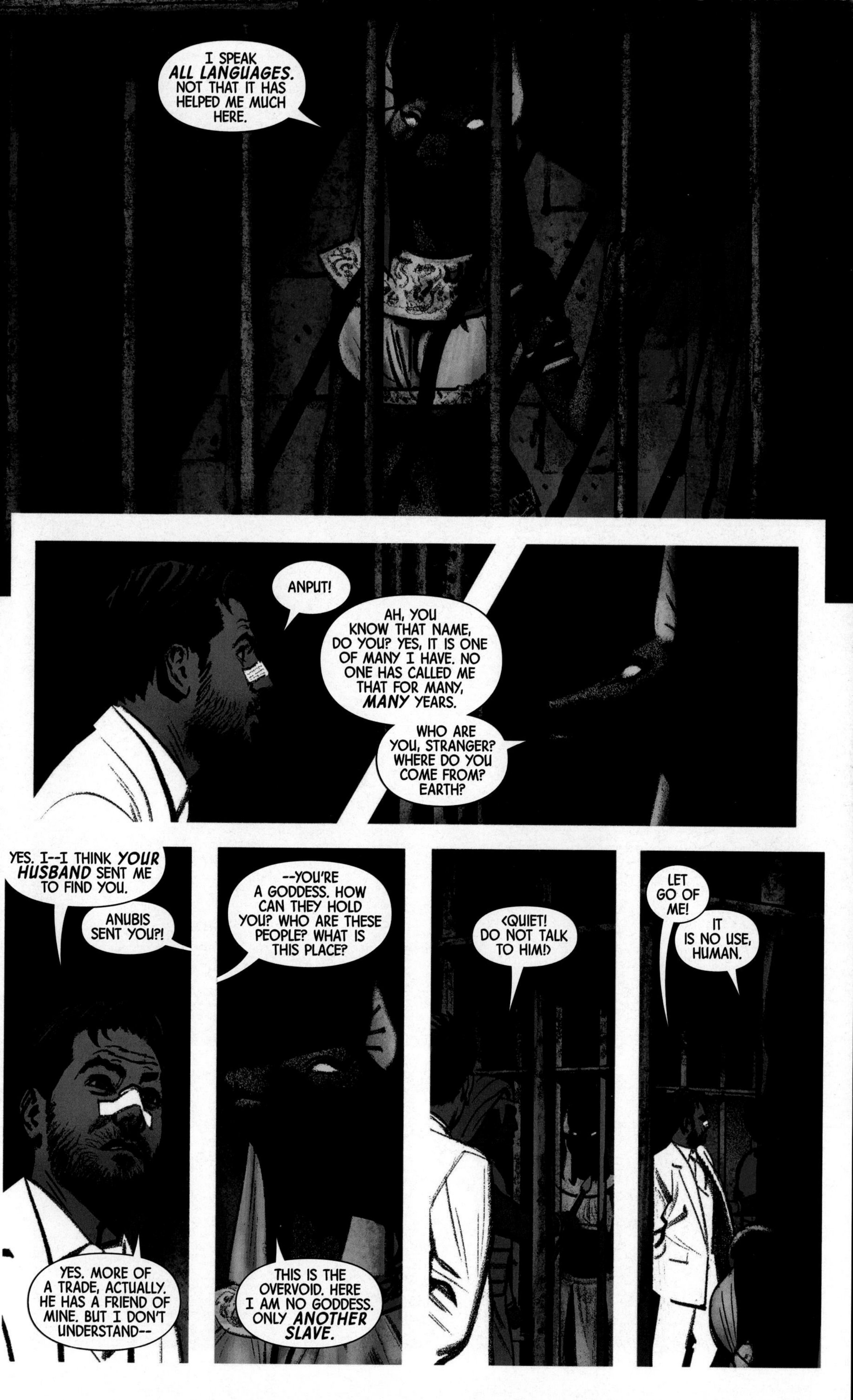

I SPEAK ALL LANGUAGES. NOT THAT IT HAS HELPED ME MUCH HERE.
ANPUT!
AH, YOU KNOW THAT NAME, DO YOU? YES, IT IS ONE OF MANY I HAVE. NO ONE HAS CALLED ME THAT FOR MANY, MANY YEARS.
WHO ARE YOU, STRANGER? WHERE DO YOU COME FROM? EARTH?
YES. I--I THINK YOUR HUSBAND SENT ME TO FIND YOU.
ANUBIS SENT YOU?!
YES. MORE OF A TRADE, ACTUALLY. HE HAS A FRIEND OF MINE. BUT I DON'T UNDERSTAND--
--YOU'RE A GODDESS. HOW CAN THEY HOLD YOU? WHO ARE THESE PEOPLE? WHAT IS THIS PLACE?
THIS IS THE OVERVOID. HERE I AM NO GODDESS. ONLY ANOTHER SLAVE.
<QUIET! DO NOT TALK TO HIM!>
LET GO OF ME!
IT IS NO USE, HUMAN.

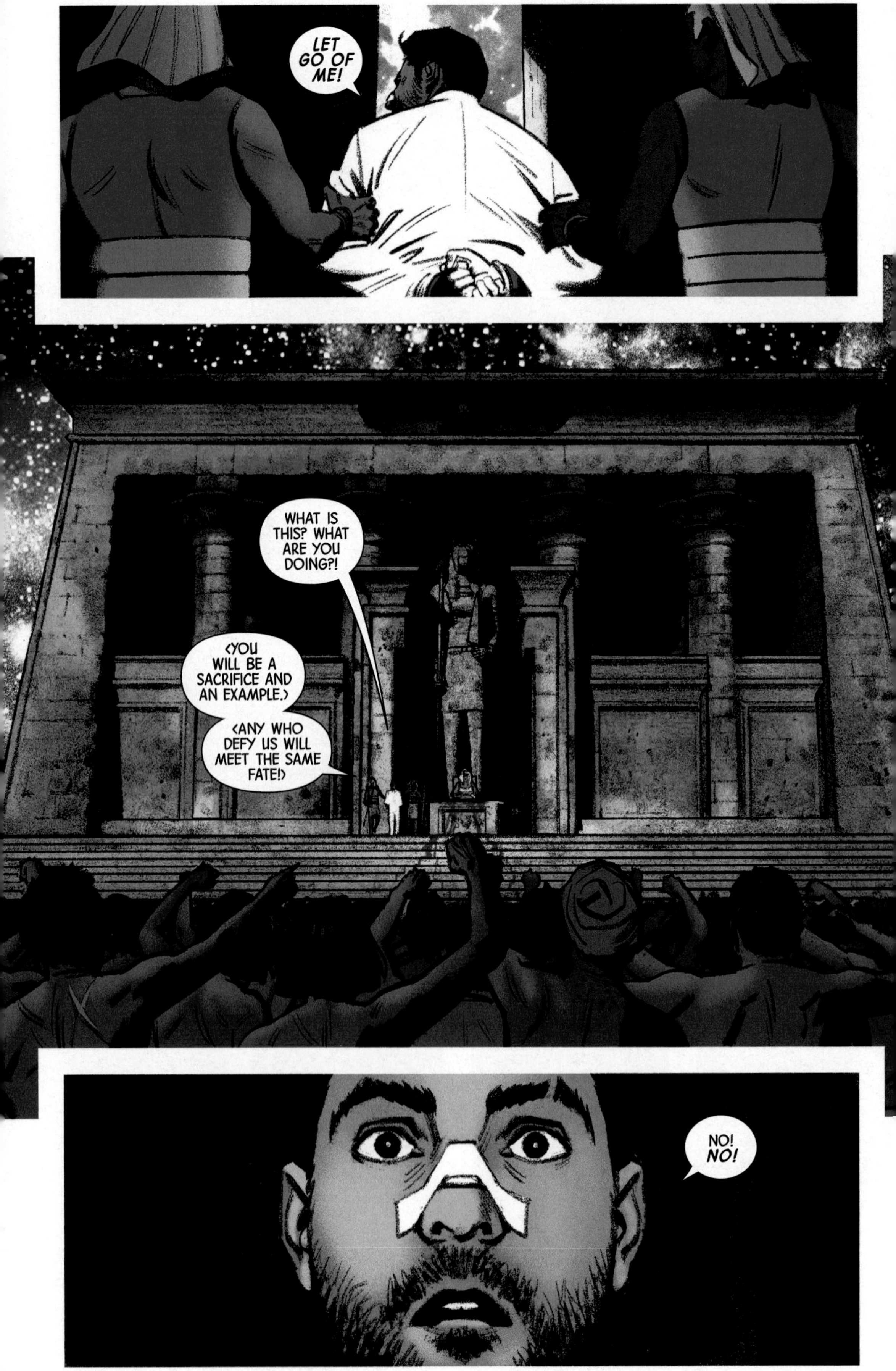
LET GO OF ME!
WHAT IS THIS? WHAT ARE YOU DOING?!
<YOU WILL BE A SACRIFICE AND AN EXAMPLE.>
<ANY WHO DEFY US WILL MEET THE SAME FATE!>
NO! NO!

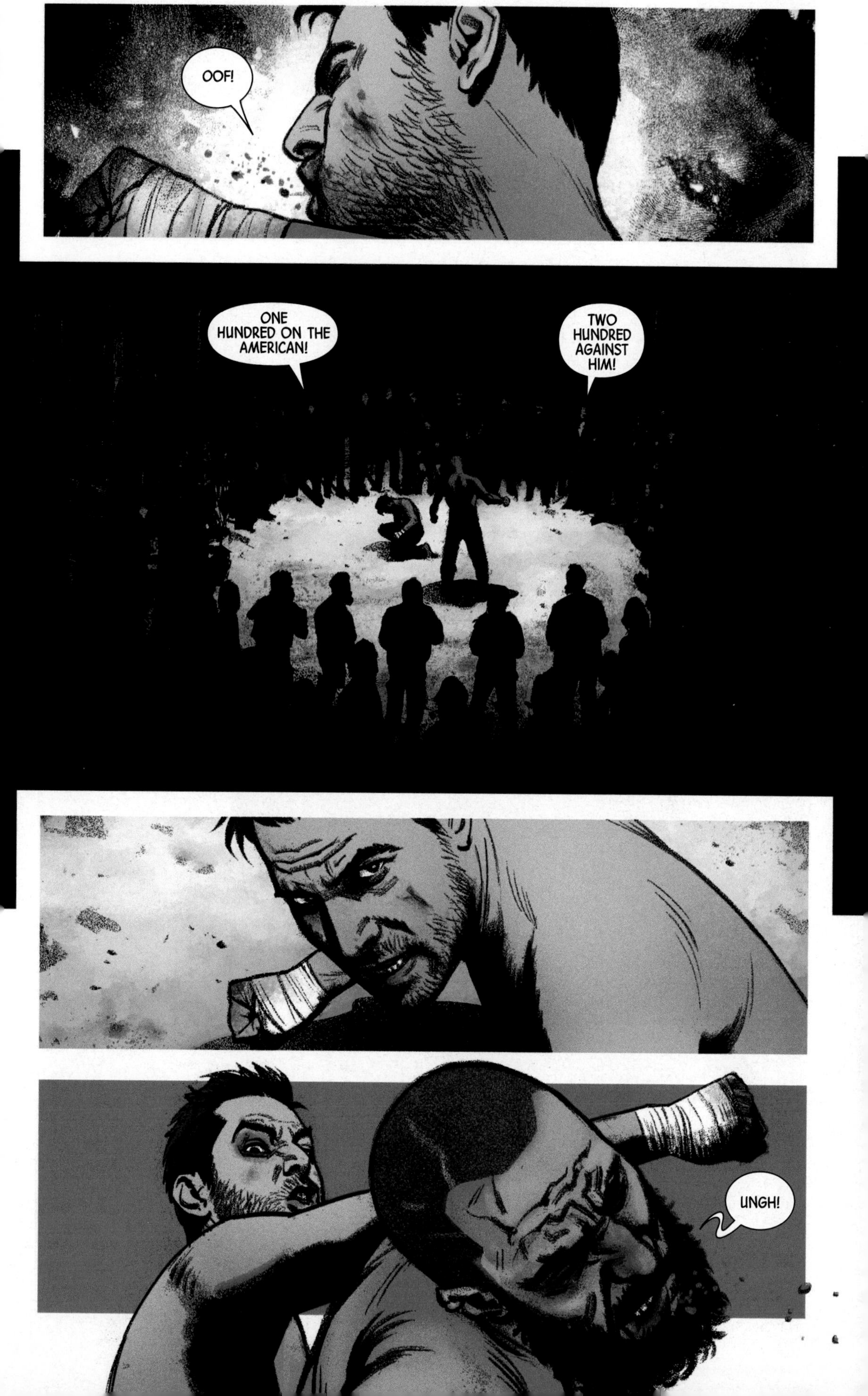
OOF!
ONE HUNDRED ON THE AMERICAN!
TWO HUNDRED AGAINST HIM!
UNGH!

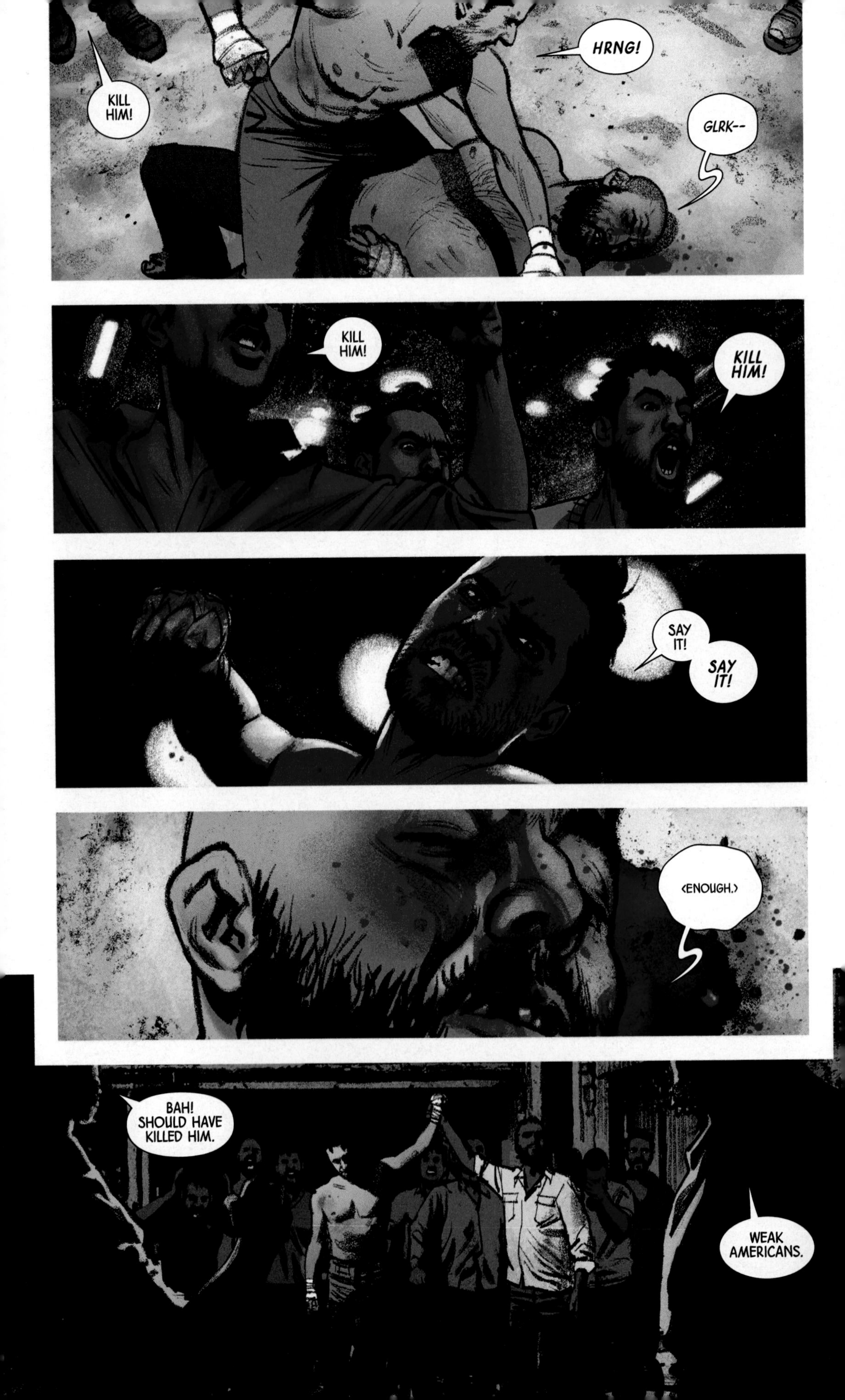
KILL HIM!
HRNG!
GLRK--
KILL HIM!
KILL HIM!
SAY IT!
SAY IT!
<ENOUGH.>
BAH! SHOULD HAVE KILLED HIM.
WEAK AMERICANS.

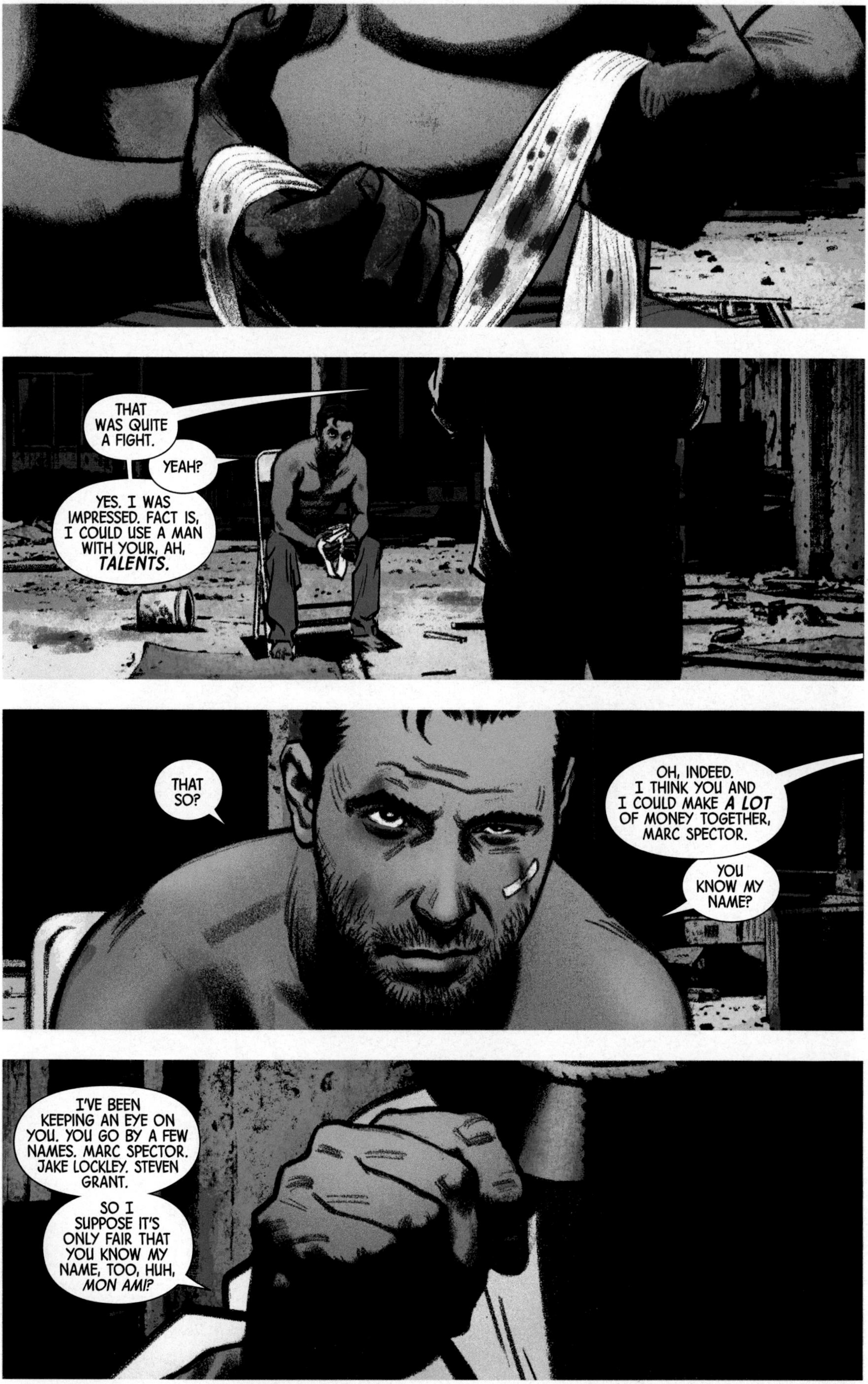
THAT WAS QUITE A FIGHT.
YEAH?
YES. I WAS IMPRESSED. FACT IS, I COULD USE A MAN WITH YOUR, AH, TALENTS.
THAT SO?
OH, INDEED. I THINK YOU AND I COULD MAKE A LOT OF MONEY TOGETHER, MARC SPECTOR.
YOU KNOW MY NAME?
I'VE BEEN KEEPING AN EYE ON YOU. YOU GO BY A FEW NAMES. MARC SPECTOR. JAKE LOCKLEY. STEVEN GRANT.
SO I SUPPOSE IT'S ONLY FAIR THAT YOU KNOW MY NAME, TOO, HUH, MON AMI?

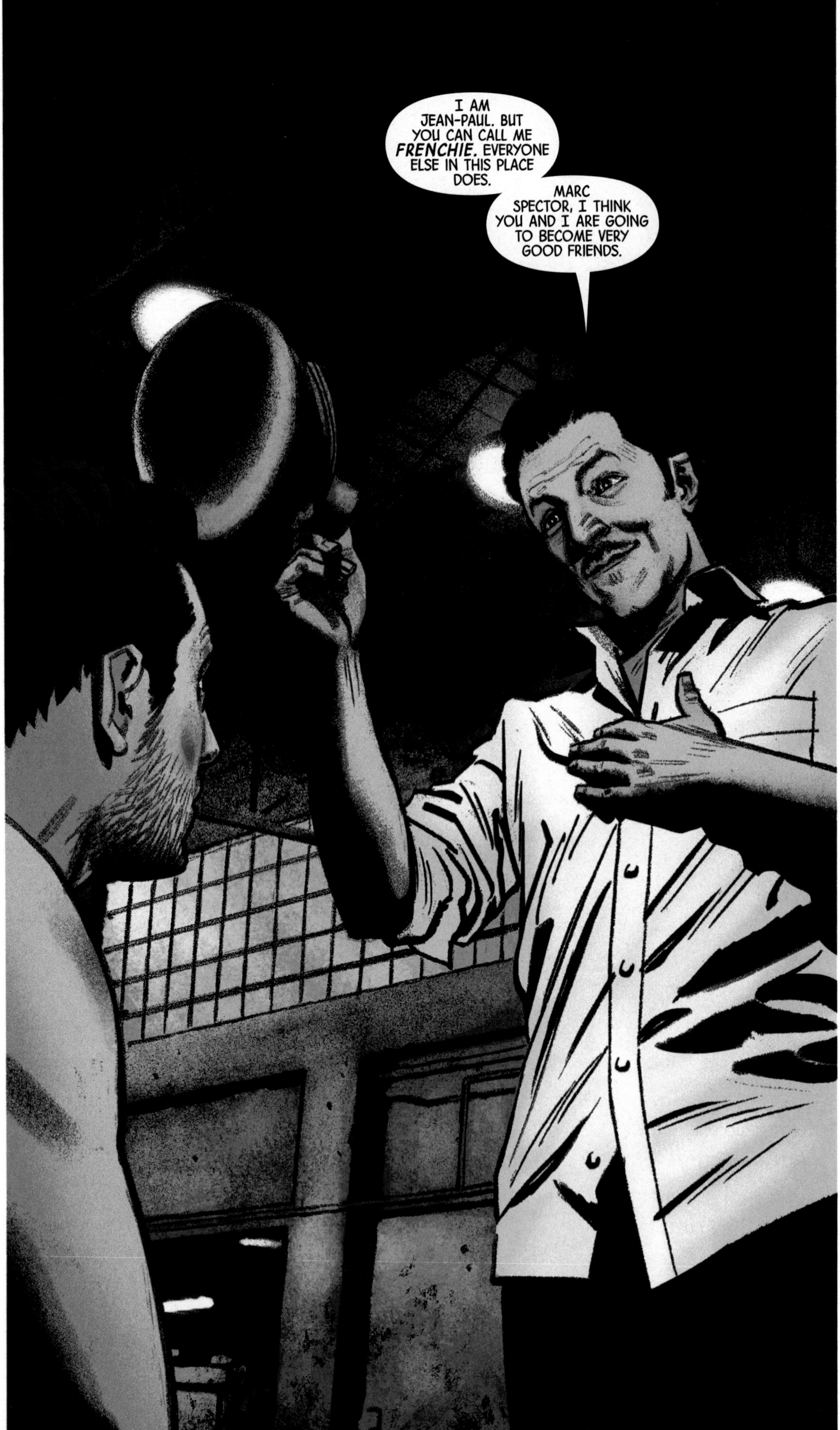
I AM JEAN-PAUL. BUT YOU CAN CALL ME FRENCHIE. EVERYONE ELSE IN THIS PLACE DOES.
MARC SPECTOR, I THINK YOU AND I ARE GOING TO BECOME VERY GOOD FRIENDS.

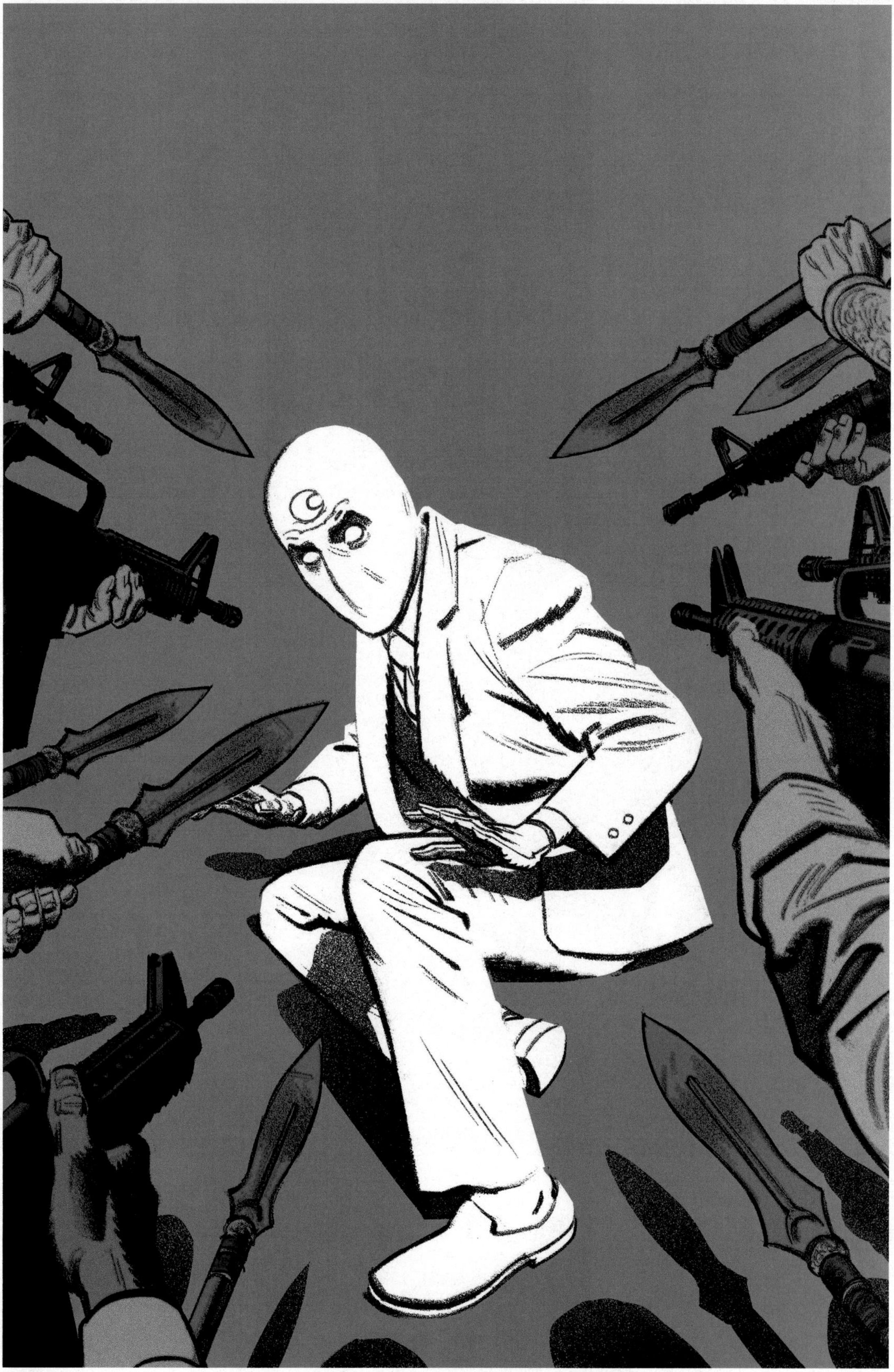

BIRTH AND DEATH
PART THREE

12

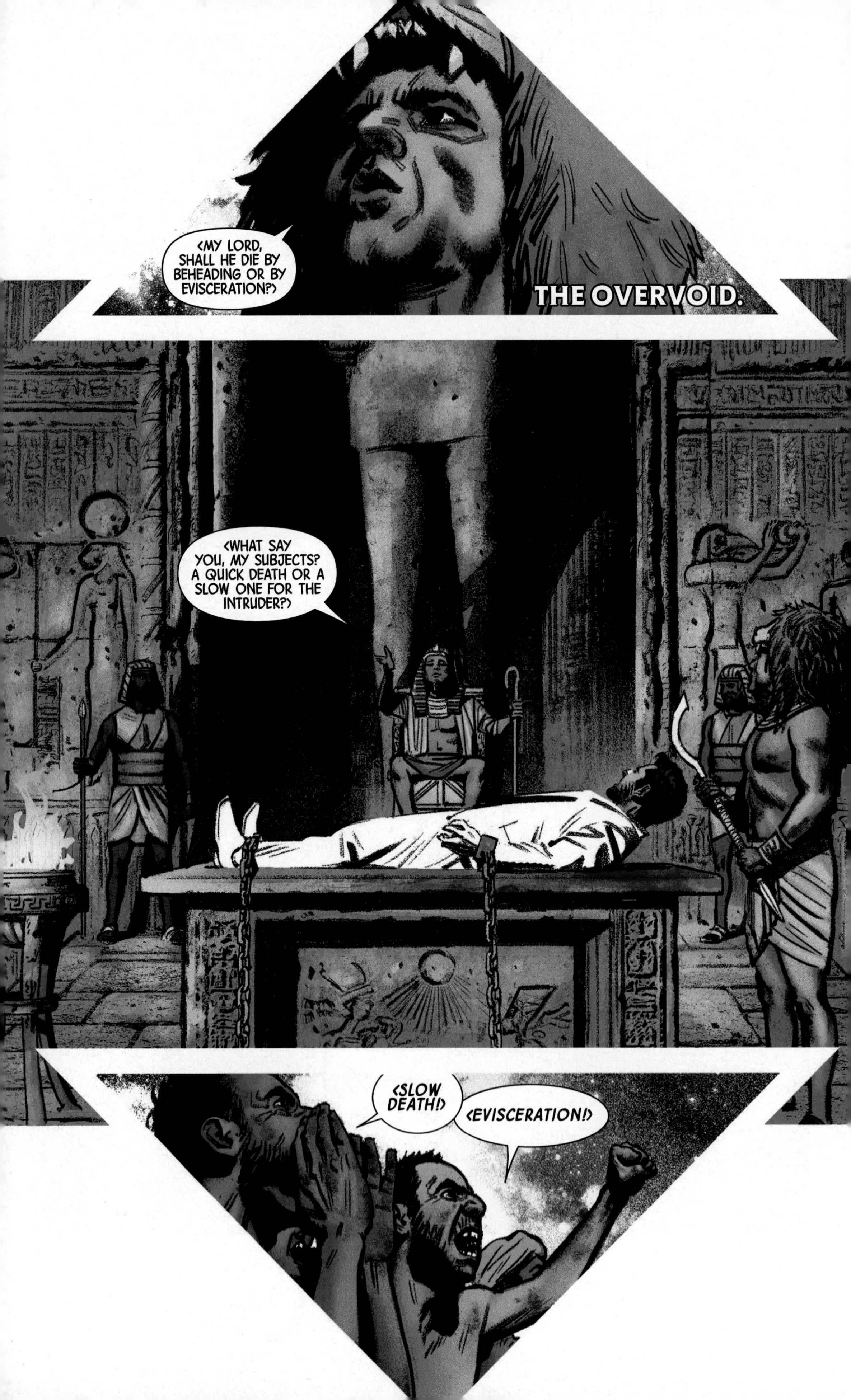

<MY LORD, SHALL HE DIE BY BEHEADING OR BY EVISCERATION?>
THE OVERVOID.
<WHAT SAY YOU, MY SUBJECTS? A QUICK DEATH OR A SLOW ONE FOR THE INTRUDER?>
<SLOW DEATH!>
<EVISCERATION!>

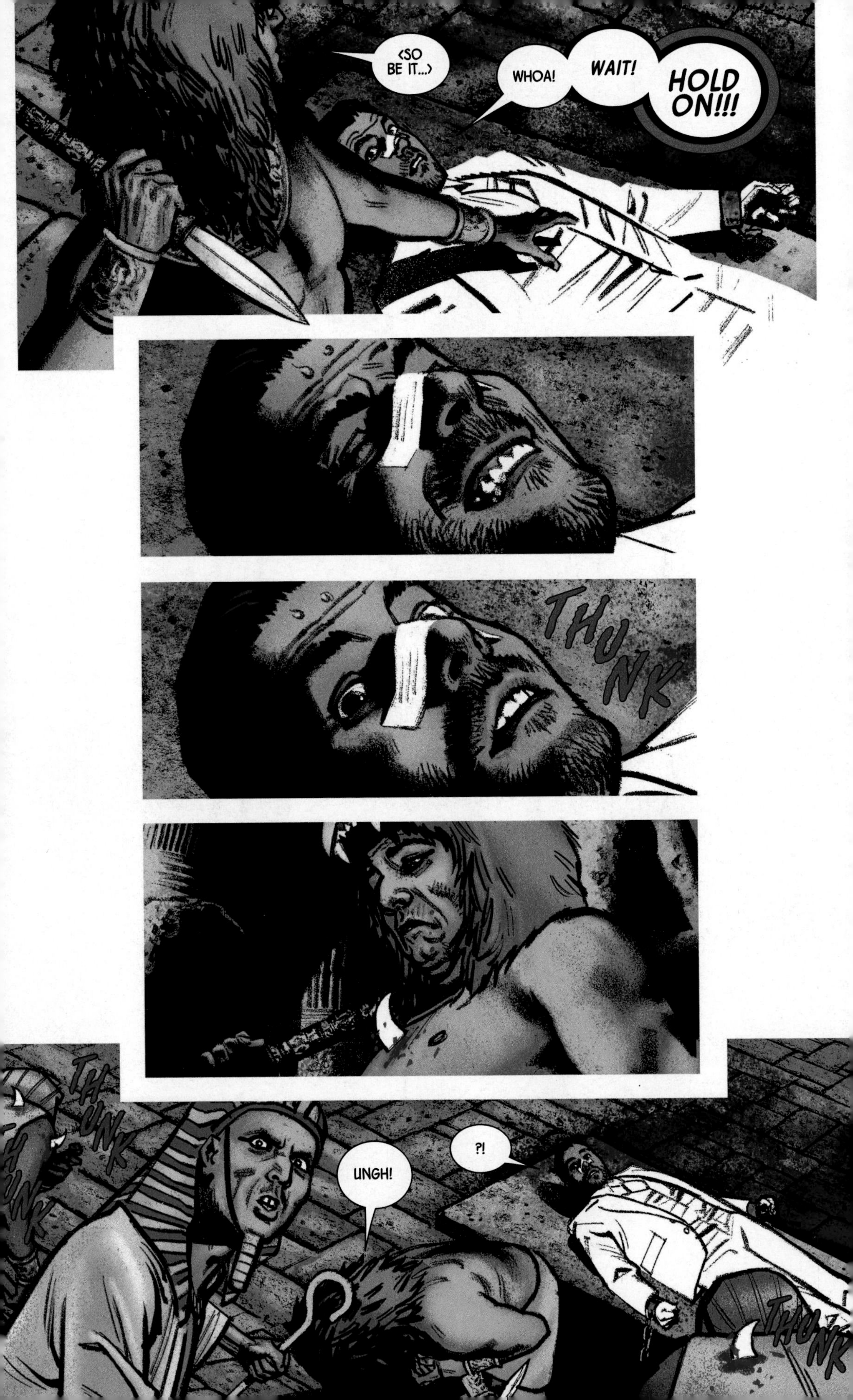

<SO BE IT...>
WHOA!
WAIT!
HOLD ON!!!
THUNK
THUNK
THUNK
UNGH!
?!
THUNK

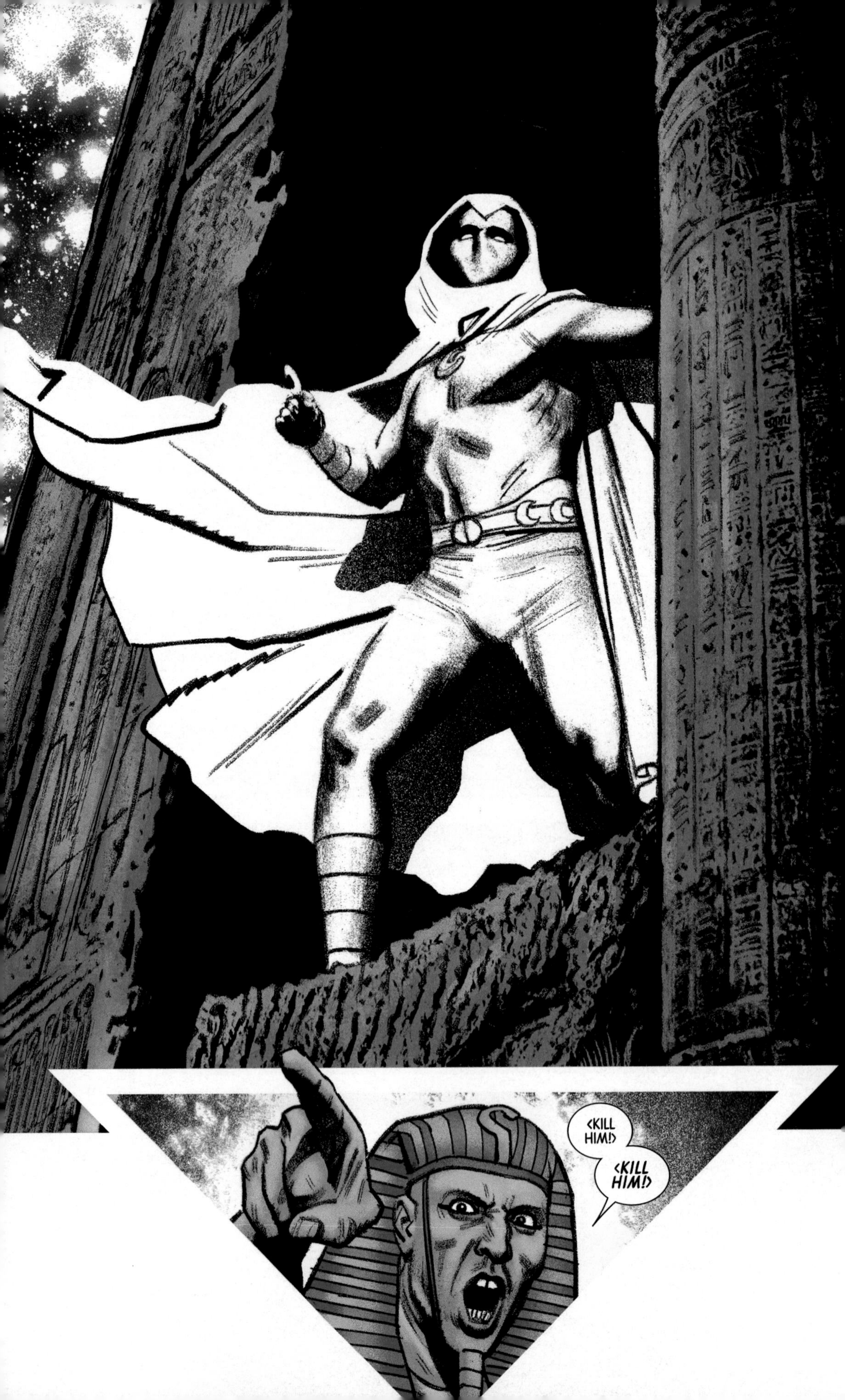
<KILL HIM!>
<KILL HIM!>

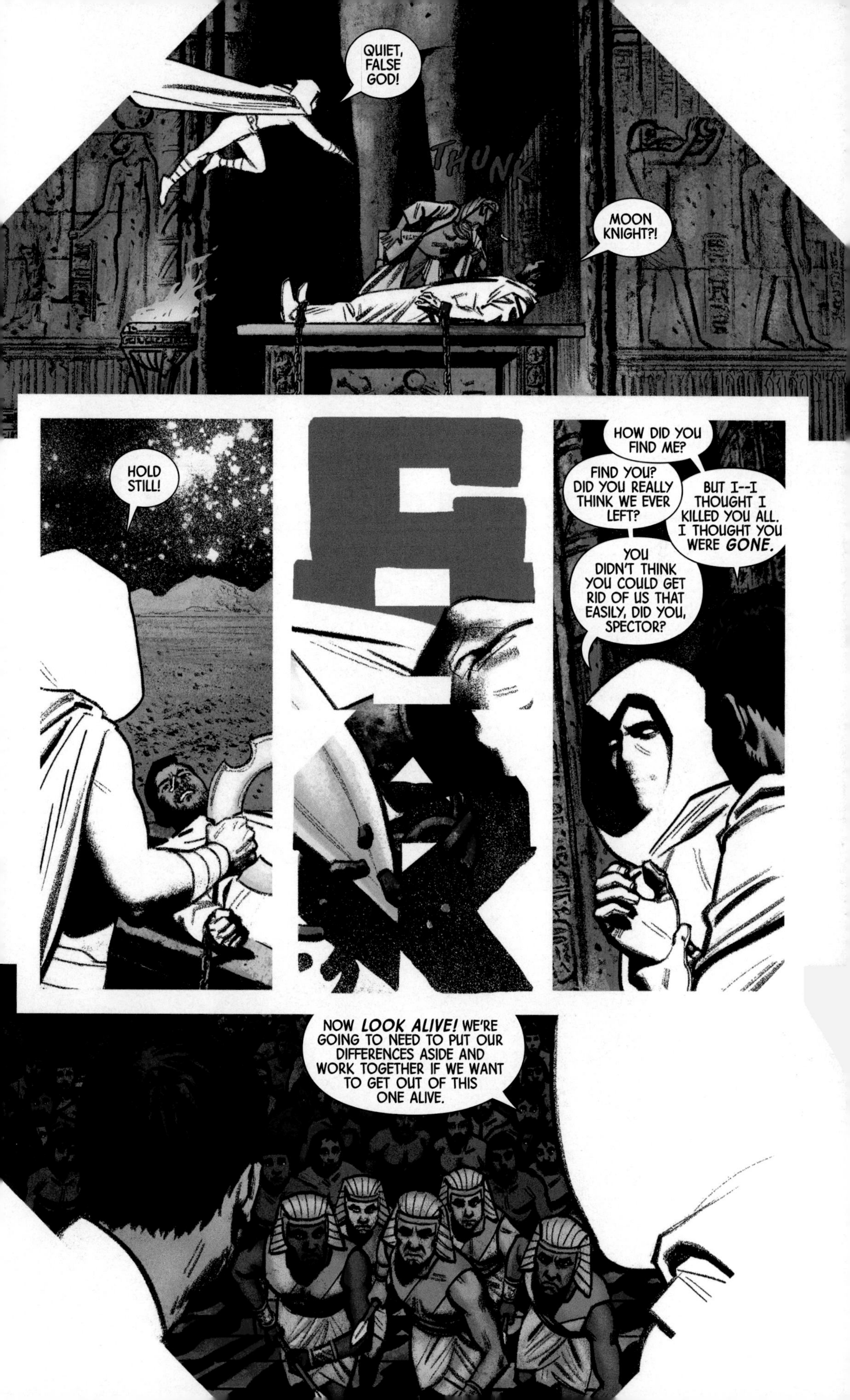
QUIET, FALSE GOD!
THUNK
MOON KNIGHT?!
HOLD STILL!
HOW DID YOU FIND ME?
FIND YOU? DID YOU REALLY THINK WE EVER LEFT?
BUT I--I THOUGHT I KILLED YOU ALL. I THOUGHT YOU WERE GONE.
YOU DIDN'T THINK YOU COULD GET RID OF US THAT EASILY, DID YOU, SPECTOR?
NOW LOOK ALIVE! WE'RE GOING TO NEED TO PUT OUR DIFFERENCES ASIDE AND WORK TOGETHER IF WE WANT TO GET OUT OF THIS ONE ALIVE.

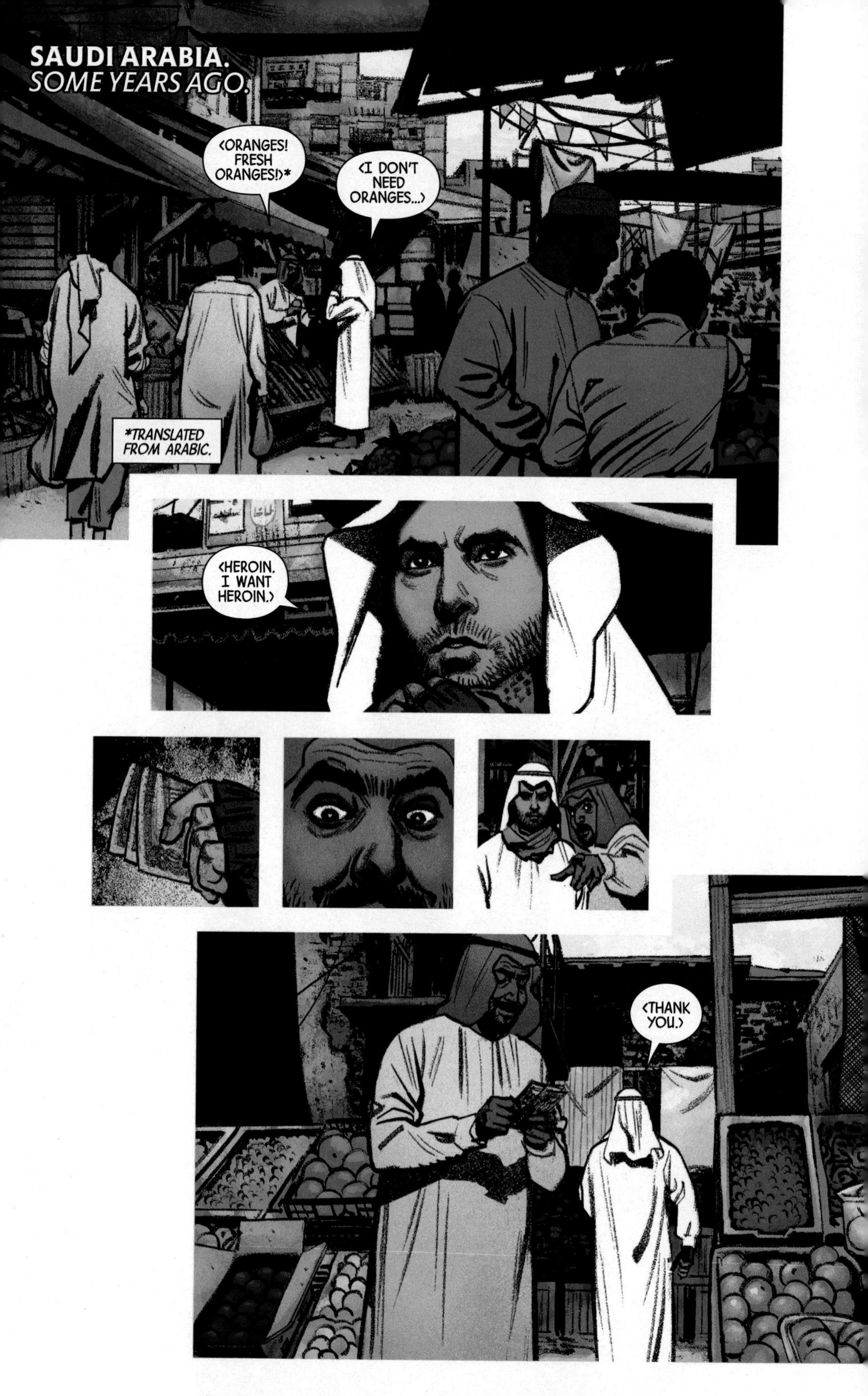
SAUDI ARABIA.
SOME YEARS AGO.
<ORANGES! FRESH ORANGES!>*
<I DON'T NEED ORANGES...>
*TRANSLATED FROM ARABIC.
<HEROIN. I WANT HEROIN.>
<THANK YOU.>

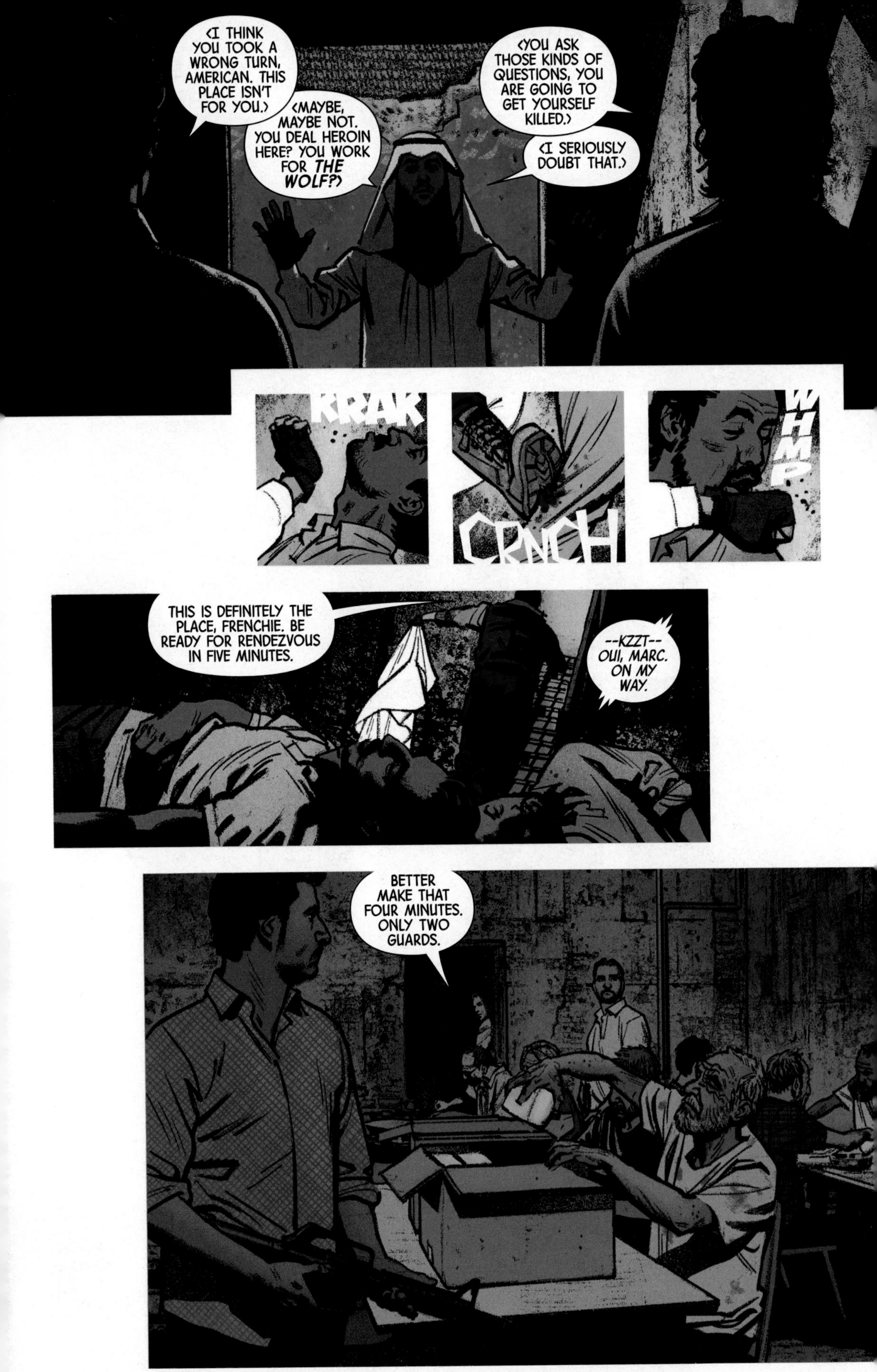
<I THINK YOU TOOK A WRONG TURN, AMERICAN. THIS PLACE ISN'T FOR YOU.>
<MAYBE, MAYBE NOT. YOU DEAL HEROIN HERE? YOU WORK FOR *THE WOLF*?>
<YOU ASK THOSE KINDS OF QUESTIONS, YOU ARE GOING TO GET YOURSELF KILLED.>
<I SERIOUSLY DOUBT THAT.>
KRAK
CRNCH
WHMP
THIS IS DEFINITELY THE PLACE, FRENCHIE. BE READY FOR RENDEZVOUS IN FIVE MINUTES.
--KZZT-- OUI, MARC. ON MY WAY.
BETTER MAKE THAT FOUR MINUTES. ONLY TWO GUARDS.

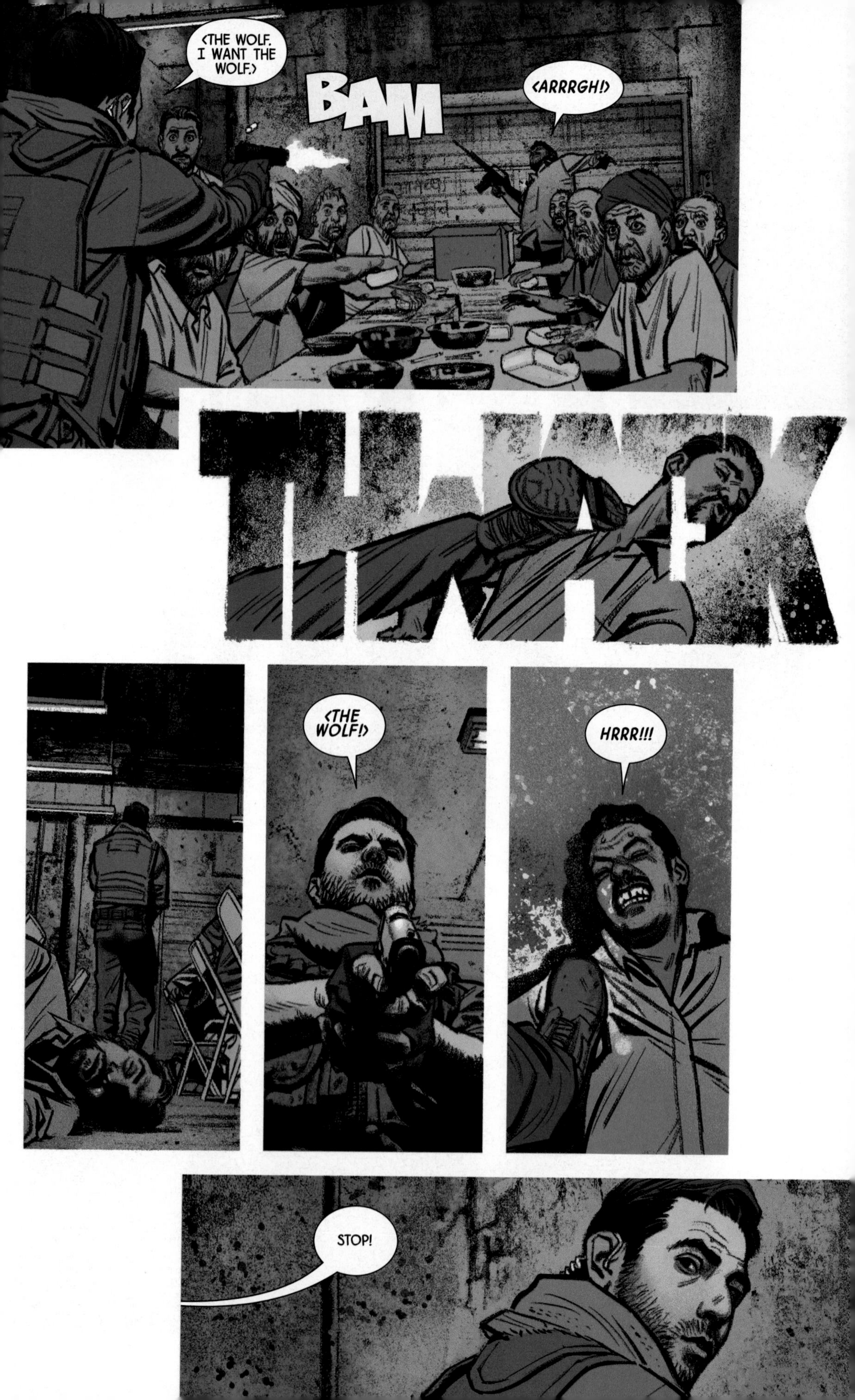
<THE WOLF. I WANT THE WOLF.>
BAM
<ARRRGH!>
THWAK
<THE WOLF!>
HRRR!!!
STOP!

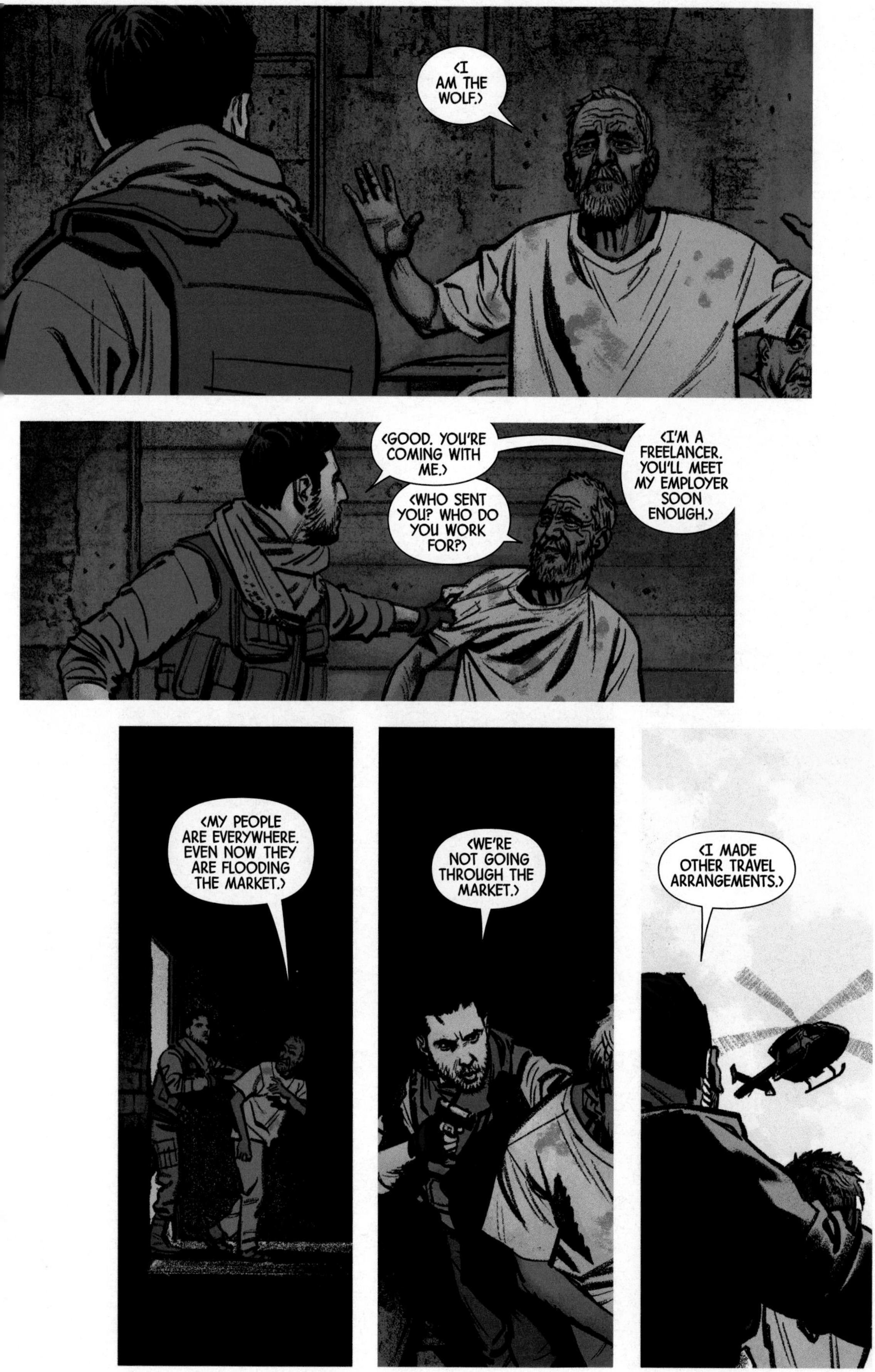
<I AM THE WOLF.>
<GOOD. YOU'RE COMING WITH ME.>
<WHO SENT YOU? WHO DO YOU WORK FOR?>
<I'M A FREELANCER. YOU'LL MEET MY EMPLOYER SOON ENOUGH.>
<MY PEOPLE ARE EVERYWHERE. EVEN NOW THEY ARE FLOODING THE MARKET.>
<WE'RE NOT GOING THROUGH THE MARKET.>
<I MADE OTHER TRAVEL ARRANGEMENTS.>

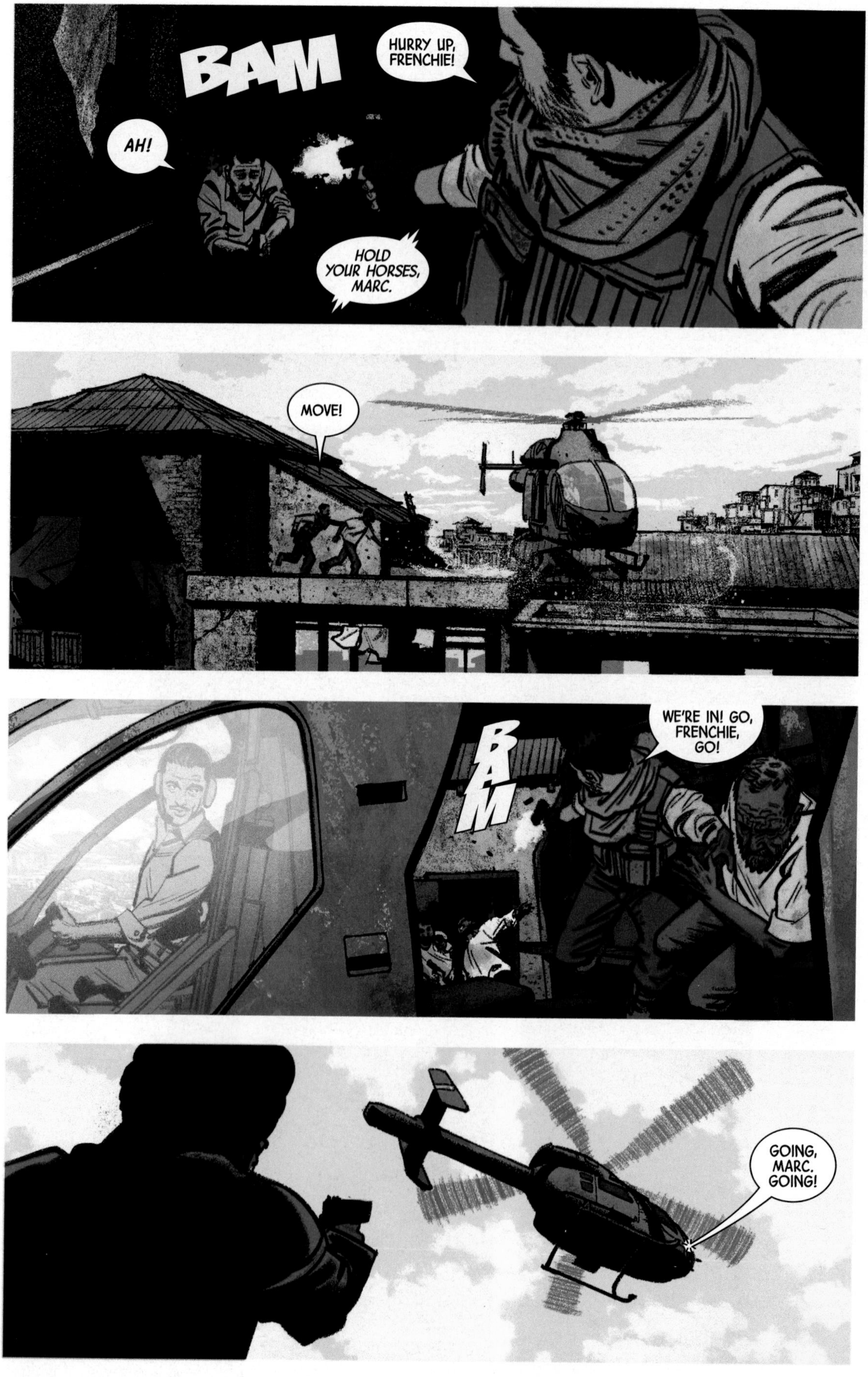
BAM
HURRY UP, FRENCHIE!
AH!
HOLD YOUR HORSES, MARC.
MOVE!
BAM
WE'RE IN! GO, FRENCHIE, GO!
GOING, MARC. GOING!

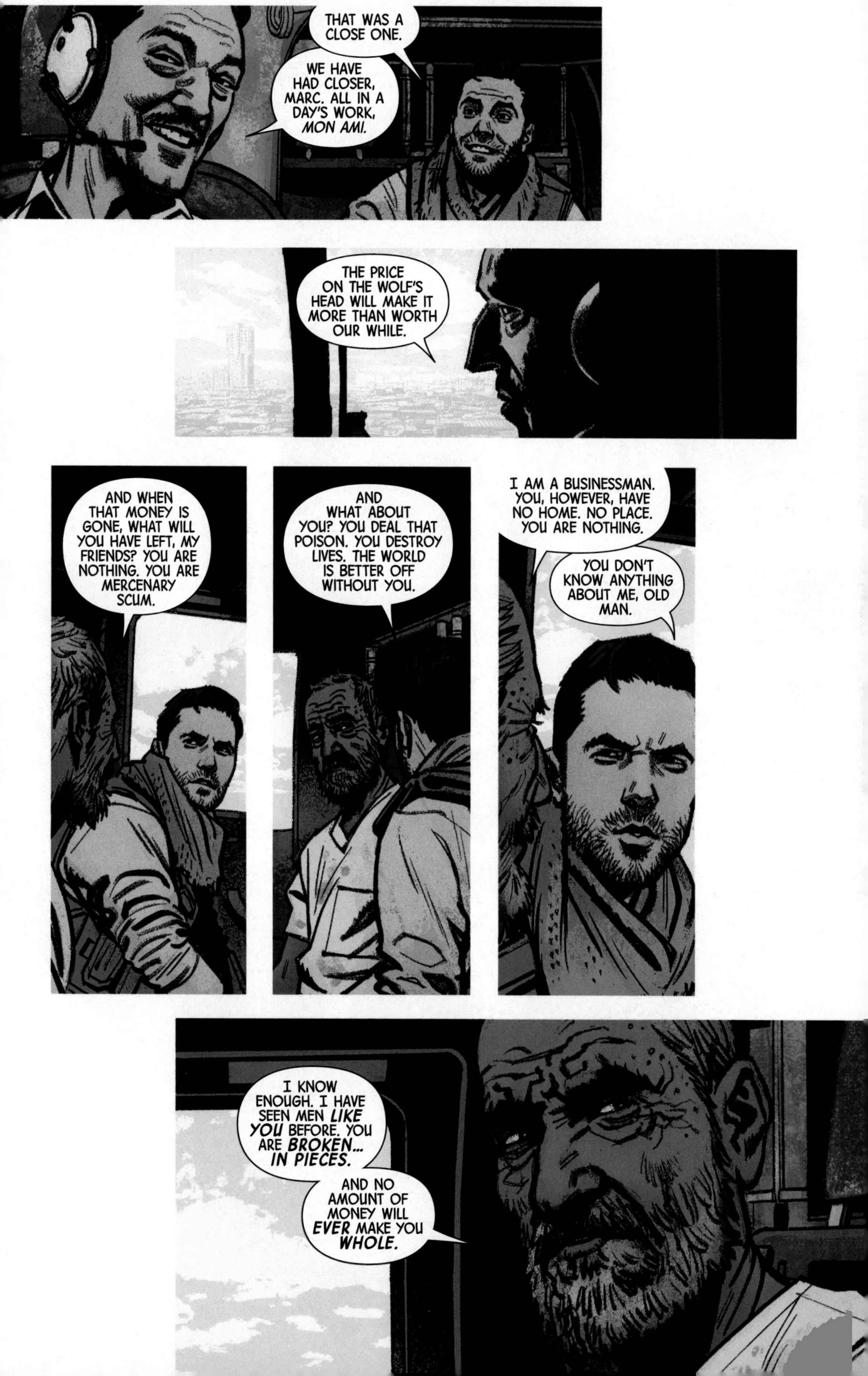
THAT WAS A CLOSE ONE.
WE HAVE HAD CLOSER, MARC. ALL IN A DAY'S WORK, *MON AMI.*
THE PRICE ON THE WOLF'S HEAD WILL MAKE IT MORE THAN WORTH OUR WHILE.
AND WHEN THAT MONEY IS GONE, WHAT WILL YOU HAVE LEFT, MY FRIENDS? YOU ARE NOTHING. YOU ARE MERCENARY SCUM.
AND WHAT ABOUT YOU? YOU DEAL THAT POISON. YOU DESTROY LIVES. THE WORLD IS BETTER OFF WITHOUT YOU.
I AM A BUSINESSMAN. YOU, HOWEVER, HAVE NO HOME. NO PLACE. YOU ARE NOTHING.
YOU DON'T KNOW ANYTHING ABOUT ME, OLD MAN.
I KNOW ENOUGH. I HAVE SEEN MEN ***LIKE YOU*** BEFORE. YOU ARE ***BROKEN... IN PIECES.***
AND NO AMOUNT OF MONEY WILL ***EVER*** MAKE YOU ***WHOLE.***

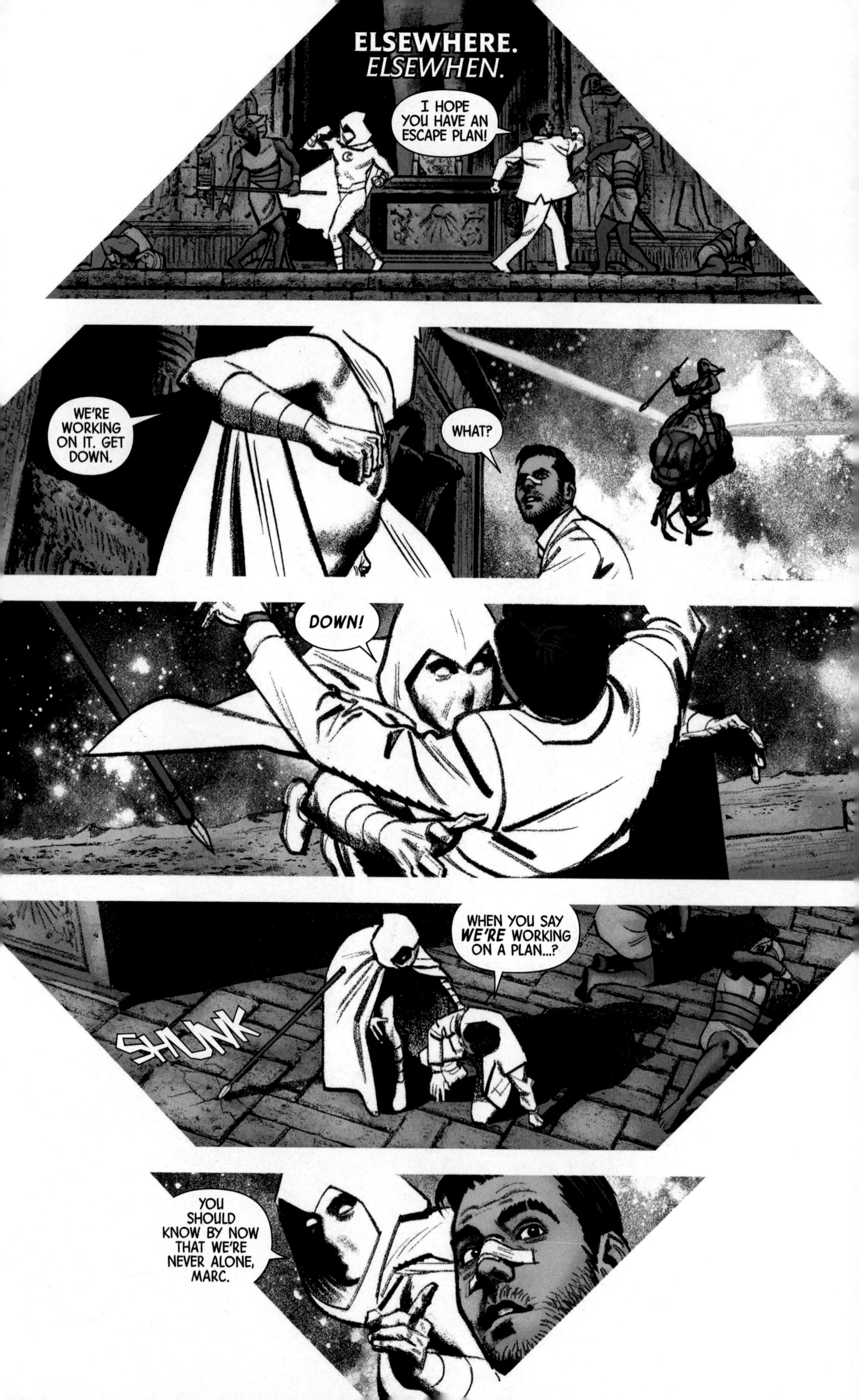
ELSEWHERE.
ELSEWHEN.
I HOPE YOU HAVE AN ESCAPE PLAN!
WE'RE WORKING ON IT. GET DOWN.
WHAT?
DOWN!
SHUNK
WHEN YOU SAY ***WE'RE*** WORKING ON A PLAN...?
YOU SHOULD KNOW BY NOW THAT WE'RE NEVER ALONE, MARC.

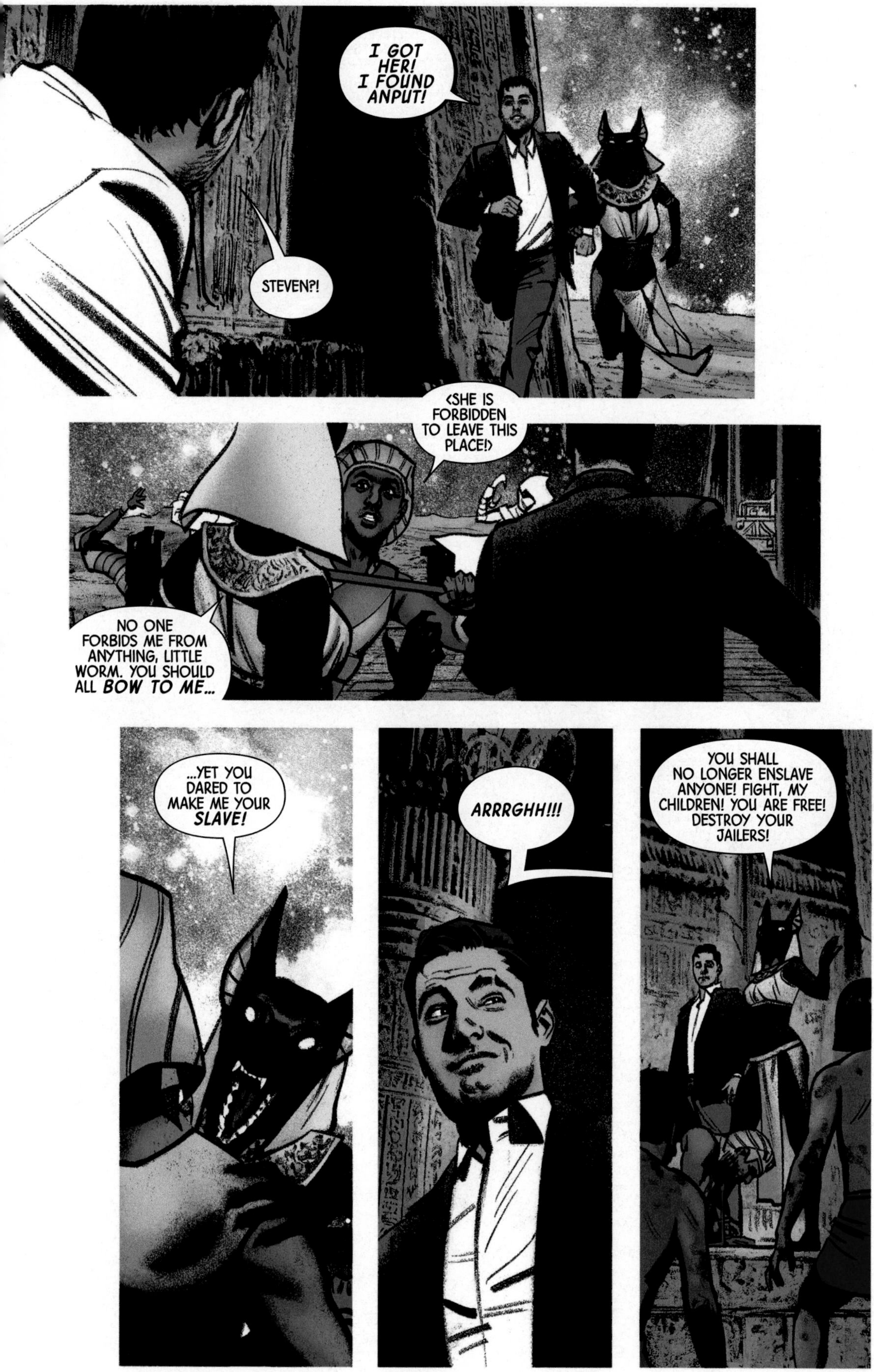
I GOT HER! I FOUND ANPUT!
STEVEN?!
<SHE IS FORBIDDEN TO LEAVE THIS PLACE!>
NO ONE FORBIDS ME FROM ANYTHING, LITTLE WORM. YOU SHOULD ALL BOW TO ME...
...YET YOU DARED TO MAKE ME YOUR SLAVE!
ARRRGHH!!!
YOU SHALL NO LONGER ENSLAVE ANYONE! FIGHT, MY CHILDREN! YOU ARE FREE! DESTROY YOUR JAILERS!

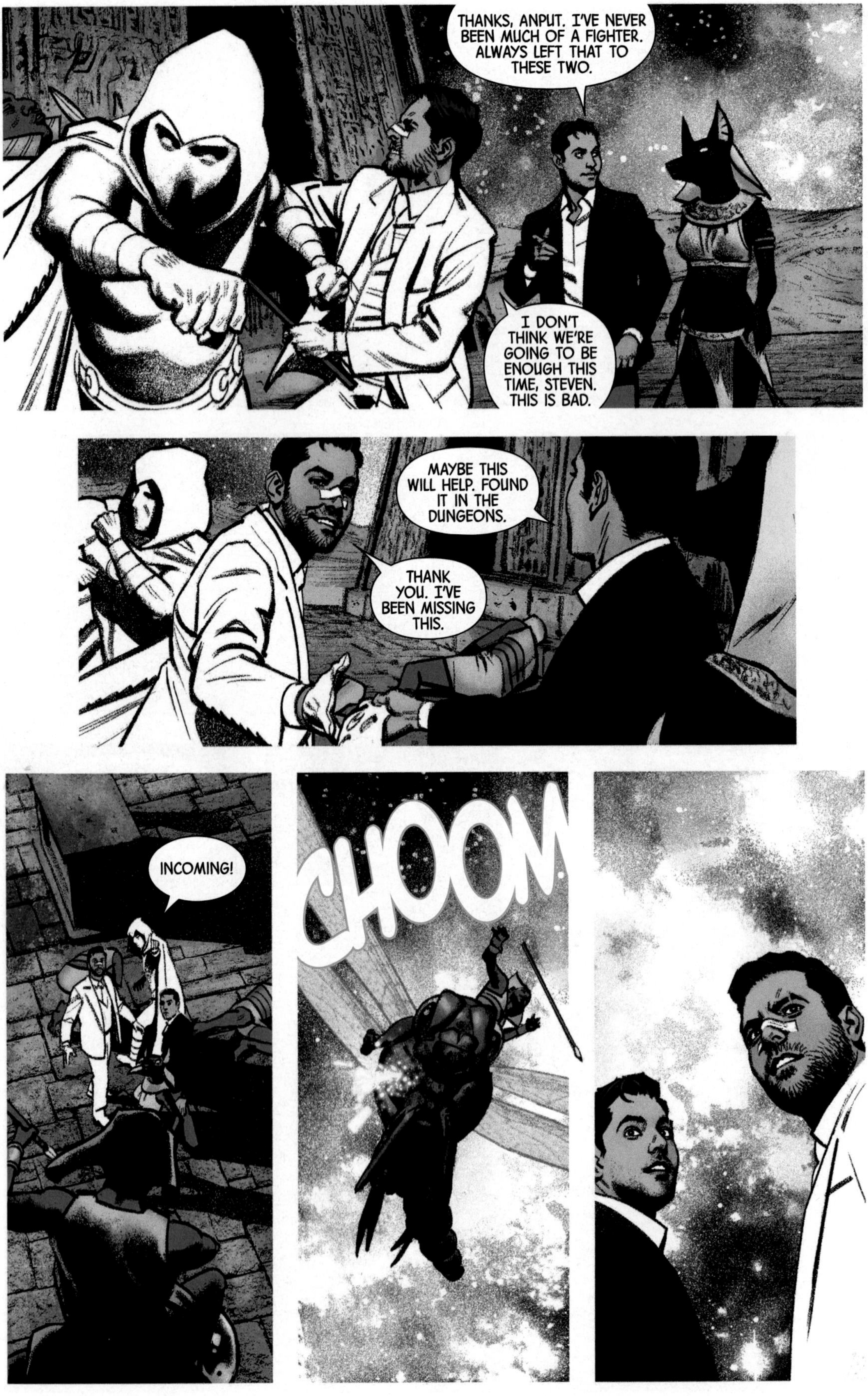
THANKS, ANPUT. I'VE NEVER BEEN MUCH OF A FIGHTER. ALWAYS LEFT THAT TO THESE TWO.
I DON'T THINK WE'RE GOING TO BE ENOUGH THIS TIME, STEVEN. THIS IS BAD.
MAYBE THIS WILL HELP. FOUND IT IN THE DUNGEONS.
THANK YOU. I'VE BEEN MISSING THIS.
INCOMING!
CHOOM

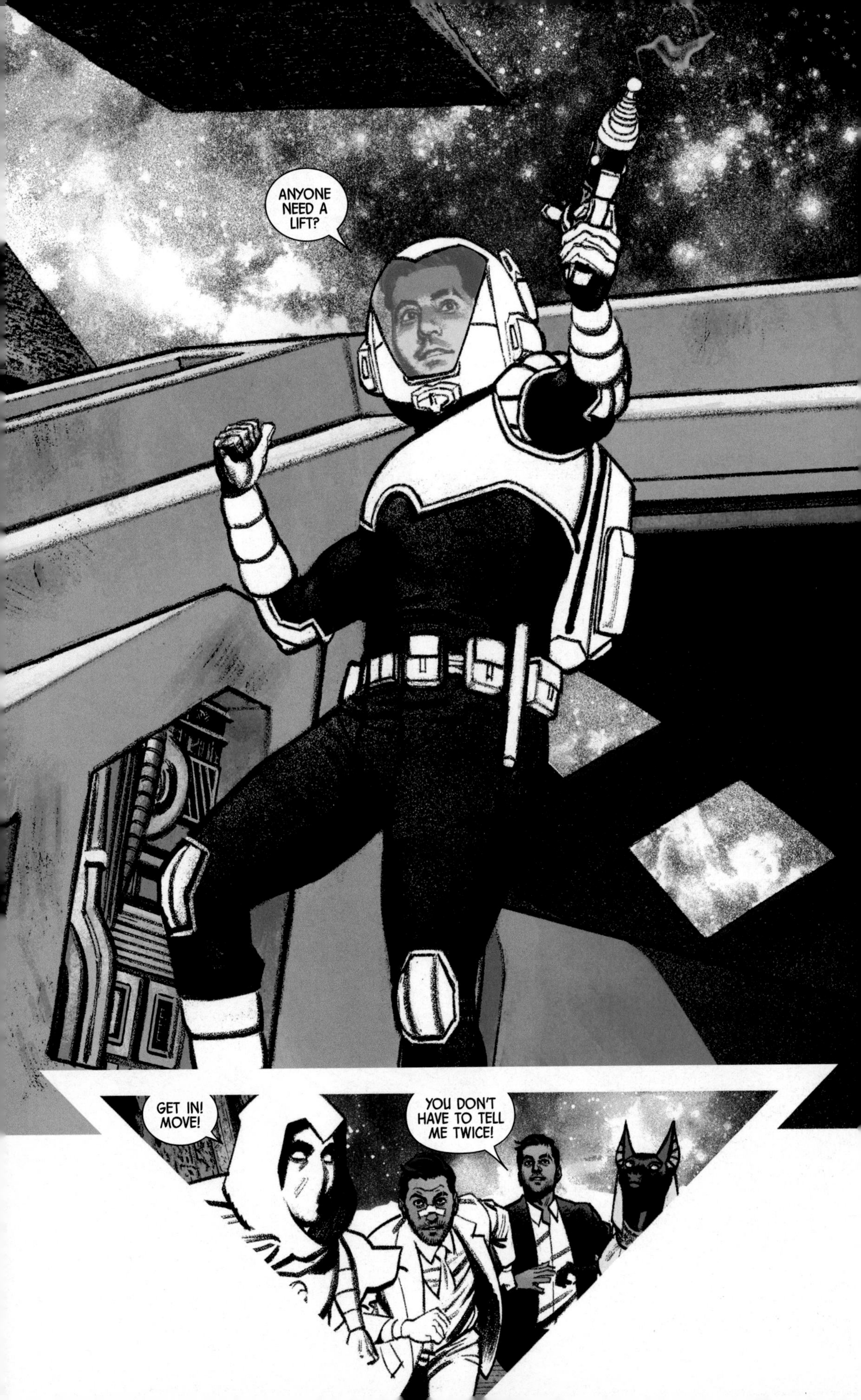
ANYONE NEED A LIFT?
GET IN! MOVE!
YOU DON'T HAVE TO TELL ME TWICE!

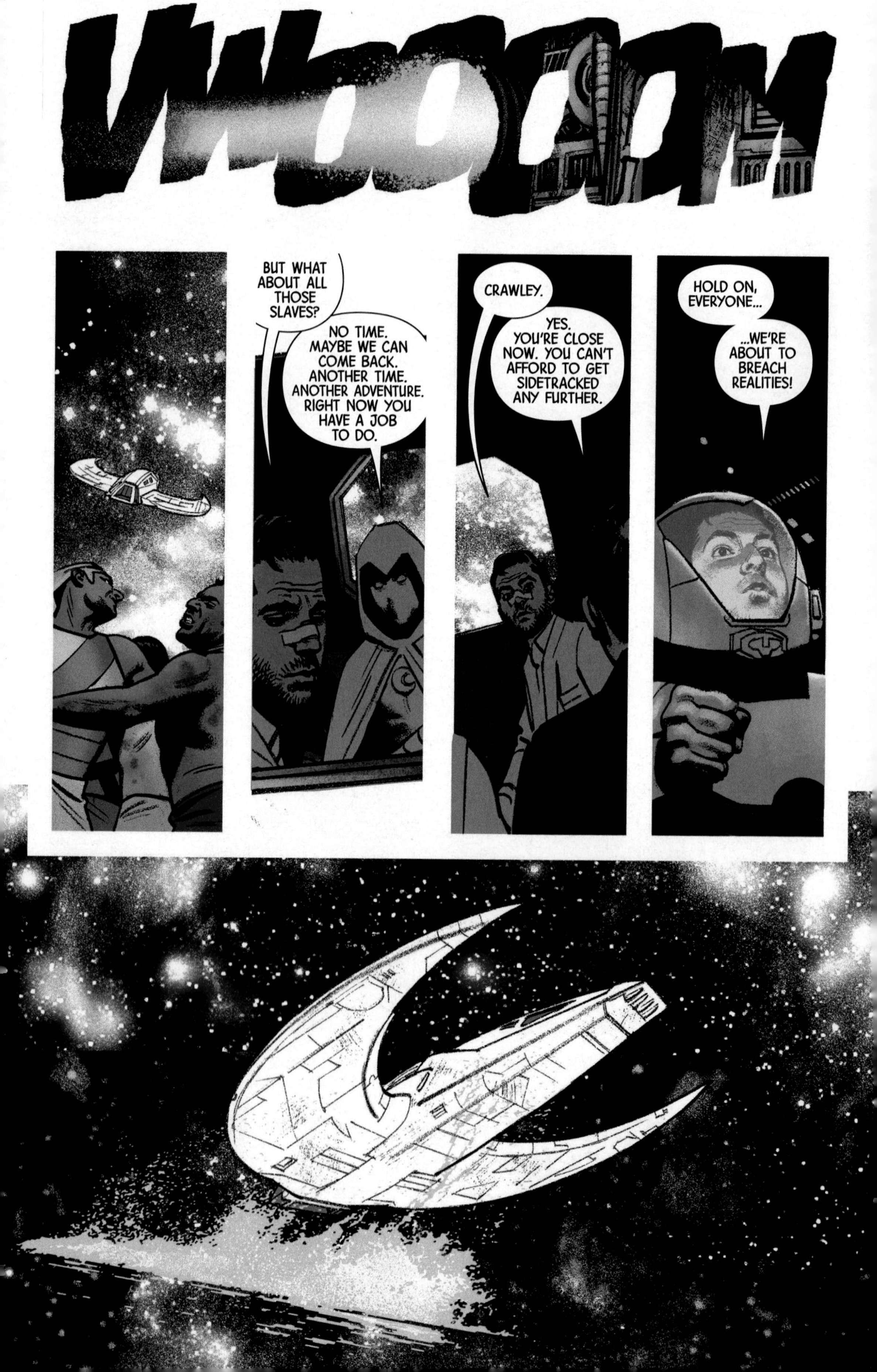
VHOOOOM
BUT WHAT ABOUT ALL THOSE SLAVES?
NO TIME. MAYBE WE CAN COME BACK. ANOTHER TIME. ANOTHER ADVENTURE. RIGHT NOW YOU HAVE A JOB TO DO.
CRAWLEY.
YES. YOU'RE CLOSE NOW. YOU CAN'T AFFORD TO GET SIDETRACKED ANY FURTHER.
HOLD ON, EVERYONE...
...WE'RE ABOUT TO BREACH REALITIES!

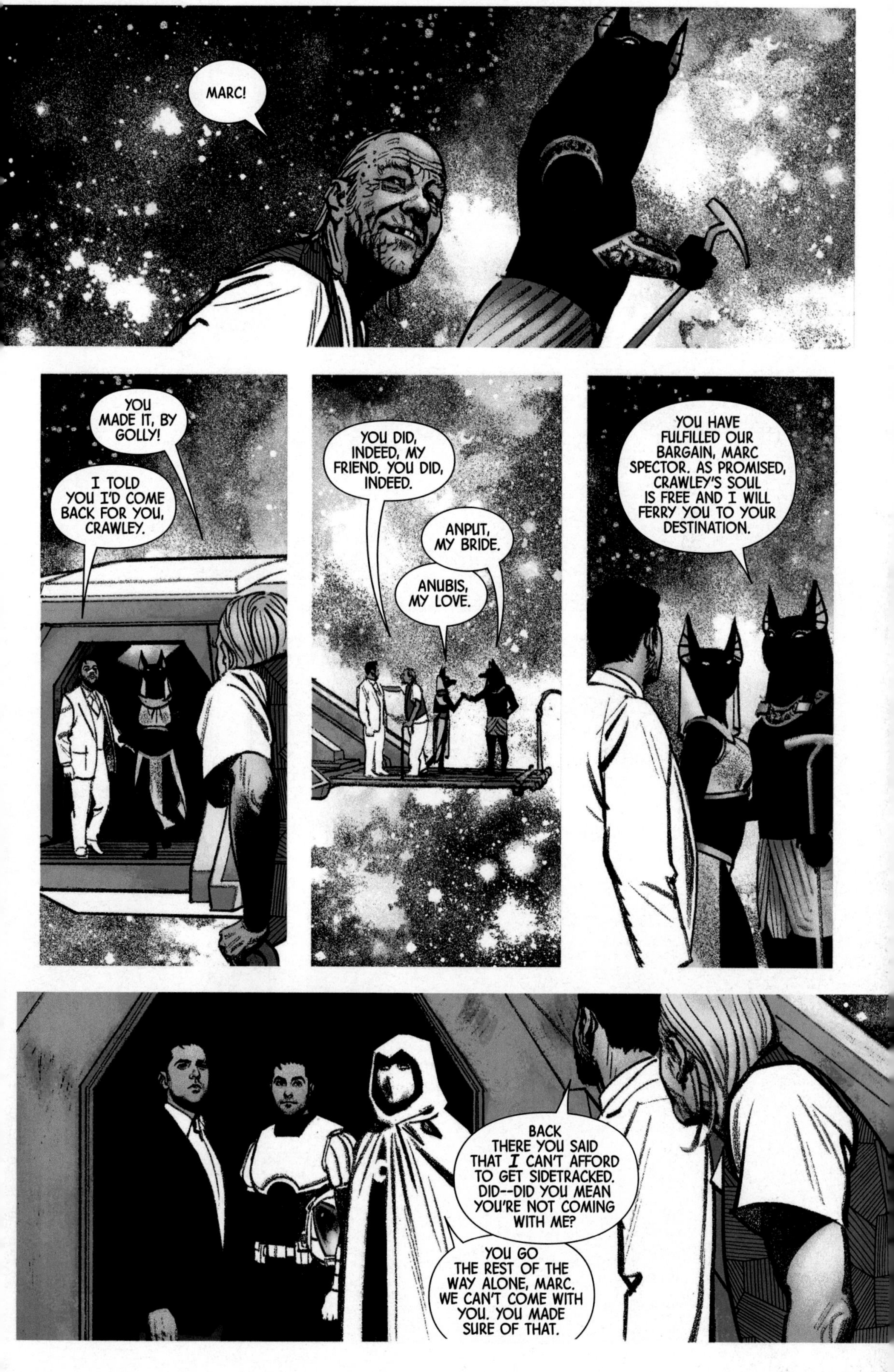
MARC!
YOU MADE IT, BY GOLLY!
I TOLD YOU I'D COME BACK FOR YOU, CRAWLEY.
YOU DID, INDEED, MY FRIEND. YOU DID, INDEED.
ANPUT, MY BRIDE.
ANUBIS, MY LOVE.
YOU HAVE FULFILLED OUR BARGAIN, MARC SPECTOR. AS PROMISED, CRAWLEY'S SOUL IS FREE AND I WILL FERRY YOU TO YOUR DESTINATION.
BACK THERE YOU SAID THAT I CAN'T AFFORD TO GET SIDETRACKED. DID--DID YOU MEAN YOU'RE NOT COMING WITH ME?
YOU GO THE REST OF THE WAY ALONE, MARC. WE CAN'T COME WITH YOU. YOU MADE SURE OF THAT.

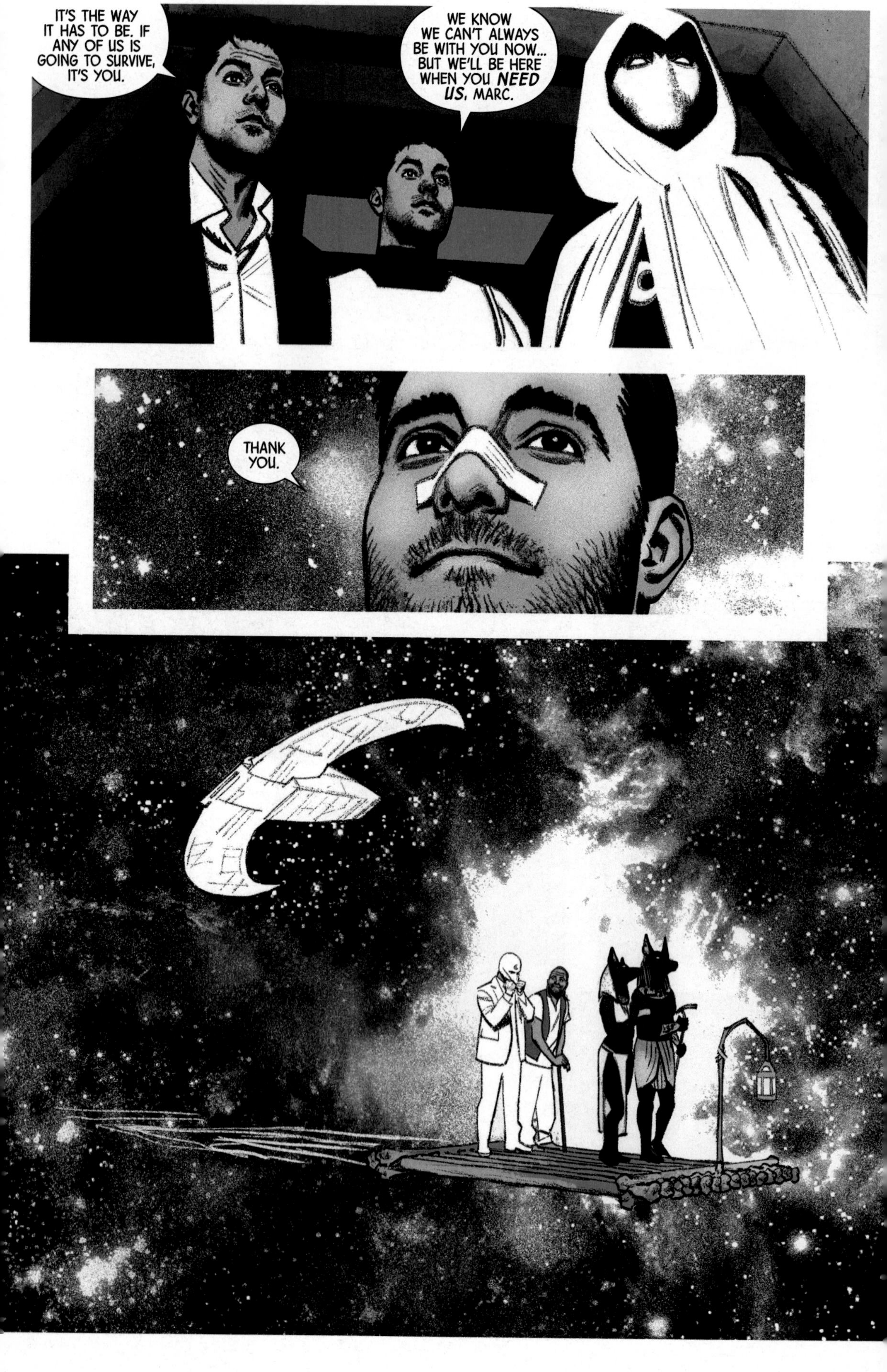
IT'S THE WAY IT HAS TO BE. IF ANY OF US IS GOING TO SURVIVE, IT'S YOU.
WE KNOW WE CAN'T ALWAYS BE WITH YOU NOW... BUT WE'LL BE HERE WHEN YOU NEED US, MARC.
THANK YOU.

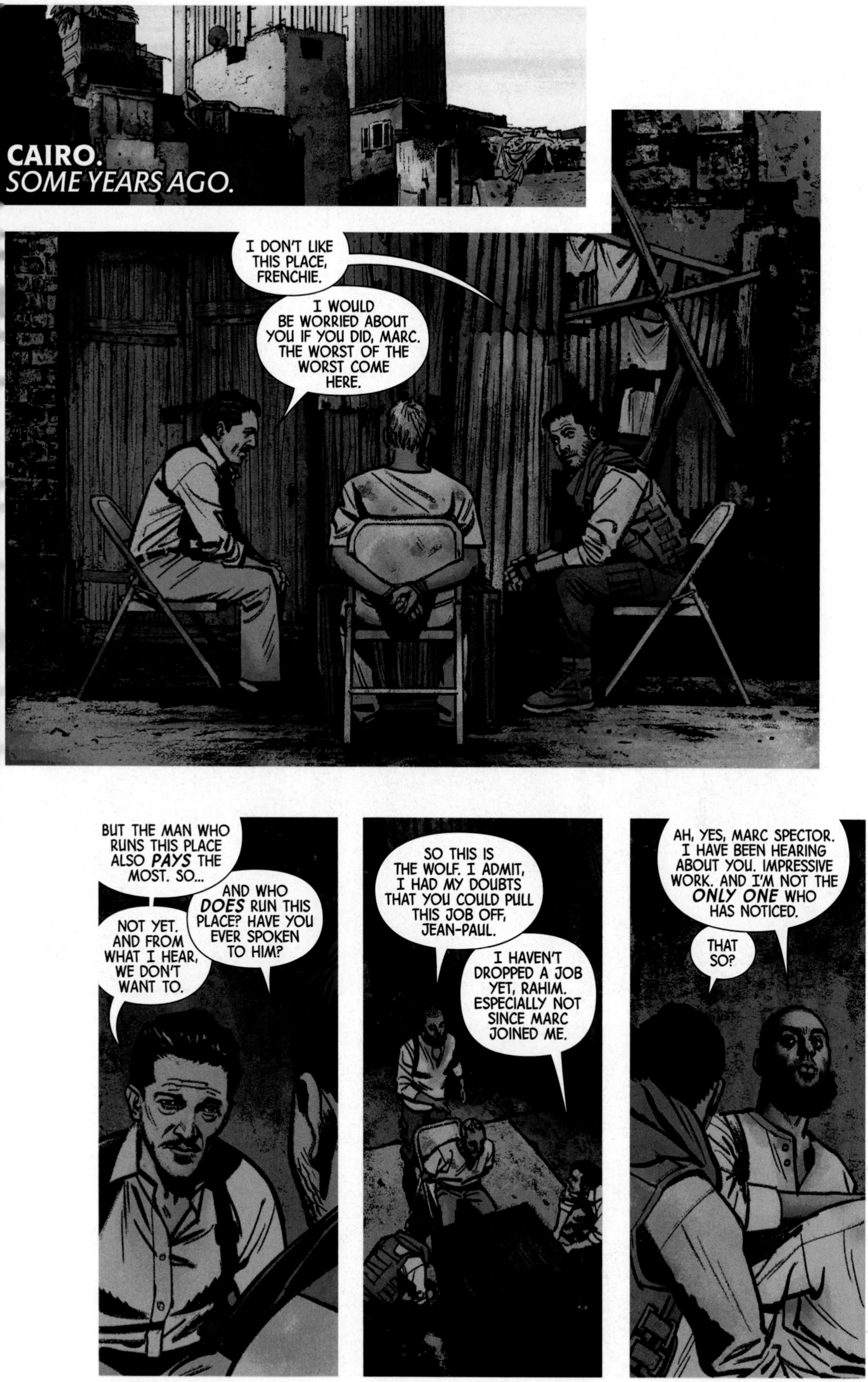
CAIRO.
SOME YEARS AGO.
I DON'T LIKE THIS PLACE, FRENCHIE.
I WOULD BE WORRIED ABOUT YOU IF YOU DID, MARC. THE WORST OF THE WORST COME HERE.
BUT THE MAN WHO RUNS THIS PLACE ALSO PAYS THE MOST. SO...
AND WHO DOES RUN THIS PLACE? HAVE YOU EVER SPOKEN TO HIM?
NOT YET. AND FROM WHAT I HEAR, WE DON'T WANT TO.
SO THIS IS THE WOLF. I ADMIT, I HAD MY DOUBTS THAT YOU COULD PULL THIS JOB OFF, JEAN-PAUL.
I HAVEN'T DROPPED A JOB YET, RAHIM. ESPECIALLY NOT SINCE MARC JOINED ME.
AH, YES, MARC SPECTOR. I HAVE BEEN HEARING ABOUT YOU. IMPRESSIVE WORK. AND I'M NOT THE ONLY ONE WHO HAS NOTICED.
THAT SO?

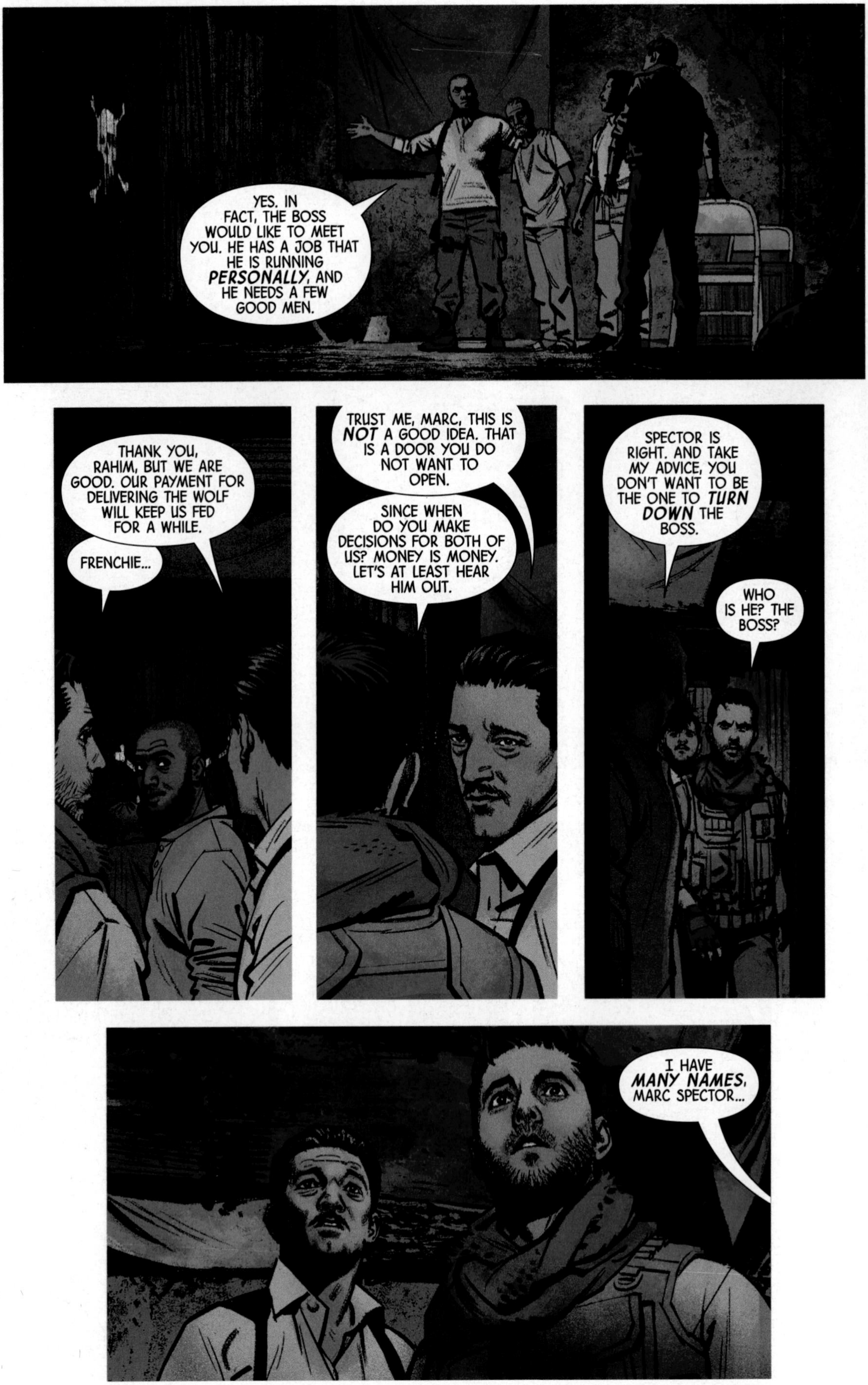
YES. IN FACT, THE BOSS WOULD LIKE TO MEET YOU. HE HAS A JOB THAT HE IS RUNNING PERSONALLY, AND HE NEEDS A FEW GOOD MEN.
THANK YOU, RAHIM, BUT WE ARE GOOD. OUR PAYMENT FOR DELIVERING THE WOLF WILL KEEP US FED FOR A WHILE.
FRENCHIE...
TRUST ME, MARC, THIS IS NOT A GOOD IDEA. THAT IS A DOOR YOU DO NOT WANT TO OPEN.
SINCE WHEN DO YOU MAKE DECISIONS FOR BOTH OF US? MONEY IS MONEY. LET'S AT LEAST HEAR HIM OUT.
SPECTOR IS RIGHT. AND TAKE MY ADVICE, YOU DON'T WANT TO BE THE ONE TO TURN DOWN THE BOSS.
WHO IS HE? THE BOSS?
I HAVE MANY NAMES, MARC SPECTOR...

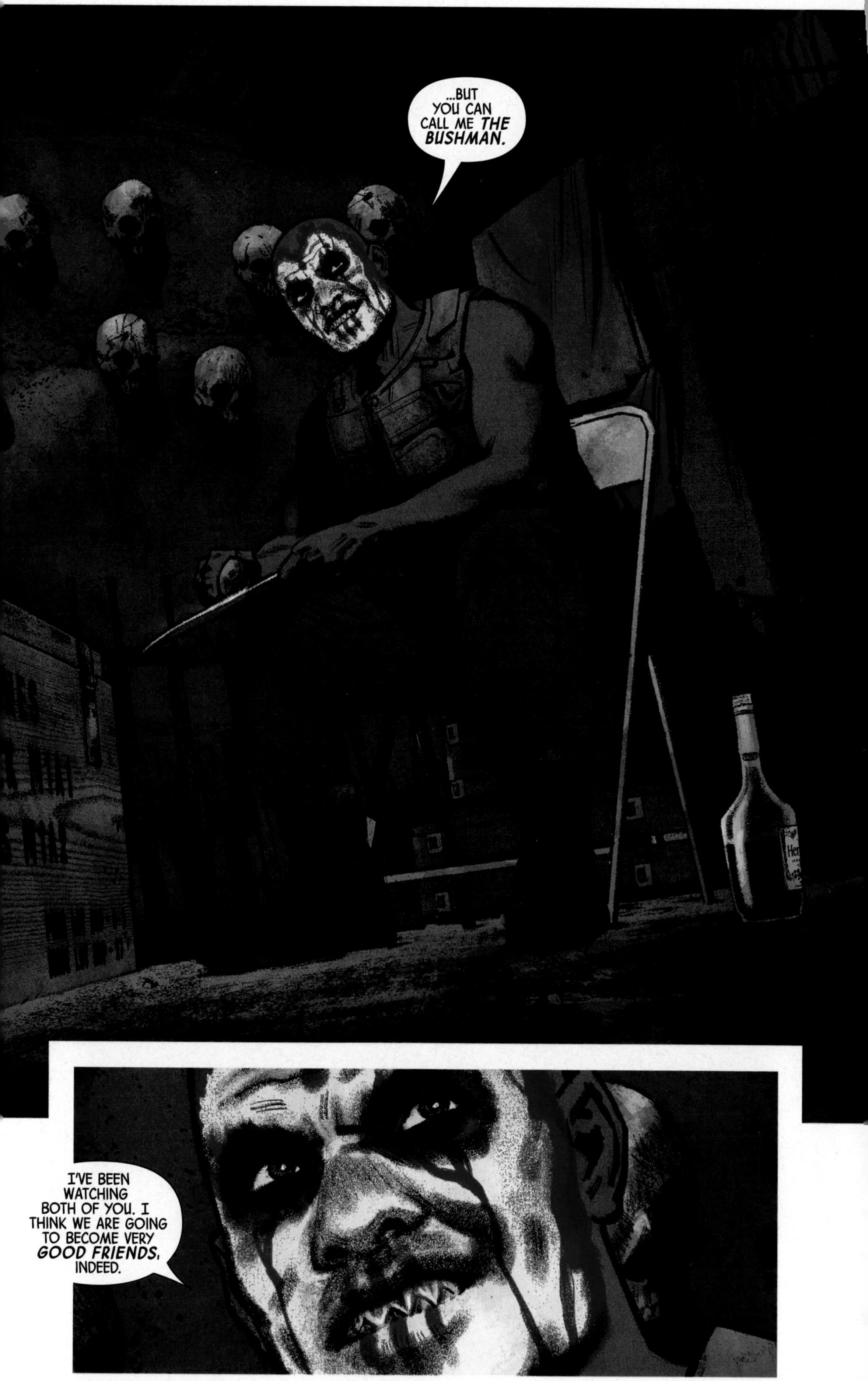
...BUT YOU CAN CALL ME *THE BUSHMAN.*
I'VE BEEN WATCHING BOTH OF YOU. I THINK WE ARE GOING TO BECOME VERY *GOOD FRIENDS,* INDEED.

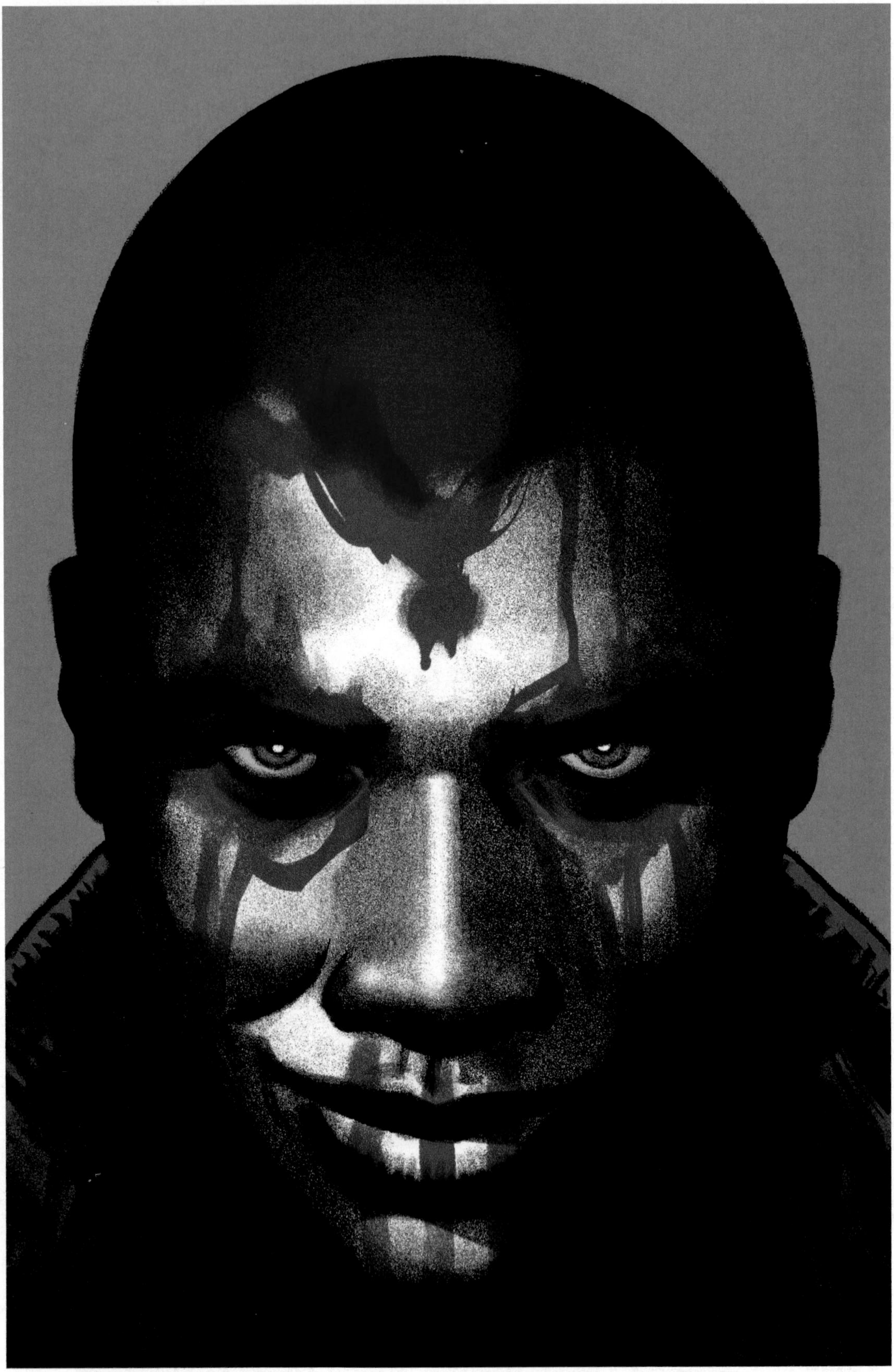

BIRTH AND DEATH
PART FOUR

13

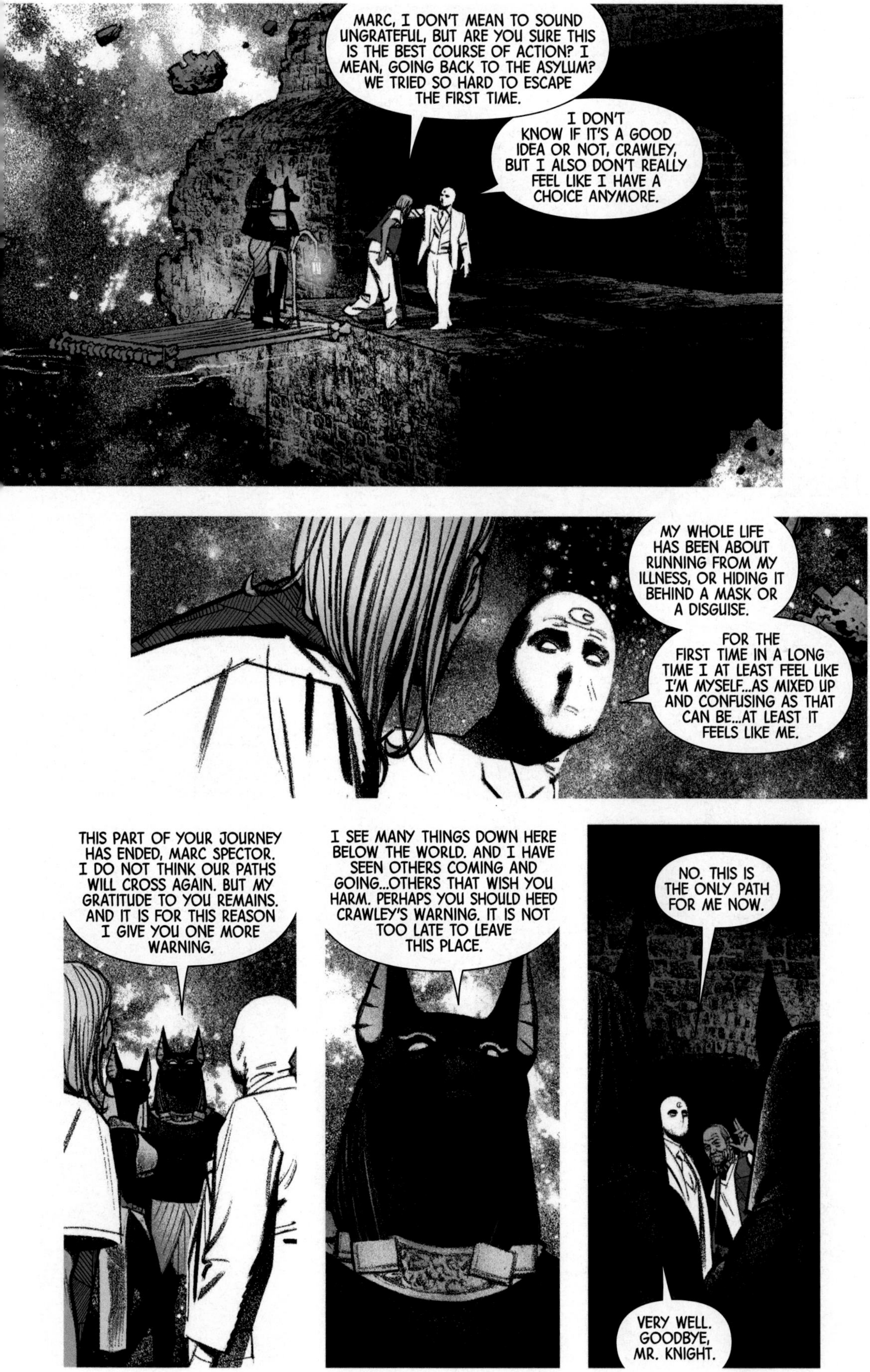
MARC, I DON'T MEAN TO SOUND UNGRATEFUL, BUT ARE YOU SURE THIS IS THE BEST COURSE OF ACTION? I MEAN, GOING BACK TO THE ASYLUM? WE TRIED SO HARD TO ESCAPE THE FIRST TIME.
I DON'T KNOW IF IT'S A GOOD IDEA OR NOT, CRAWLEY, BUT I ALSO DON'T REALLY FEEL LIKE I HAVE A CHOICE ANYMORE.
MY WHOLE LIFE HAS BEEN ABOUT RUNNING FROM MY ILLNESS, OR HIDING IT BEHIND A MASK OR A DISGUISE.
FOR THE FIRST TIME IN A LONG TIME I AT LEAST FEEL LIKE I'M MYSELF...AS MIXED UP AND CONFUSING AS THAT CAN BE...AT LEAST IT FEELS LIKE ME.
THIS PART OF YOUR JOURNEY HAS ENDED, MARC SPECTOR. I DO NOT THINK OUR PATHS WILL CROSS AGAIN. BUT MY GRATITUDE TO YOU REMAINS. AND IT IS FOR THIS REASON I GIVE YOU ONE MORE WARNING.
I SEE MANY THINGS DOWN HERE BELOW THE WORLD. AND I HAVE SEEN OTHERS COMING AND GOING...OTHERS THAT WISH YOU HARM. PERHAPS YOU SHOULD HEED CRAWLEY'S WARNING. IT IS NOT TOO LATE TO LEAVE THIS PLACE.
NO. THIS IS THE ONLY PATH FOR ME NOW.
VERY WELL. GOODBYE, MR. KNIGHT.

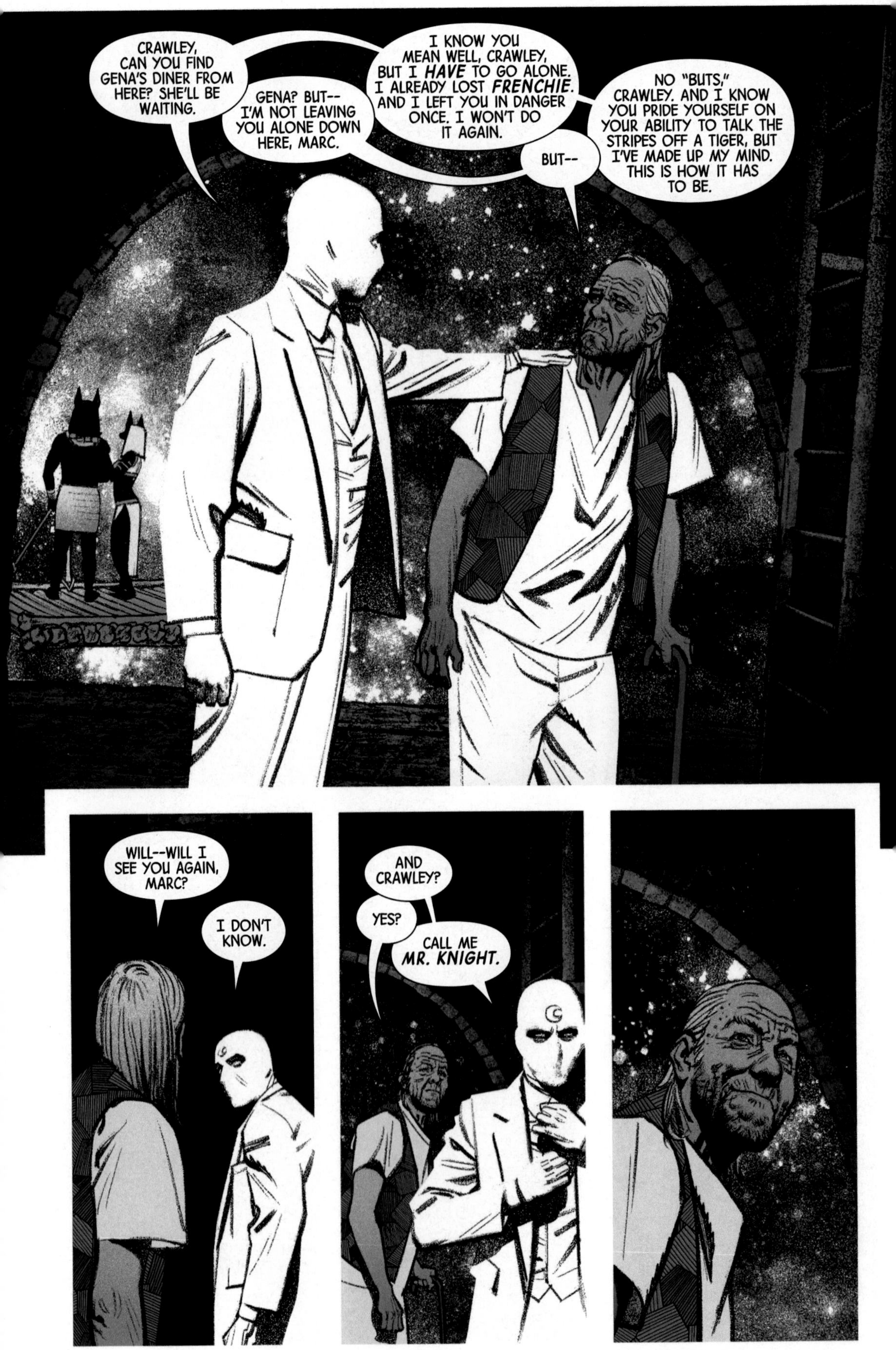
CRAWLEY, CAN YOU FIND GENA'S DINER FROM HERE? SHE'LL BE WAITING.
GENA? BUT-- I'M NOT LEAVING YOU ALONE DOWN HERE, MARC.
I KNOW YOU MEAN WELL, CRAWLEY, BUT I HAVE TO GO ALONE. I ALREADY LOST FRENCHIE. AND I LEFT YOU IN DANGER ONCE. I WON'T DO IT AGAIN.
BUT--
NO "BUTS," CRAWLEY. AND I KNOW YOU PRIDE YOURSELF ON YOUR ABILITY TO TALK THE STRIPES OFF A TIGER, BUT I'VE MADE UP MY MIND. THIS IS HOW IT HAS TO BE.
WILL--WILL I SEE YOU AGAIN, MARC?
I DON'T KNOW.
AND CRAWLEY?
YES?
CALL ME MR. KNIGHT.

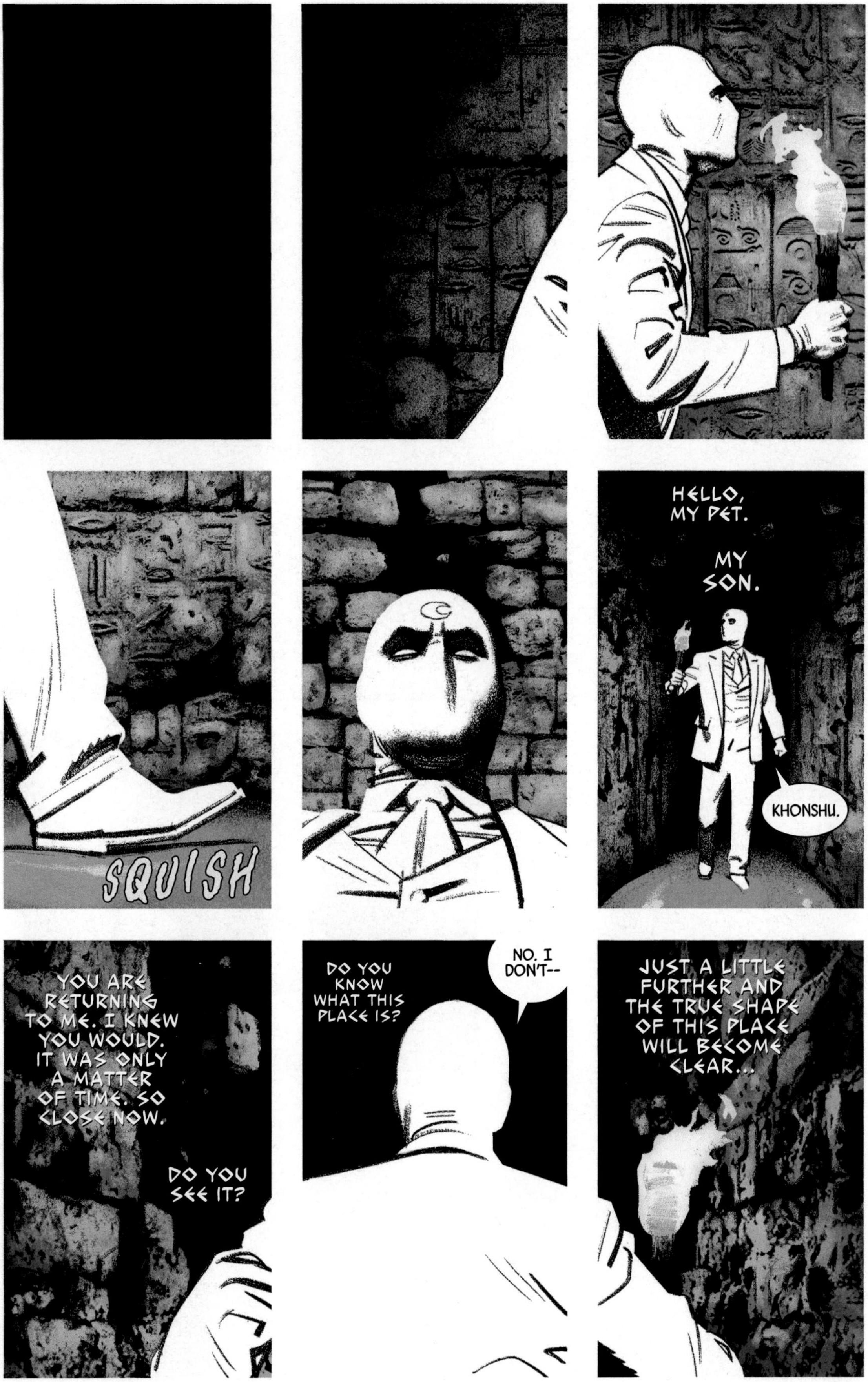
SQUISH
HELLO, MY PET.
MY SON.
KHONSHU.
YOU ARE RETURNING TO ME. I KNEW YOU WOULD. IT WAS ONLY A MATTER OF TIME. SO CLOSE NOW.
DO YOU SEE IT?
DO YOU KNOW WHAT THIS PLACE IS?
NO. I DON'T--
JUST A LITTLE FURTHER AND THE TRUE SHAPE OF THIS PLACE WILL BECOME CLEAR...

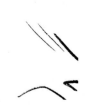

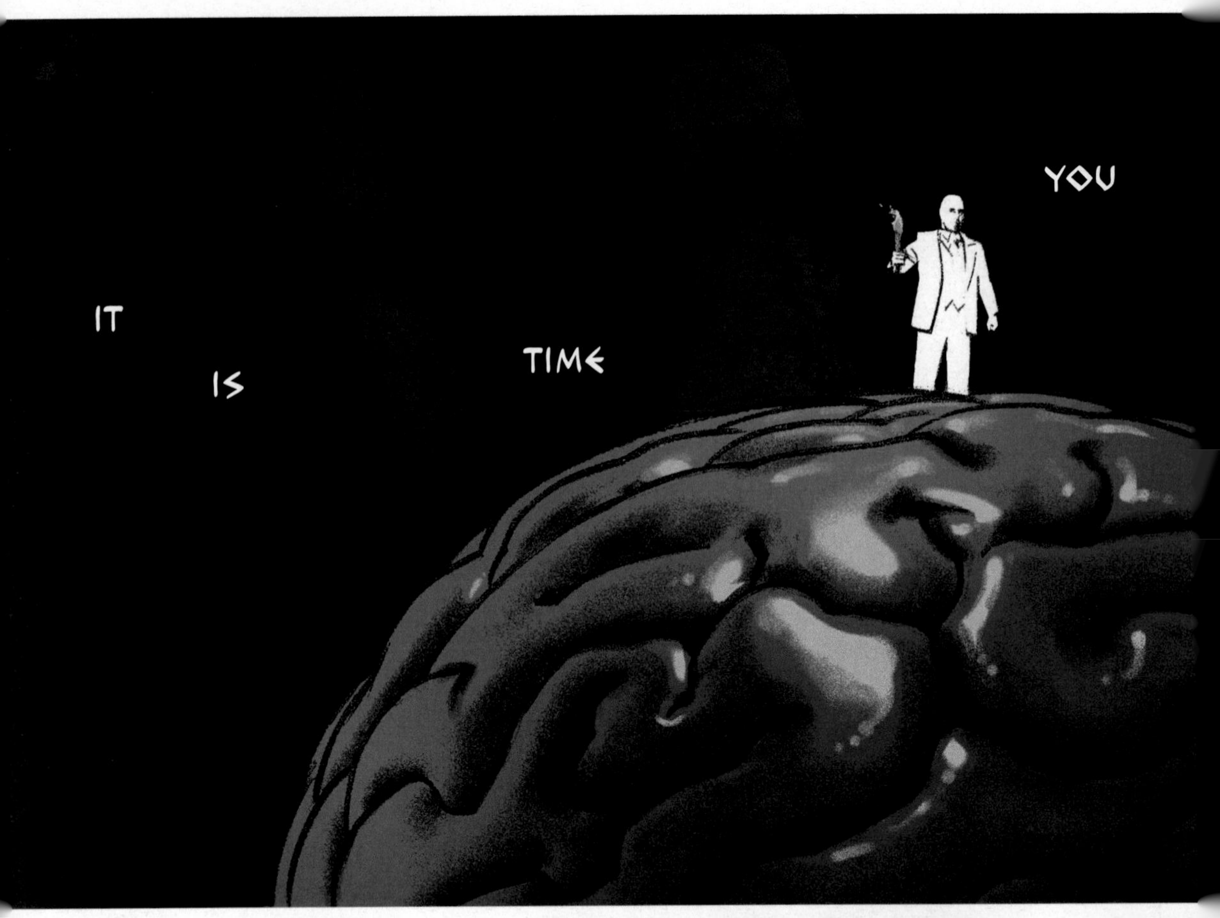
IT
IS
TIME
YOU

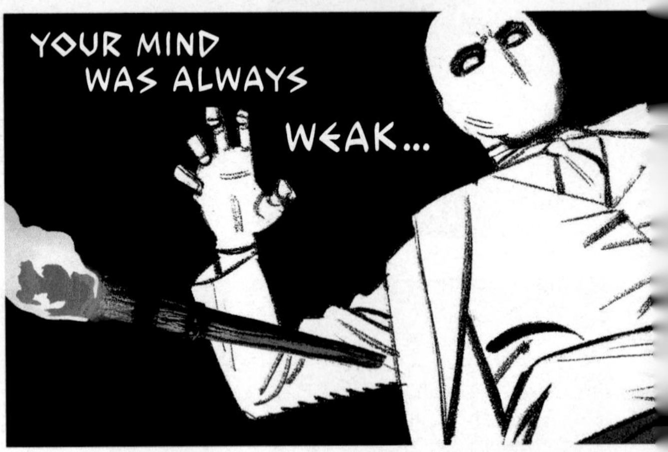
YOUR MIND WAS ALWAYS
WEAK...

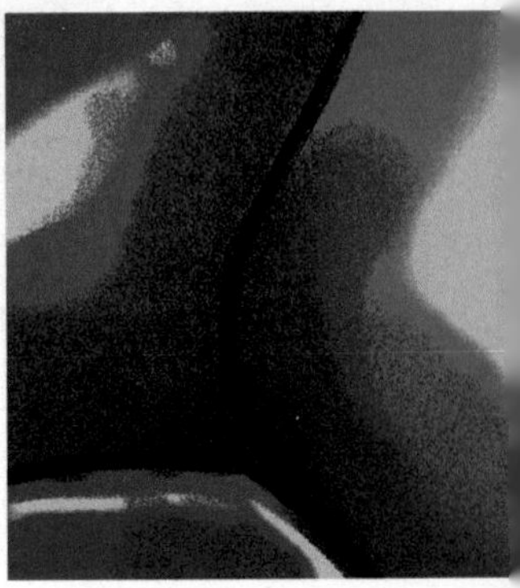

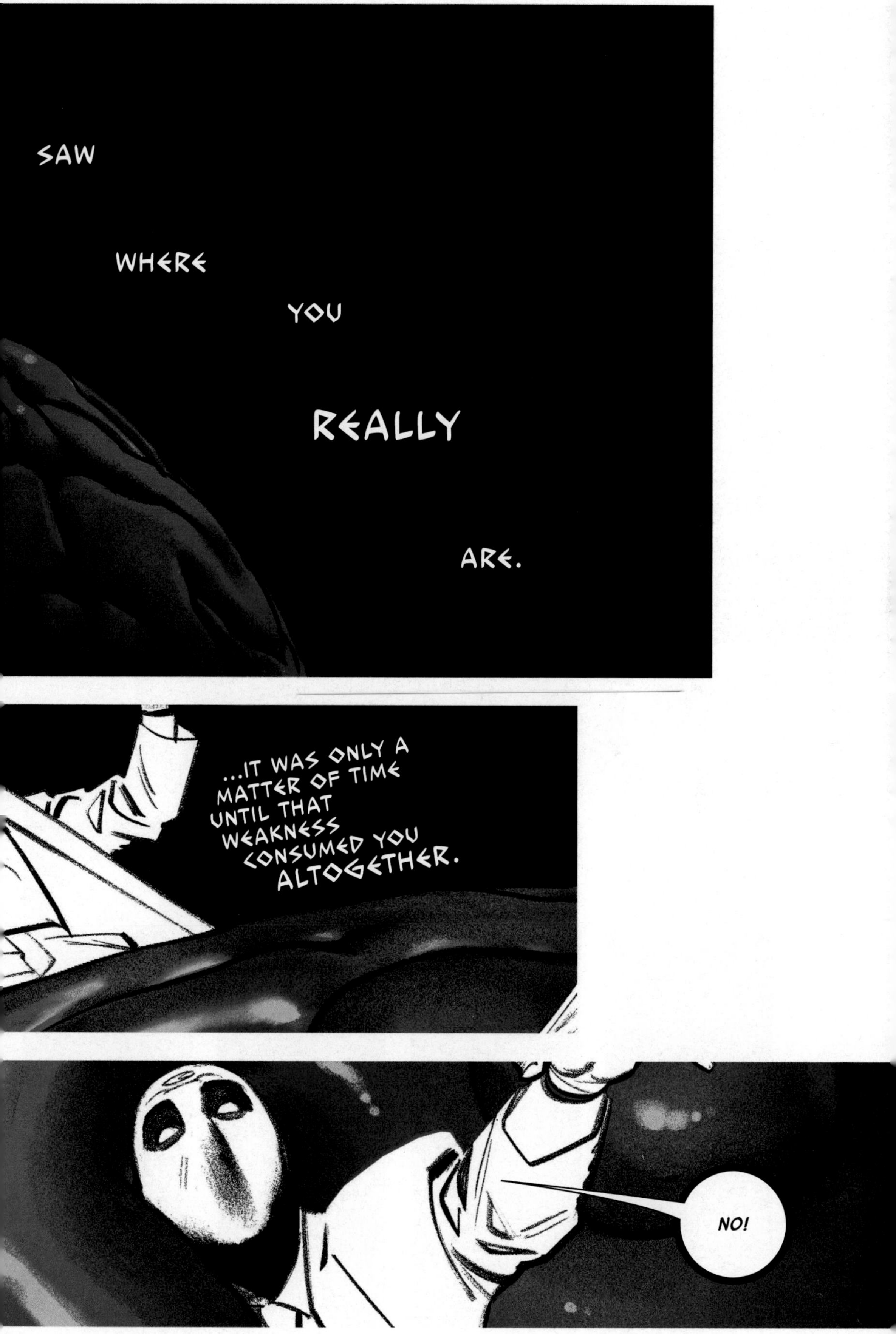
SAW
WHERE
YOU
REALLY
ARE.
...IT WAS ONLY A MATTER OF TIME UNTIL THAT WEAKNESS CONSUMED YOU ALTOGETHER.
NO!

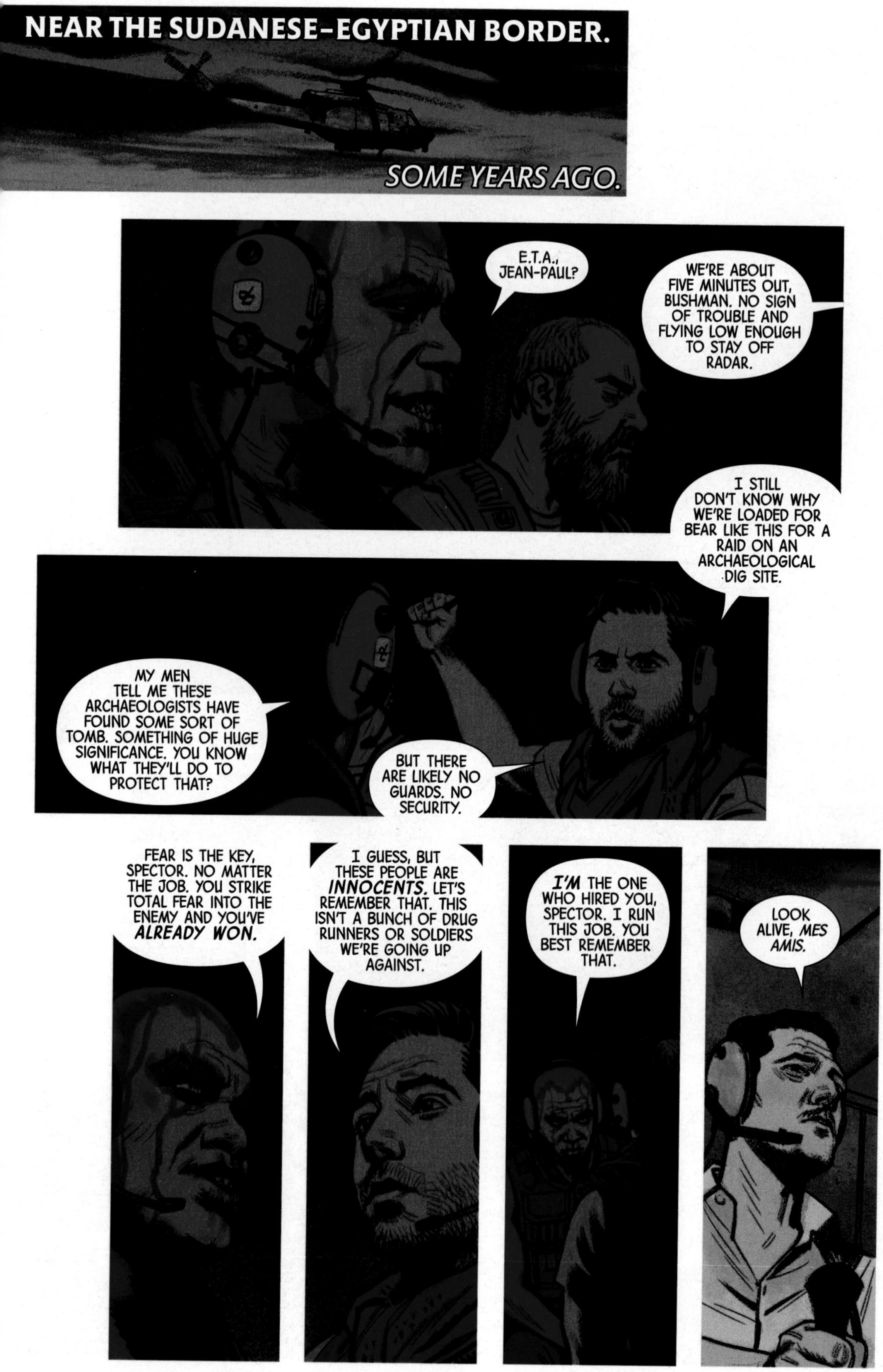
NEAR THE SUDANESE-EGYPTIAN BORDER.
SOME YEARS AGO.
E.T.A., JEAN-PAUL?
WE'RE ABOUT FIVE MINUTES OUT, BUSHMAN. NO SIGN OF TROUBLE AND FLYING LOW ENOUGH TO STAY OFF RADAR.
I STILL DON'T KNOW WHY WE'RE LOADED FOR BEAR LIKE THIS FOR A RAID ON AN ARCHAEOLOGICAL DIG SITE.
MY MEN TELL ME THESE ARCHAEOLOGISTS HAVE FOUND SOME SORT OF TOMB. SOMETHING OF HUGE SIGNIFICANCE. YOU KNOW WHAT THEY'LL DO TO PROTECT THAT?
BUT THERE ARE LIKELY NO GUARDS. NO SECURITY.
FEAR IS THE KEY, SPECTOR. NO MATTER THE JOB. YOU STRIKE TOTAL FEAR INTO THE ENEMY AND YOU'VE ALREADY WON.
I GUESS, BUT THESE PEOPLE ARE INNOCENTS. LET'S REMEMBER THAT. THIS ISN'T A BUNCH OF DRUG RUNNERS OR SOLDIERS WE'RE GOING UP AGAINST.
I'M THE ONE WHO HIRED YOU, SPECTOR. I RUN THIS JOB. YOU BEST REMEMBER THAT.
LOOK ALIVE, MES AMIS.

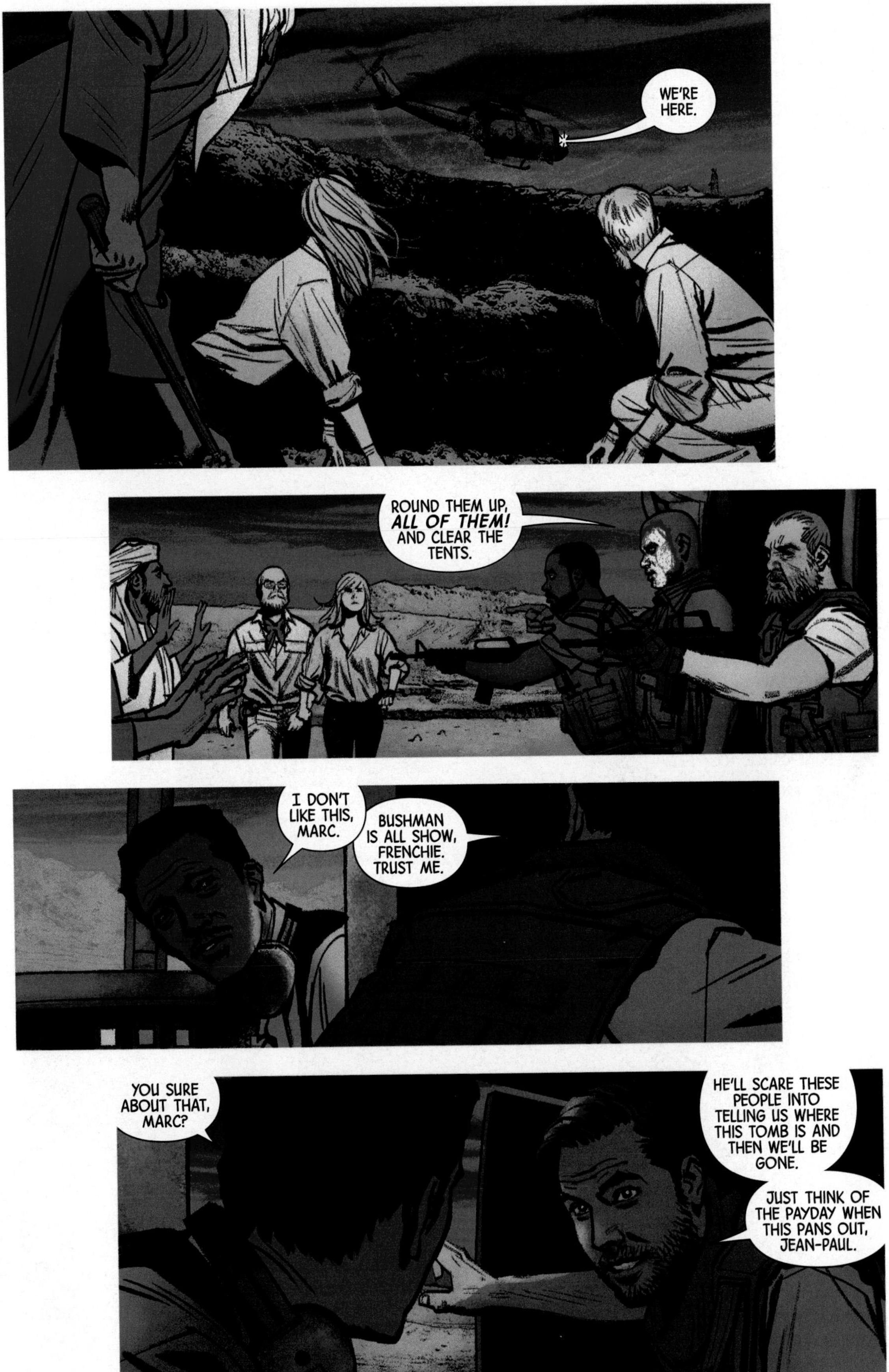
WE'RE HERE.
ROUND THEM UP, ALL OF THEM! AND CLEAR THE TENTS.
I DON'T LIKE THIS, MARC.
BUSHMAN IS ALL SHOW, FRENCHIE. TRUST ME.
YOU SURE ABOUT THAT, MARC?
HE'LL SCARE THESE PEOPLE INTO TELLING US WHERE THIS TOMB IS AND THEN WE'LL BE GONE.
JUST THINK OF THE PAYDAY WHEN THIS PANS OUT, JEAN-PAUL.

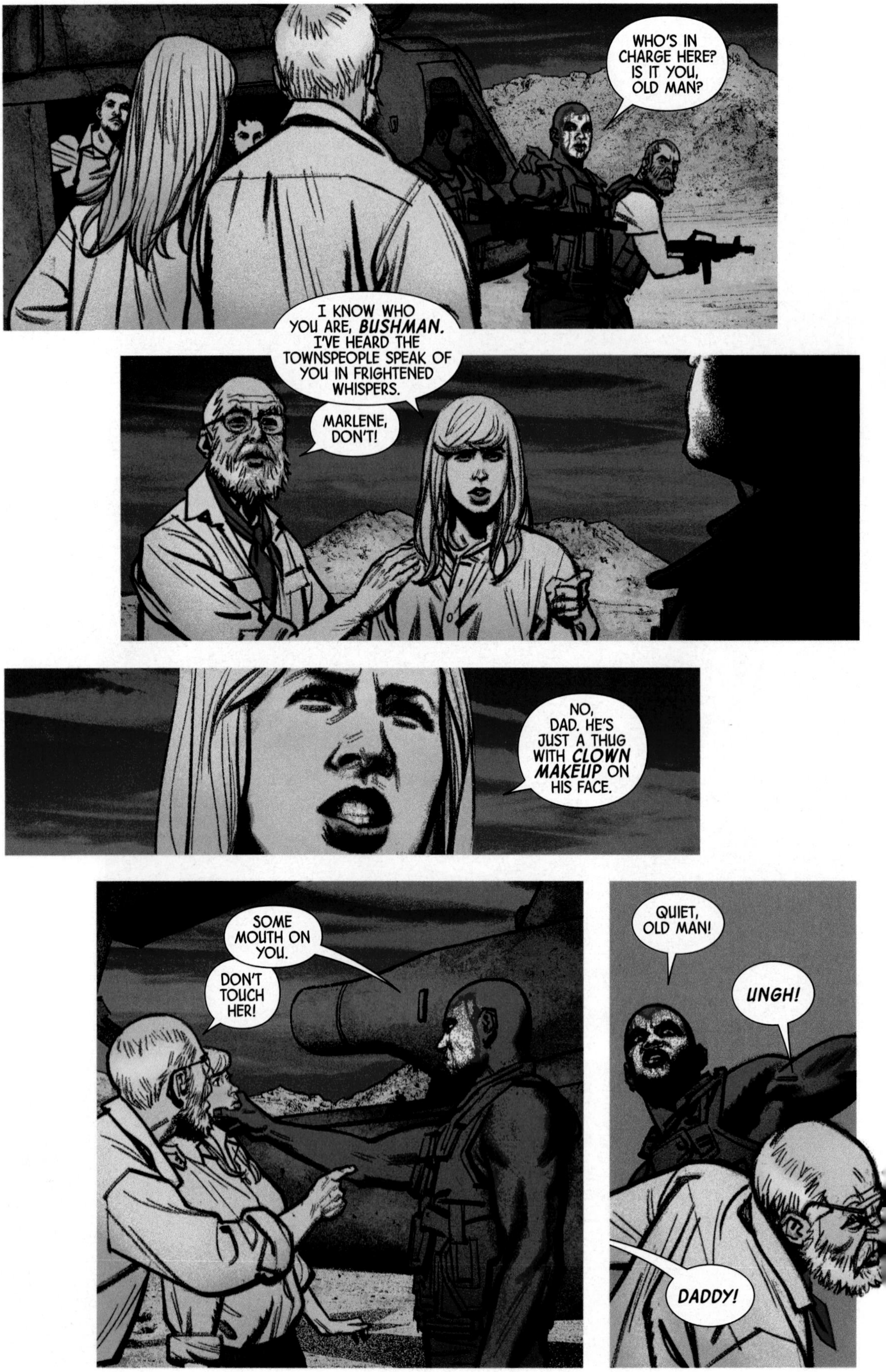
WHO'S IN CHARGE HERE? IS IT YOU, OLD MAN?
I KNOW WHO YOU ARE, BUSHMAN. I'VE HEARD THE TOWNSPEOPLE SPEAK OF YOU IN FRIGHTENED WHISPERS.
MARLENE, DON'T!
NO, DAD. HE'S JUST A THUG WITH CLOWN MAKEUP ON HIS FACE.
SOME MOUTH ON YOU.
DON'T TOUCH HER!
QUIET, OLD MAN!
UNGH!
DADDY!

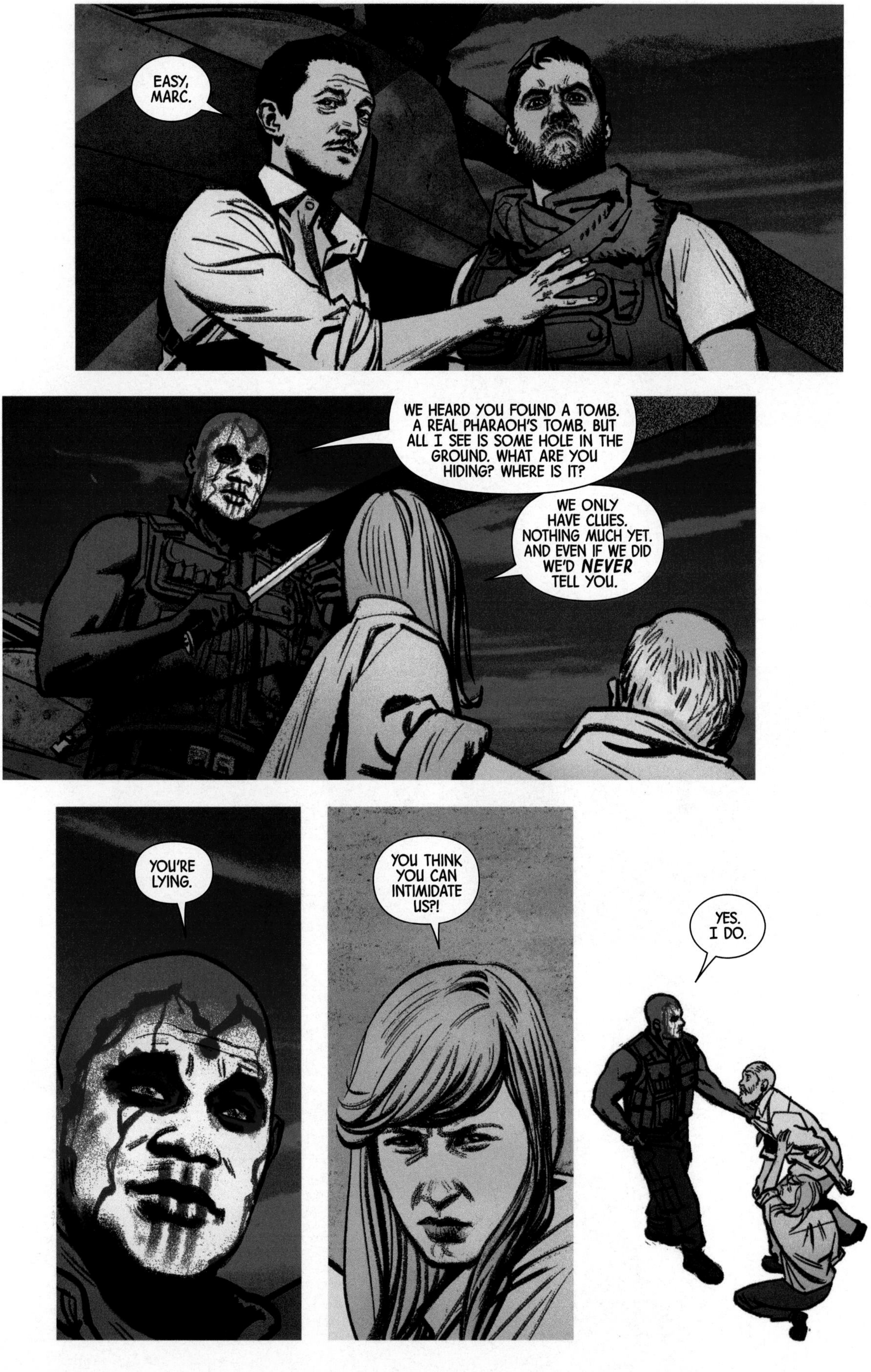
EASY, MARC.
WE HEARD YOU FOUND A TOMB. A REAL PHARAOH'S TOMB. BUT ALL I SEE IS SOME HOLE IN THE GROUND. WHAT ARE YOU HIDING? WHERE IS IT?
WE ONLY HAVE CLUES. NOTHING MUCH YET. AND EVEN IF WE DID WE'D NEVER TELL YOU.
YOU'RE LYING.
YOU THINK YOU CAN INTIMIDATE US?!
YES. I DO.

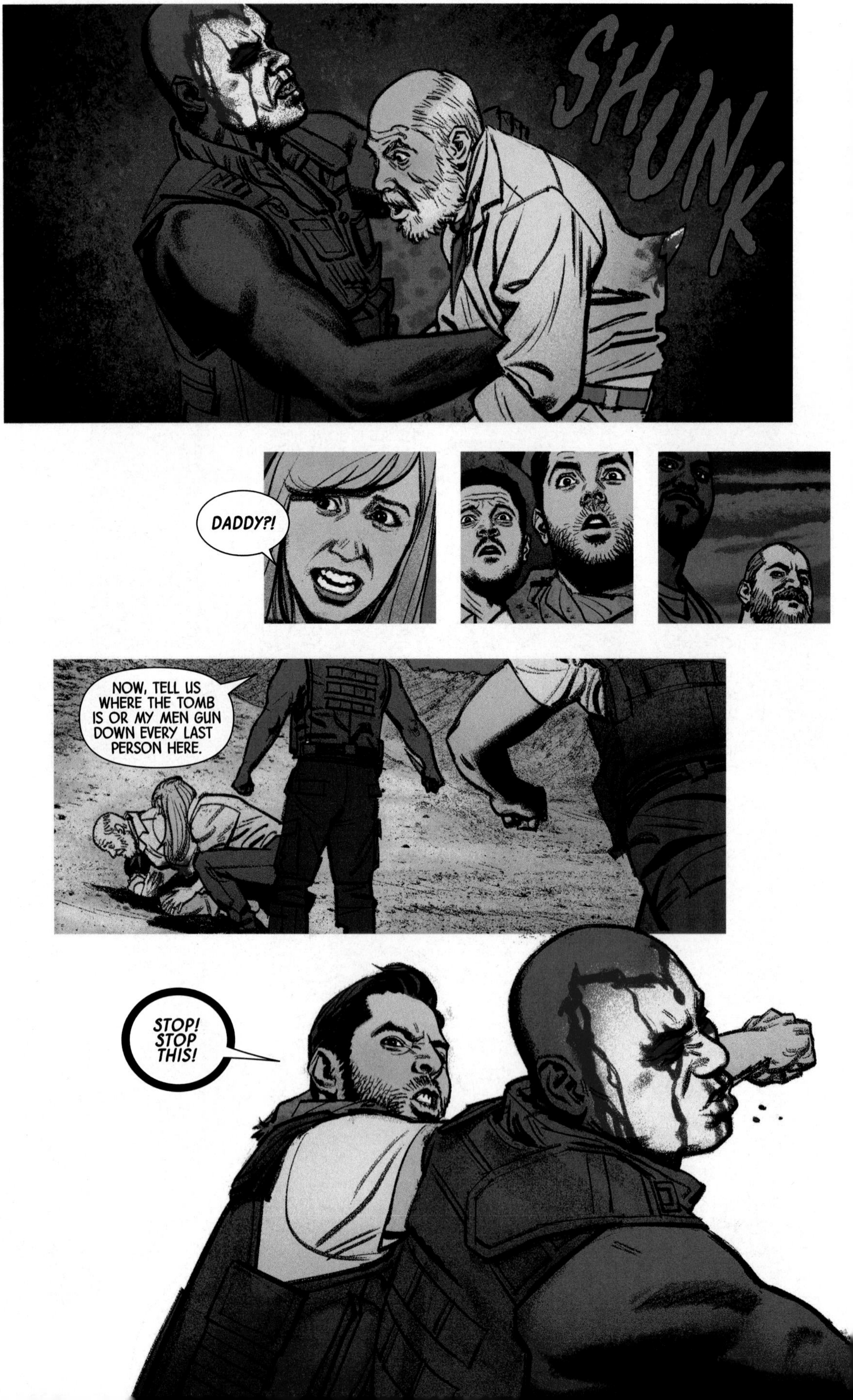
SHUNK
DADDY?!
NOW, TELL US WHERE THE TOMB IS OR MY MEN GUN DOWN EVERY LAST PERSON HERE.
STOP! STOP THIS!

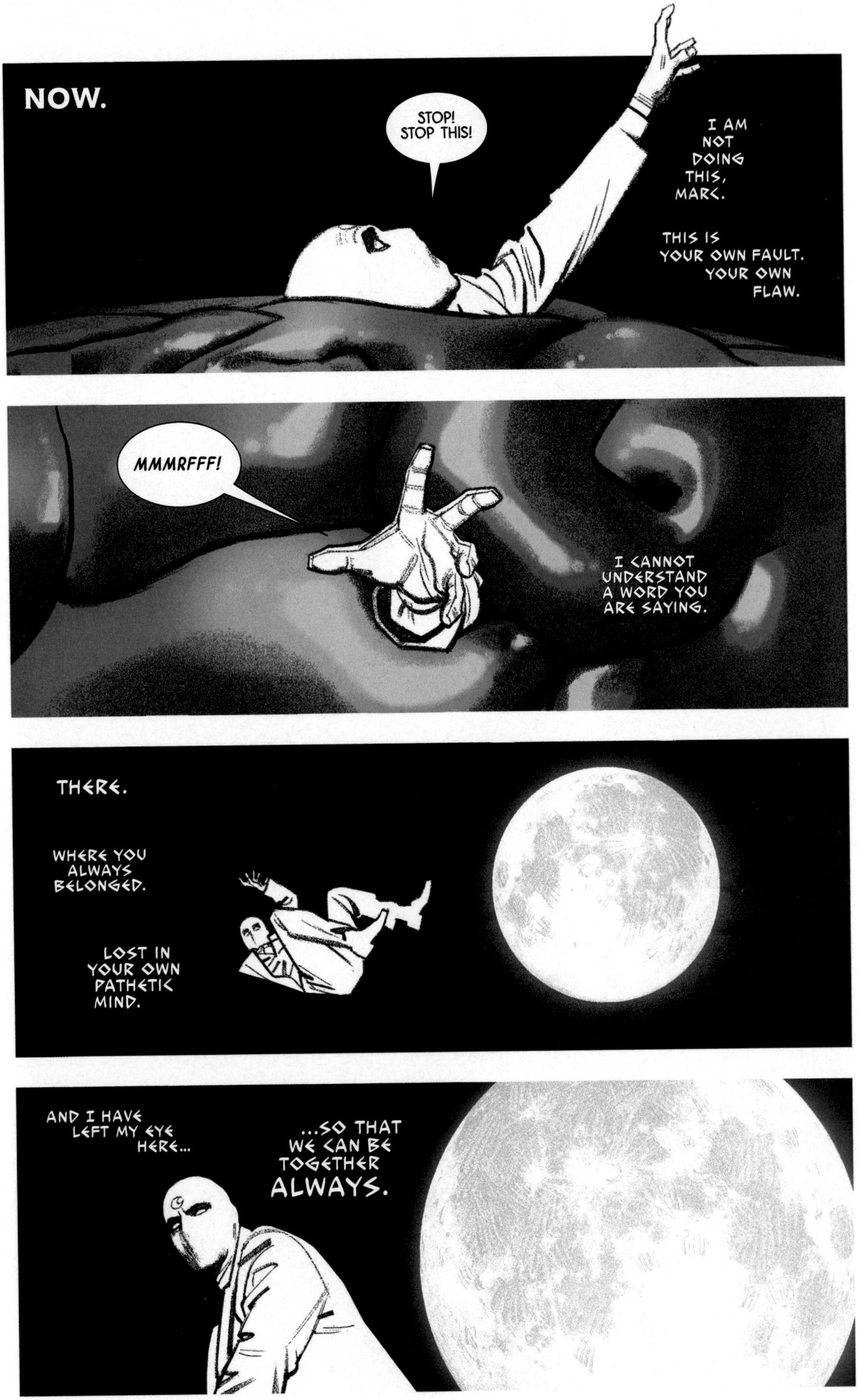
NOW.
STOP! STOP THIS!
I AM NOT DOING THIS, MARC.
THIS IS YOUR OWN FAULT. YOUR OWN FLAW.
MMMRFFF!
I CANNOT UNDERSTAND A WORD YOU ARE SAYING.
THERE.
WHERE YOU ALWAYS BELONGED.
LOST IN YOUR OWN PATHETIC MIND.
AND I HAVE LEFT MY EYE HERE...
...SO THAT WE CAN BE TOGETHER ALWAYS.

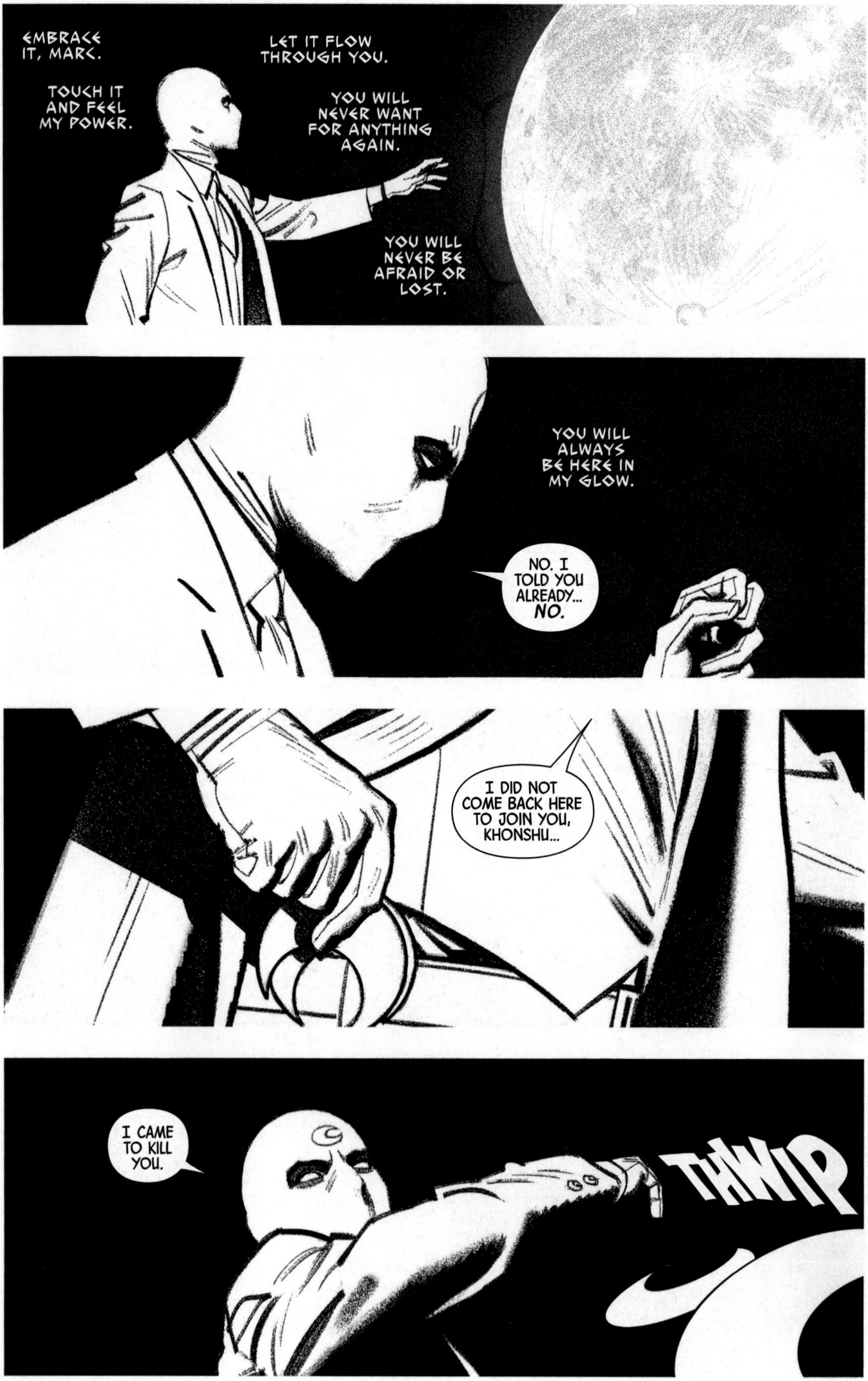
EMBRACE IT, MARC.
TOUCH IT AND FEEL MY POWER.
LET IT FLOW THROUGH YOU.
YOU WILL NEVER WANT FOR ANYTHING AGAIN.
YOU WILL NEVER BE AFRAID OR LOST.
YOU WILL ALWAYS BE HERE IN MY GLOW.
NO. I TOLD YOU ALREADY... NO.
I DID NOT COME BACK HERE TO JOIN YOU, KHONSHU...
I CAME TO KILL YOU.
THWIP

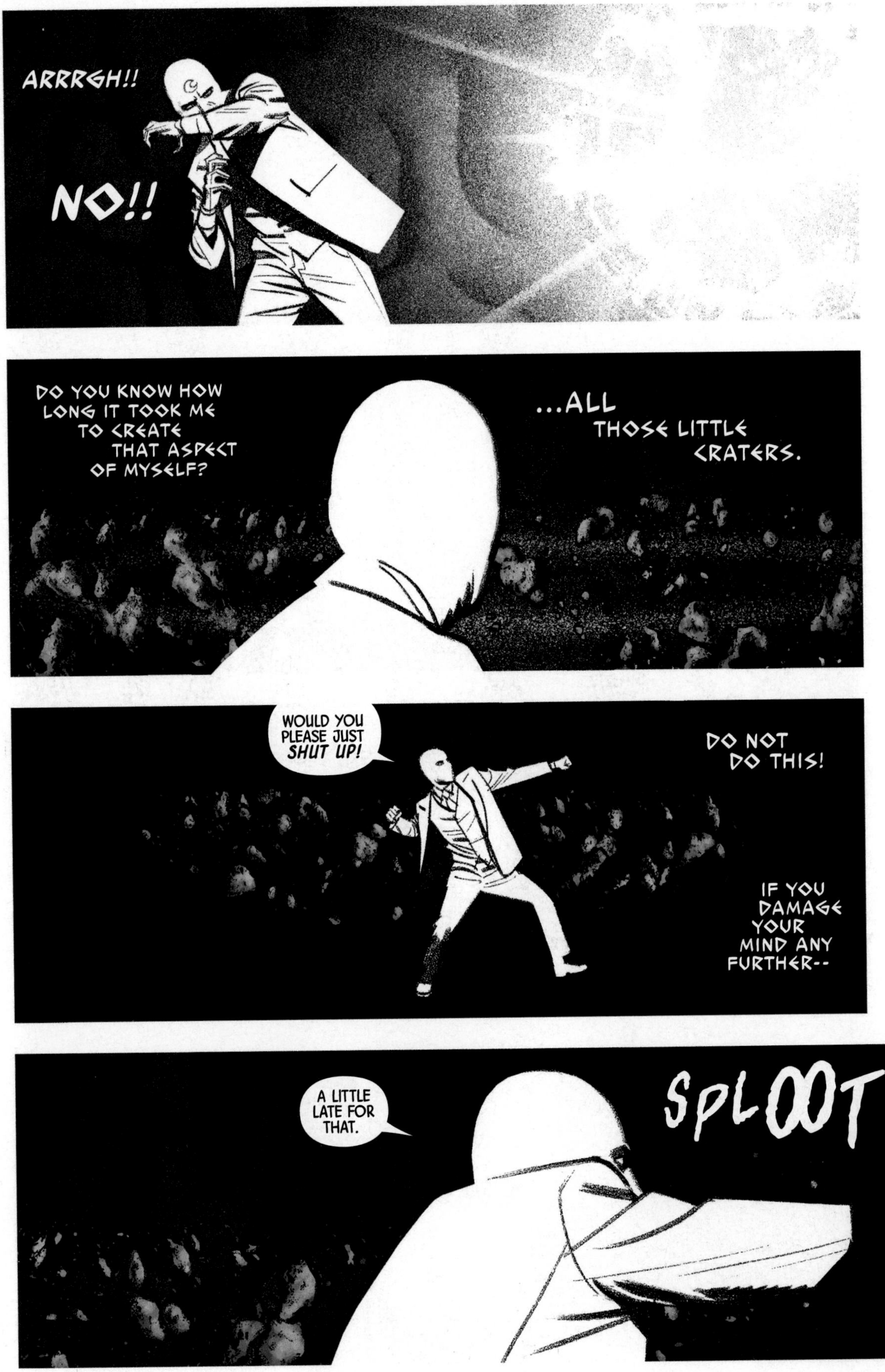
ARRRGH!!
NO!!
DO YOU KNOW HOW LONG IT TOOK ME TO CREATE THAT ASPECT OF MYSELF?
...ALL THOSE LITTLE CRATERS.
WOULD YOU PLEASE JUST SHUT UP!
DO NOT DO THIS!
IF YOU DAMAGE YOUR MIND ANY FURTHER--
A LITTLE LATE FOR THAT.
SPLOOT

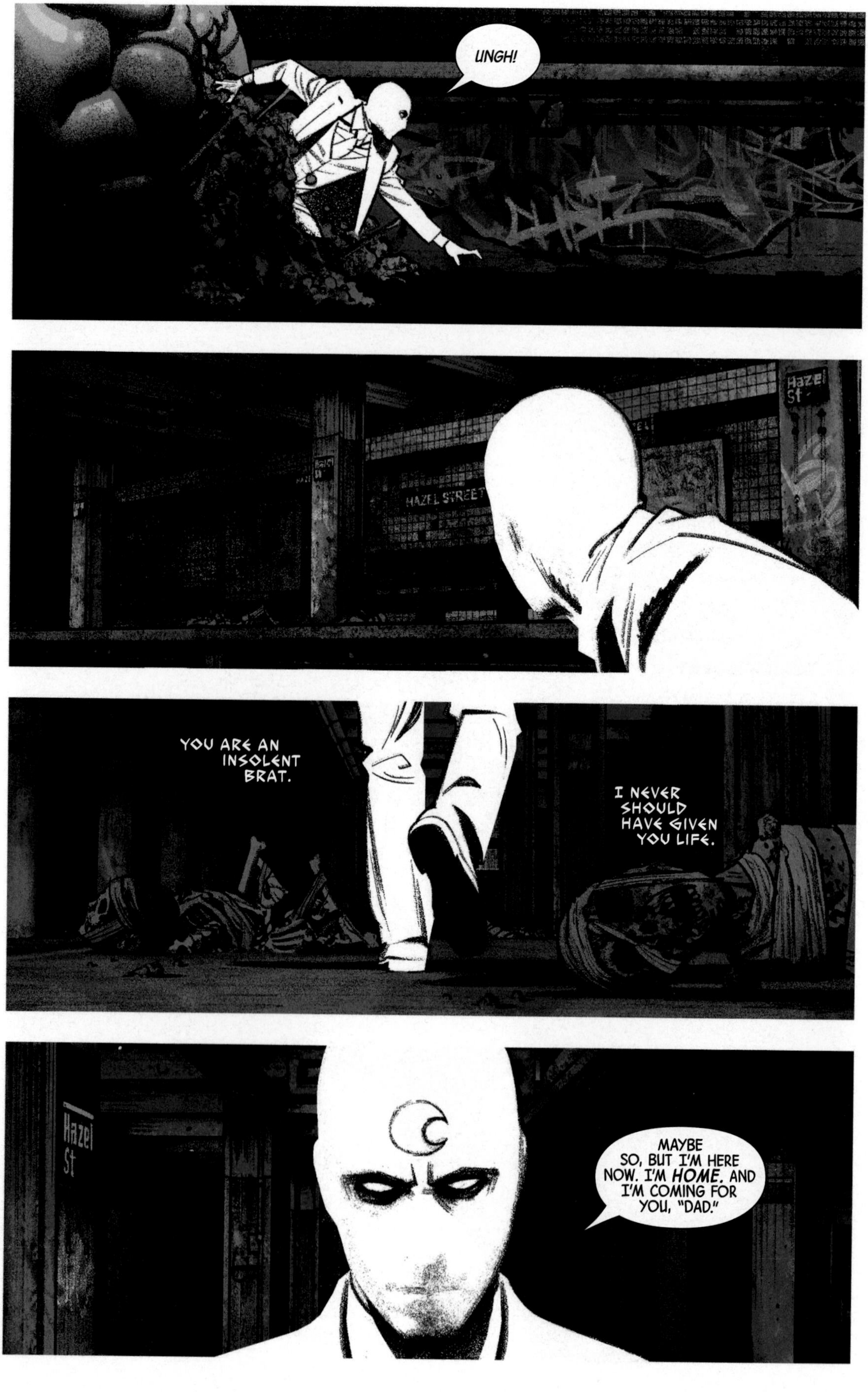
UNGH!
HAZEL STREET
Hazel St
YOU ARE AN INSOLENT BRAT.
I NEVER SHOULD HAVE GIVEN YOU LIFE.
Hazel St
MAYBE SO, BUT I'M HERE NOW. I'M *HOME.* AND I'M COMING FOR YOU, "DAD."

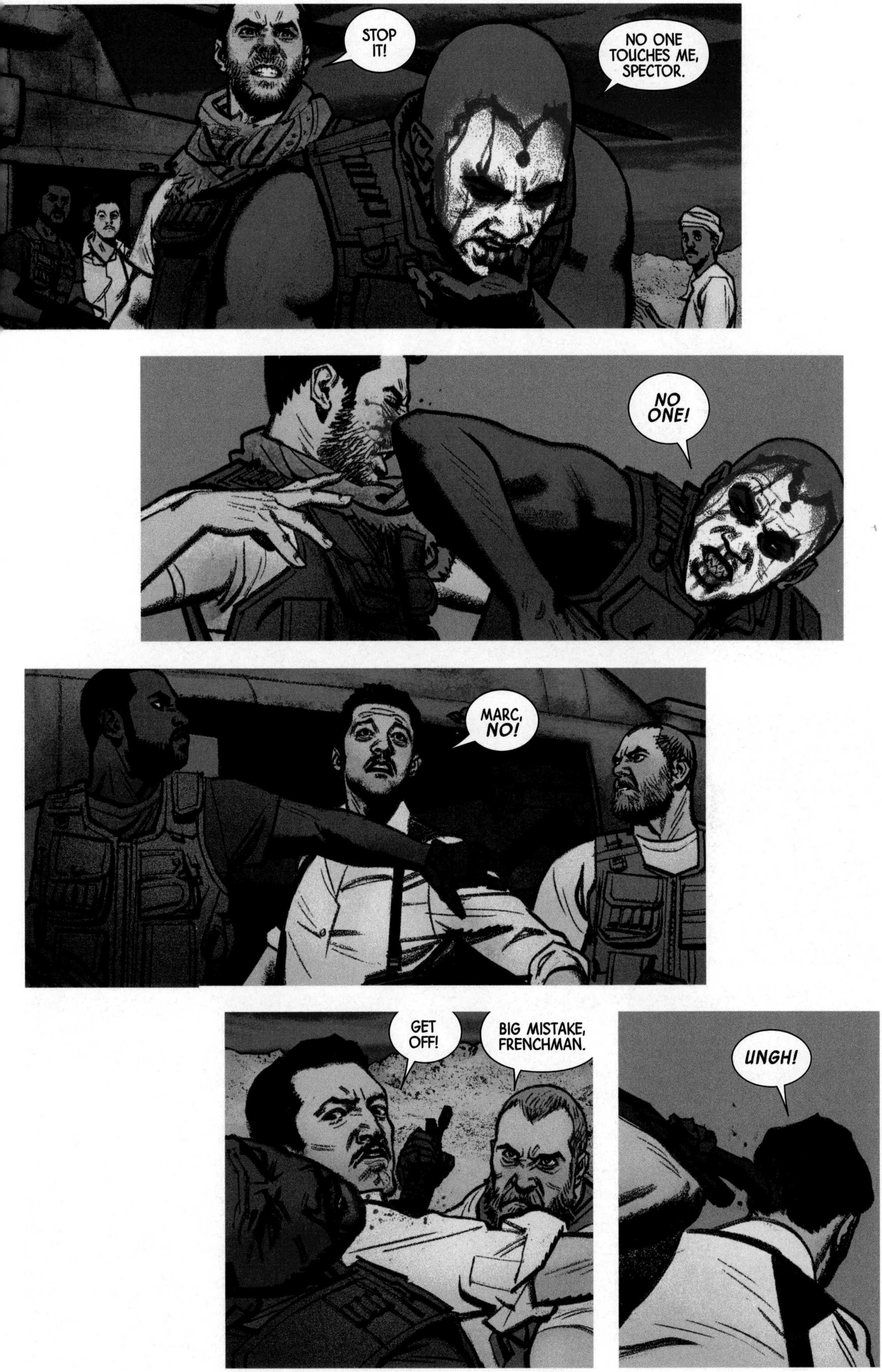
STOP IT!
NO ONE TOUCHES ME, SPECTOR.
NO ONE!
MARC, NO!
GET OFF!
BIG MISTAKE, FRENCHMAN.
UNGH!

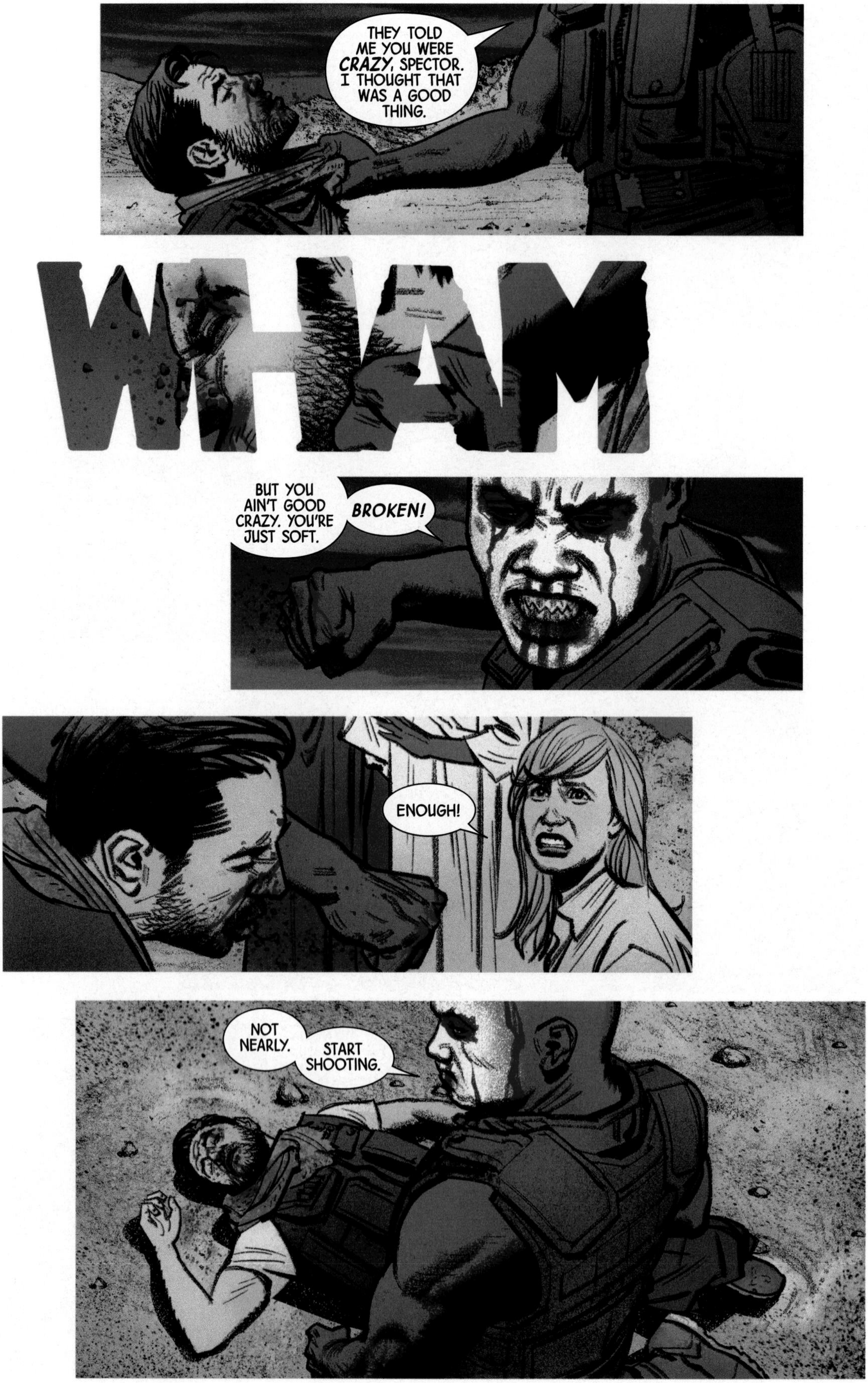
THEY TOLD ME YOU WERE *CRAZY*, SPECTOR. I THOUGHT THAT WAS A GOOD THING.
WHAM
BUT YOU AIN'T GOOD CRAZY. YOU'RE JUST SOFT.
BROKEN!
ENOUGH!
NOT NEARLY.
START SHOOTING.

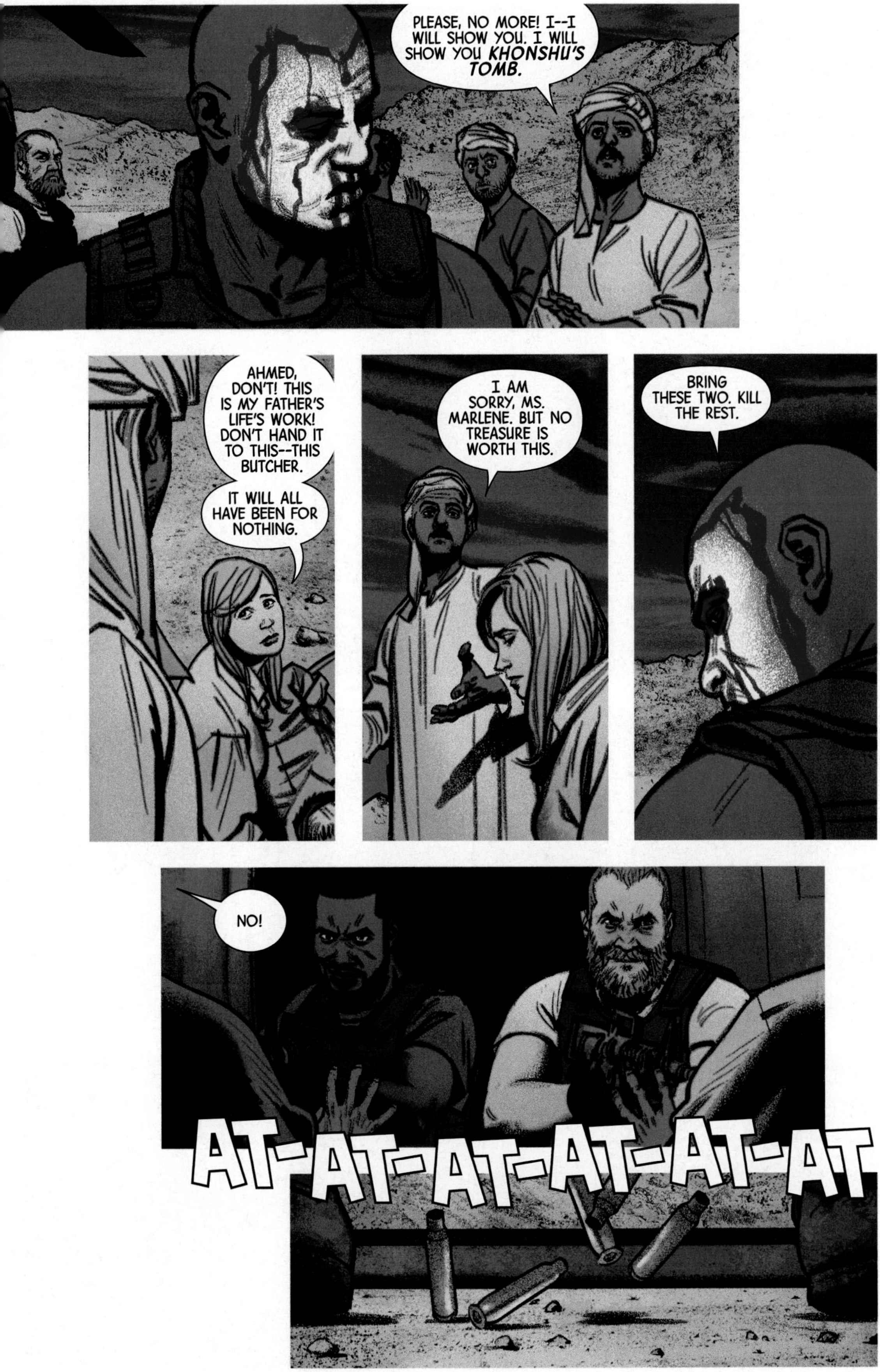
PLEASE, NO MORE! I--I WILL SHOW YOU. I WILL SHOW YOU KHONSHU'S TOMB.
AHMED, DON'T! THIS IS MY FATHER'S LIFE'S WORK! DON'T HAND IT TO THIS--THIS BUTCHER.
IT WILL ALL HAVE BEEN FOR NOTHING.
I AM SORRY, MS. MARLENE. BUT NO TREASURE IS WORTH THIS.
BRING THESE TWO. KILL THE REST.
NO!
AT-AT-AT-AT-AT-AT-AT

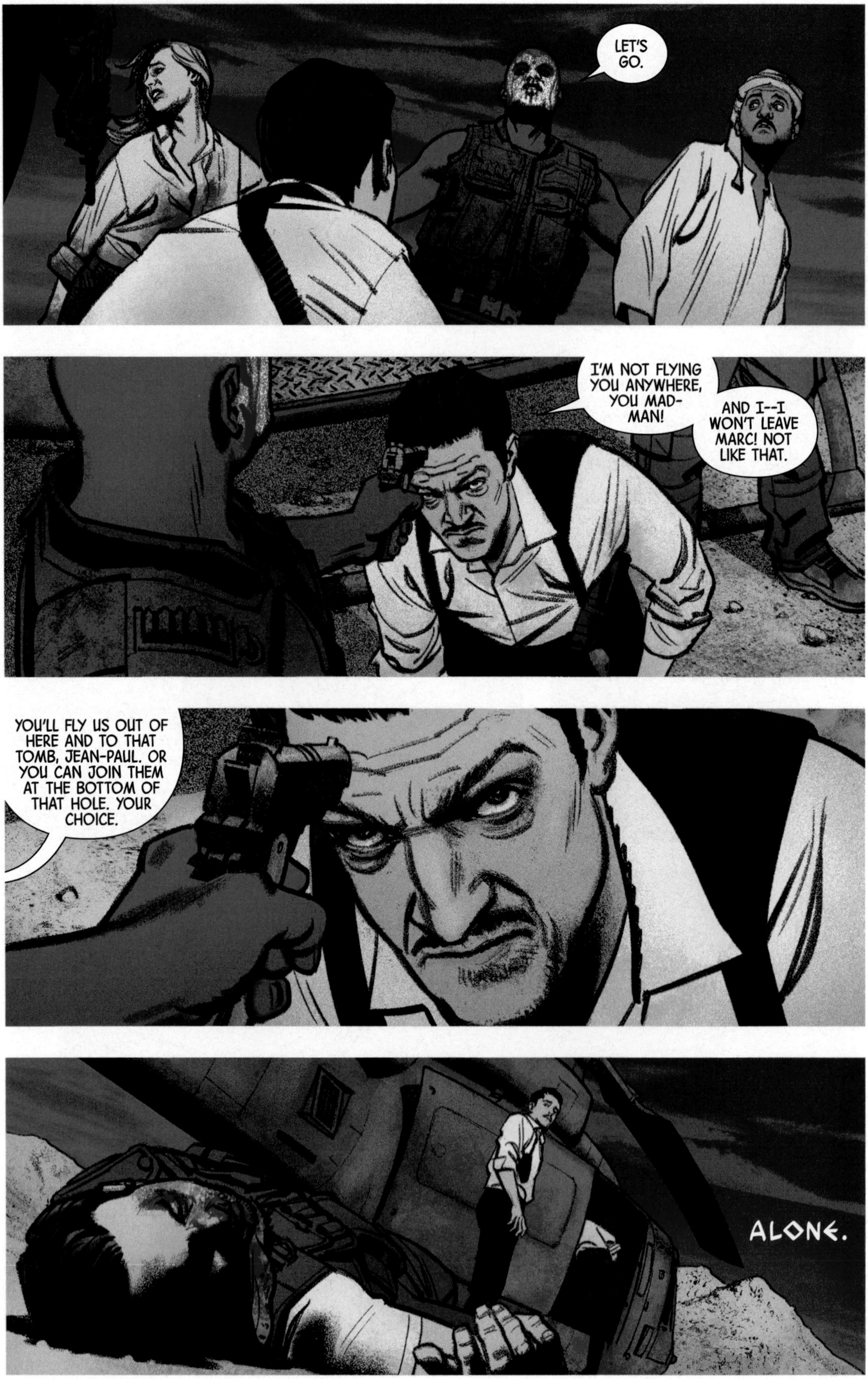
LET'S GO.
I'M NOT FLYING YOU ANYWHERE, YOU MAD-MAN!
AND I--I WON'T LEAVE MARC! NOT LIKE THAT.
YOU'LL FLY US OUT OF HERE AND TO THAT TOMB, JEAN-PAUL. OR YOU CAN JOIN THEM AT THE BOTTOM OF THAT HOLE. YOUR CHOICE.
ALONE.

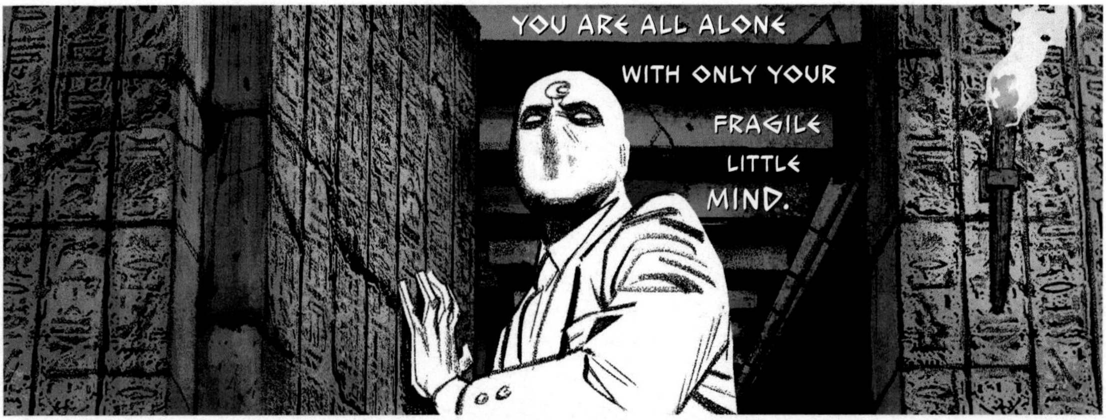
YOU ARE ALL ALONE
WITH ONLY YOUR
FRAGILE
LITTLE
MIND.

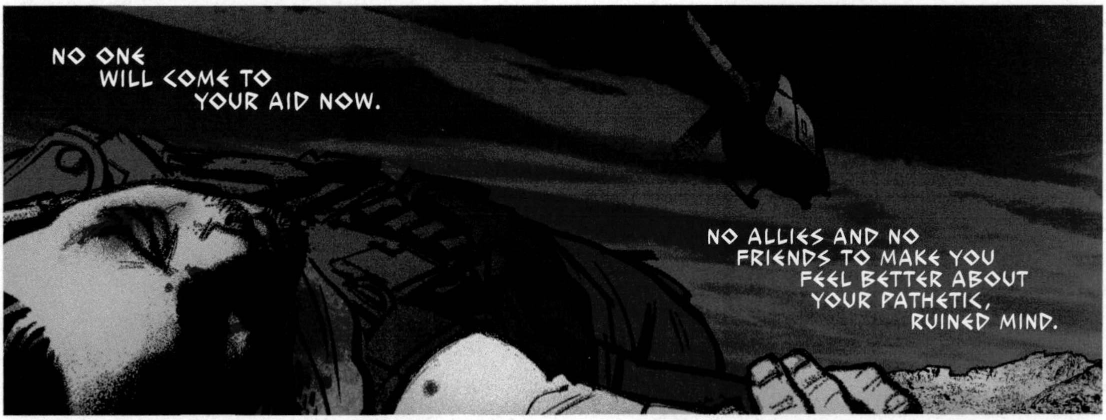
NO ONE WILL COME TO YOUR AID NOW.
NO ALLIES AND NO FRIENDS TO MAKE YOU FEEL BETTER ABOUT YOUR PATHETIC, RUINED MIND.

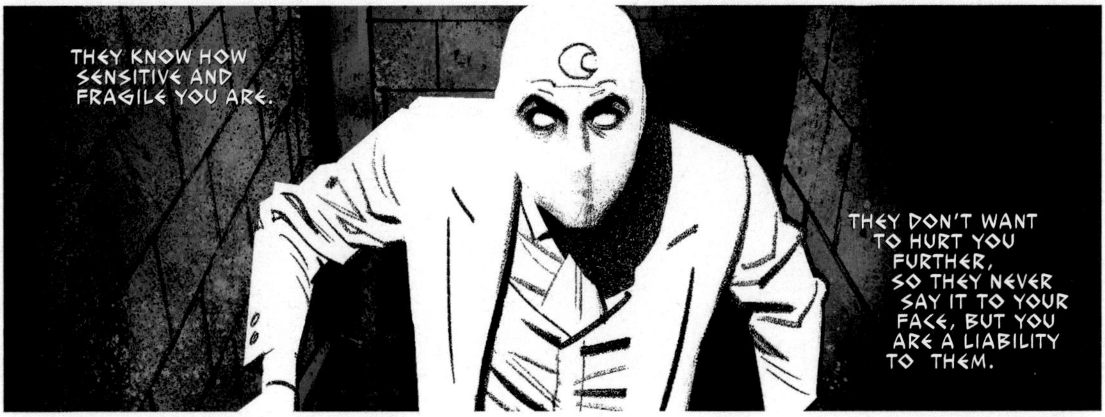
THEY KNOW HOW SENSITIVE AND FRAGILE YOU ARE.
THEY DON'T WANT TO HURT YOU FURTHER, SO THEY NEVER SAY IT TO YOUR FACE, BUT YOU ARE A LIABILITY TO THEM.

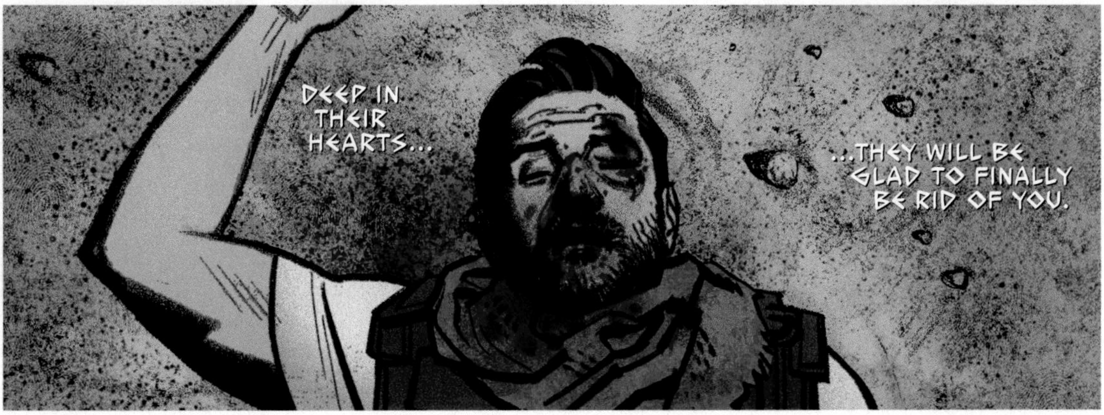
DEEP IN THEIR HEARTS...
...THEY WILL BE GLAD TO FINALLY BE RID OF YOU.

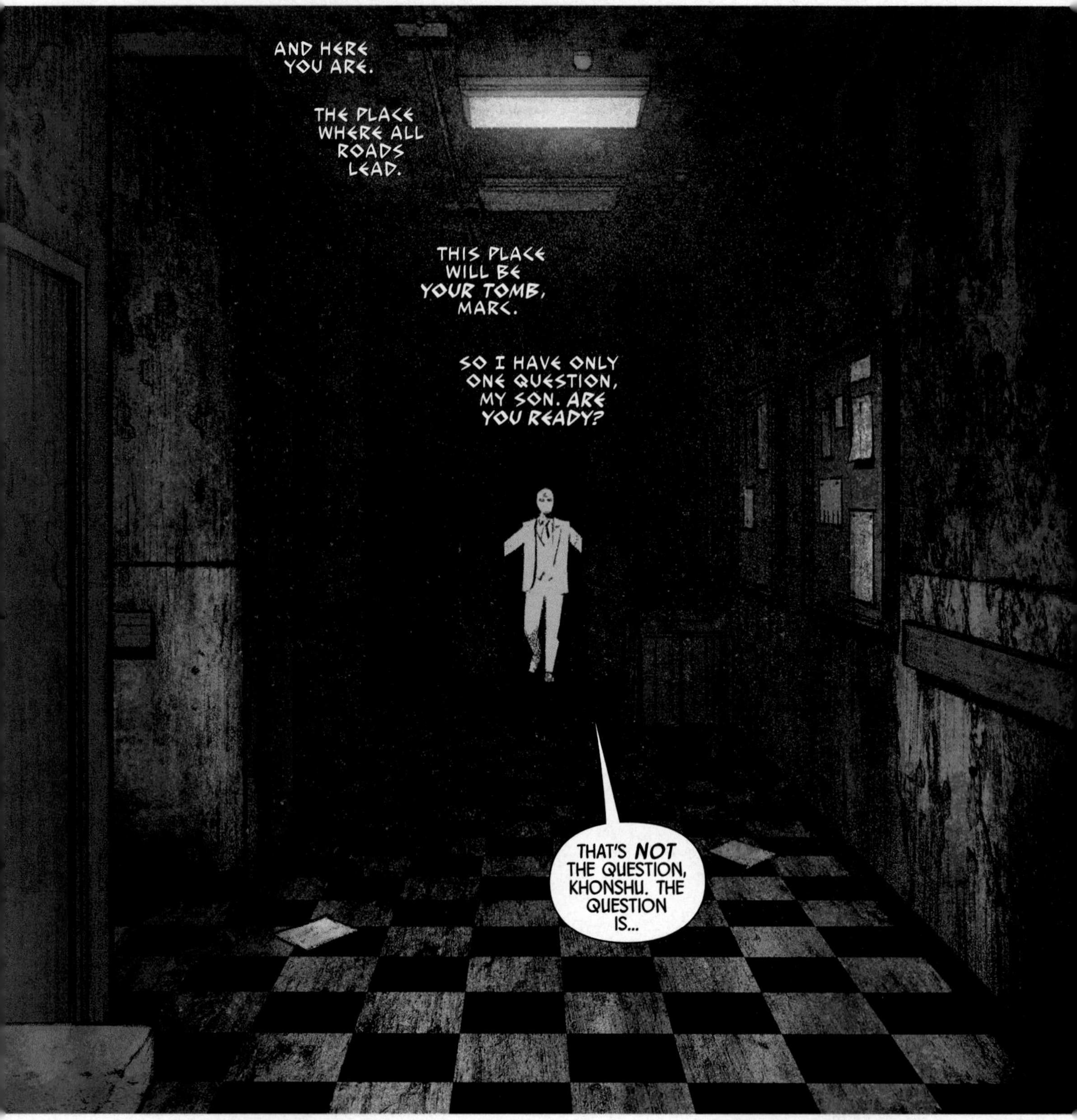
AND HERE YOU ARE.
THE PLACE WHERE ALL ROADS LEAD.
THIS PLACE WILL BE YOUR TOMB, MARC.
SO I HAVE ONLY ONE QUESTION, MY SON. ARE YOU READY?
THAT'S NOT THE QUESTION, KHONSHU. THE QUESTION IS...

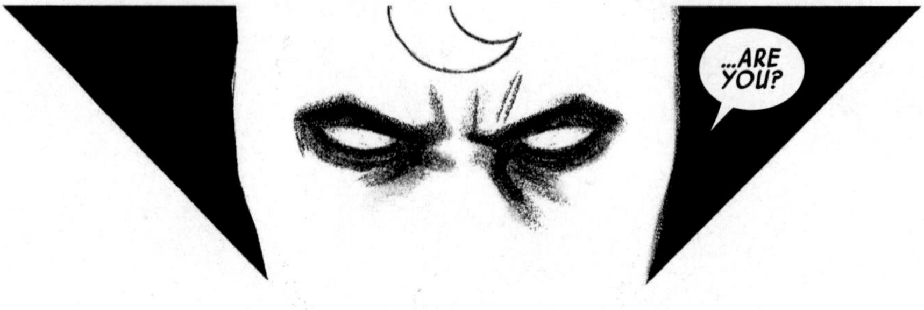
...ARE YOU?

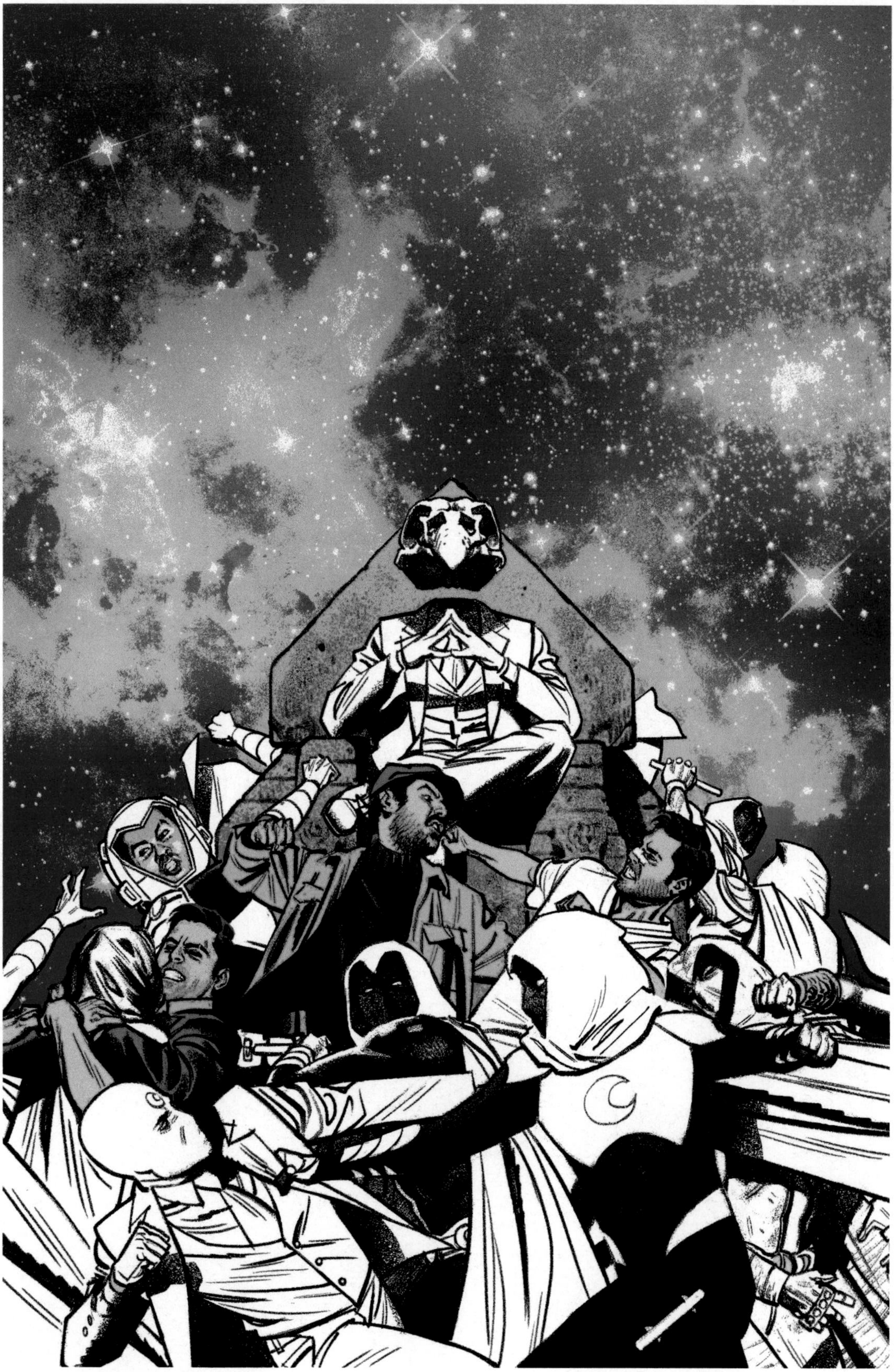

BIRTH AND DEATH
PART FIVE

14

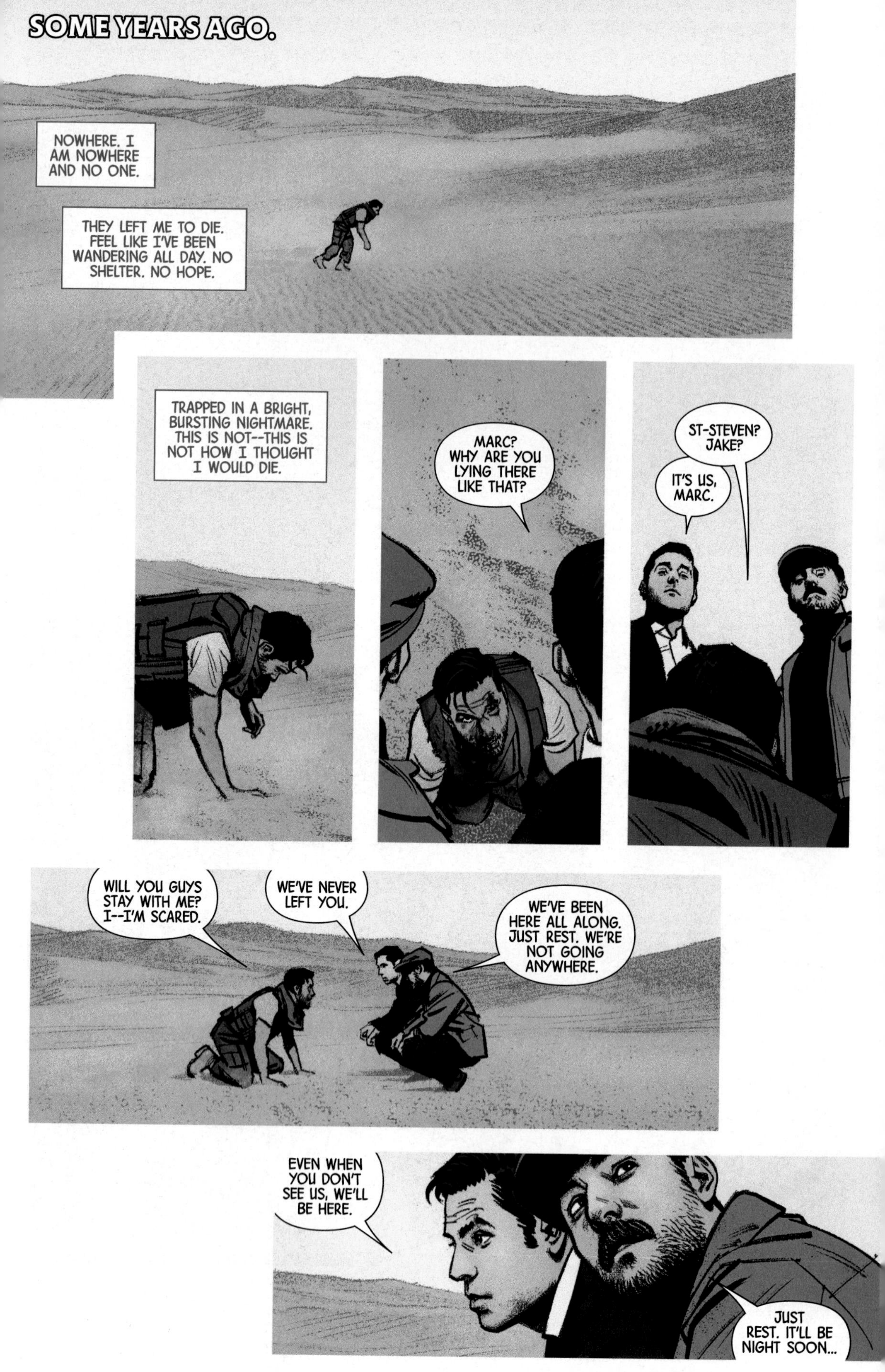
SOME YEARS AGO.
NOWHERE. I AM NOWHERE AND NO ONE.
THEY LEFT ME TO DIE. FEEL LIKE I'VE BEEN WANDERING ALL DAY. NO SHELTER. NO HOPE.
TRAPPED IN A BRIGHT, BURSTING NIGHTMARE. THIS IS NOT--THIS IS NOT HOW I THOUGHT I WOULD DIE.
MARC? WHY ARE YOU LYING THERE LIKE THAT?
ST-STEVEN? JAKE?
IT'S US, MARC.
WILL YOU GUYS STAY WITH ME? I--I'M SCARED.
WE'VE NEVER LEFT YOU.
WE'VE BEEN HERE ALL ALONG. JUST REST. WE'RE NOT GOING ANYWHERE.
EVEN WHEN YOU DON'T SEE US, WE'LL BE HERE.
JUST REST. IT'LL BE NIGHT SOON...

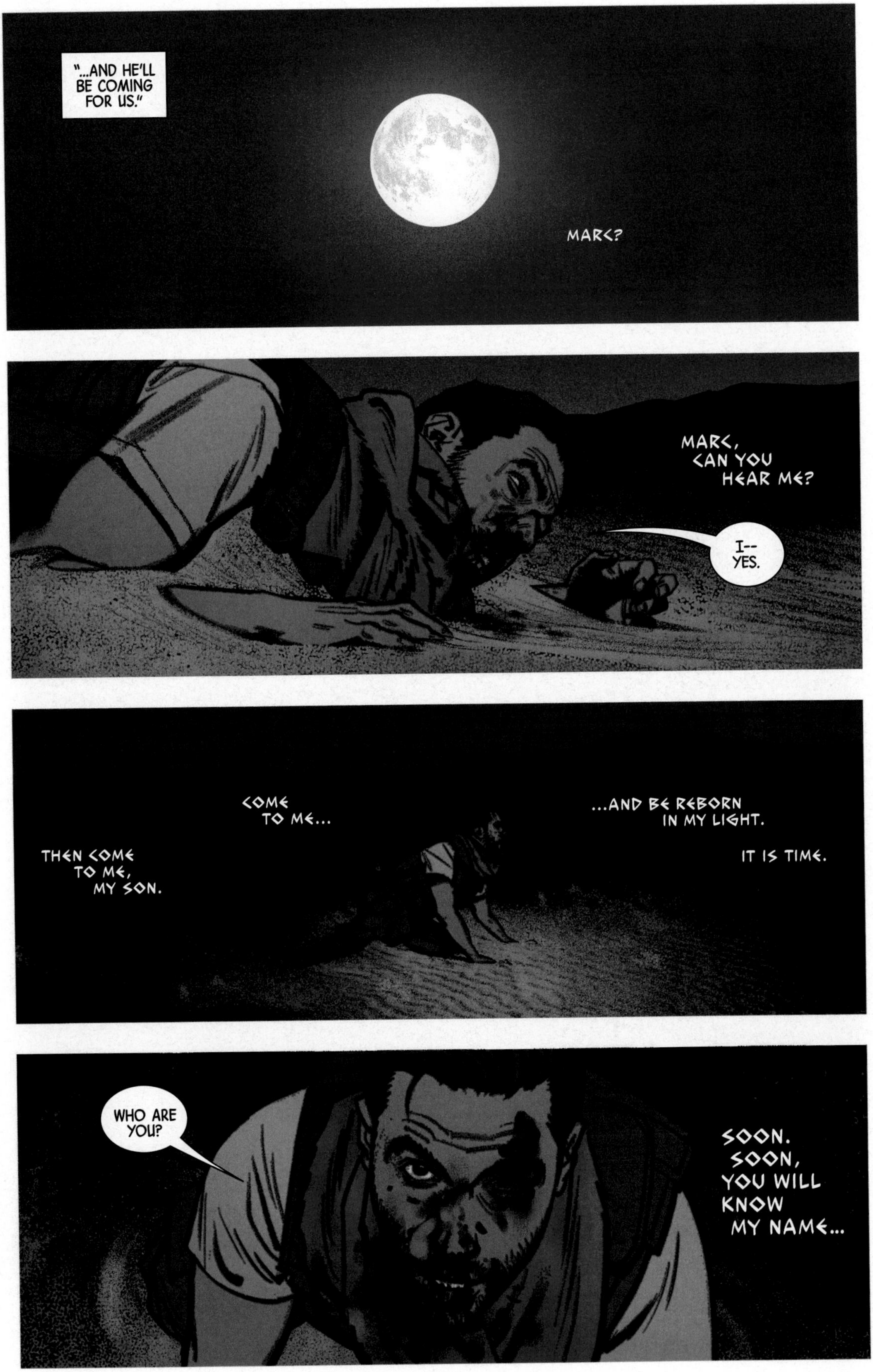

"...AND HE'LL BE COMING FOR US."
MARC?
MARC, CAN YOU HEAR ME?
I-- YES.
THEN COME TO ME, MY SON.
COME TO ME...
...AND BE REBORN IN MY LIGHT.
IT IS TIME.
WHO ARE YOU?
SOON. SOON, YOU WILL KNOW MY NAME...

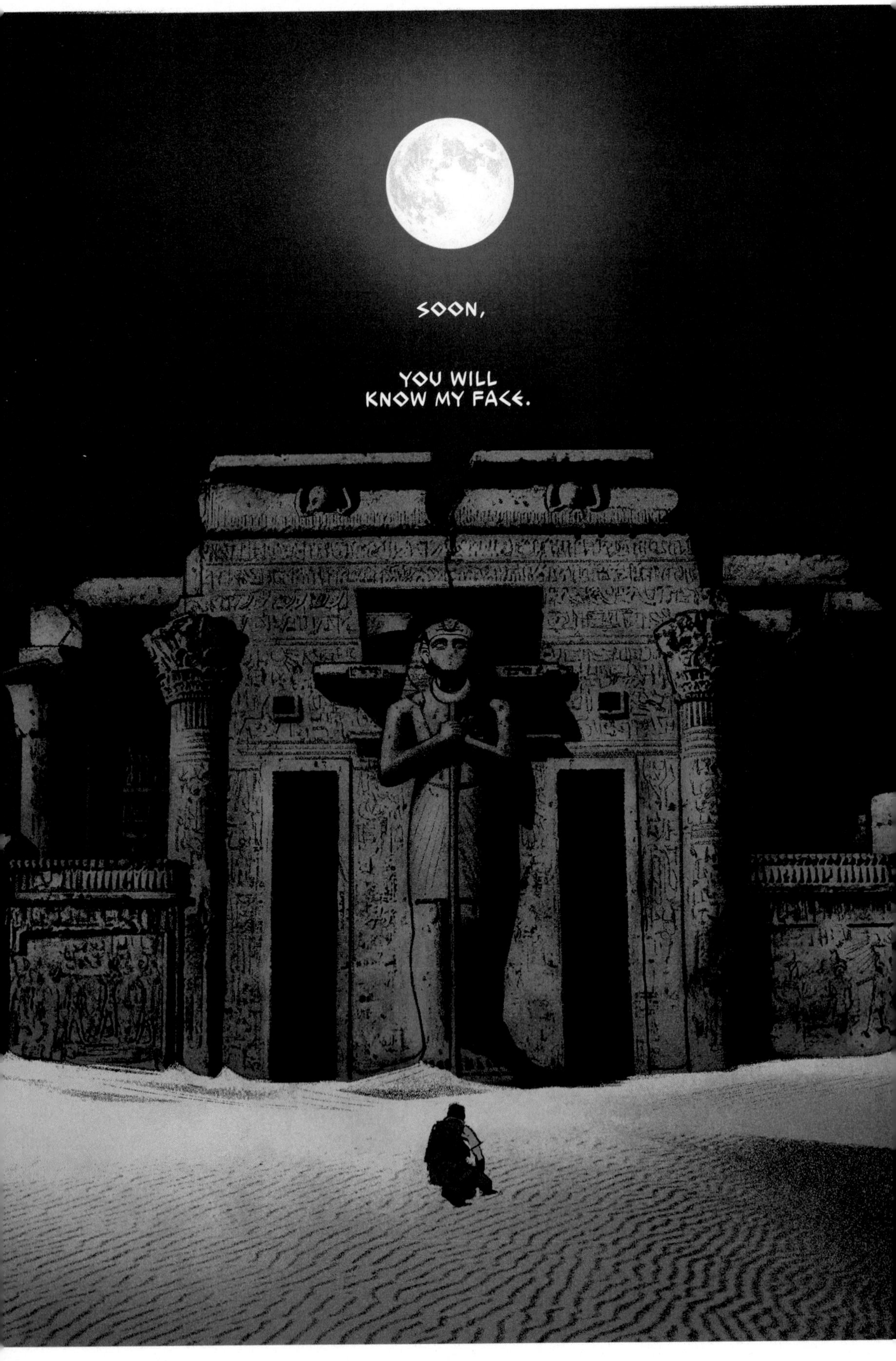
SOON,
YOU WILL KNOW MY FACE.

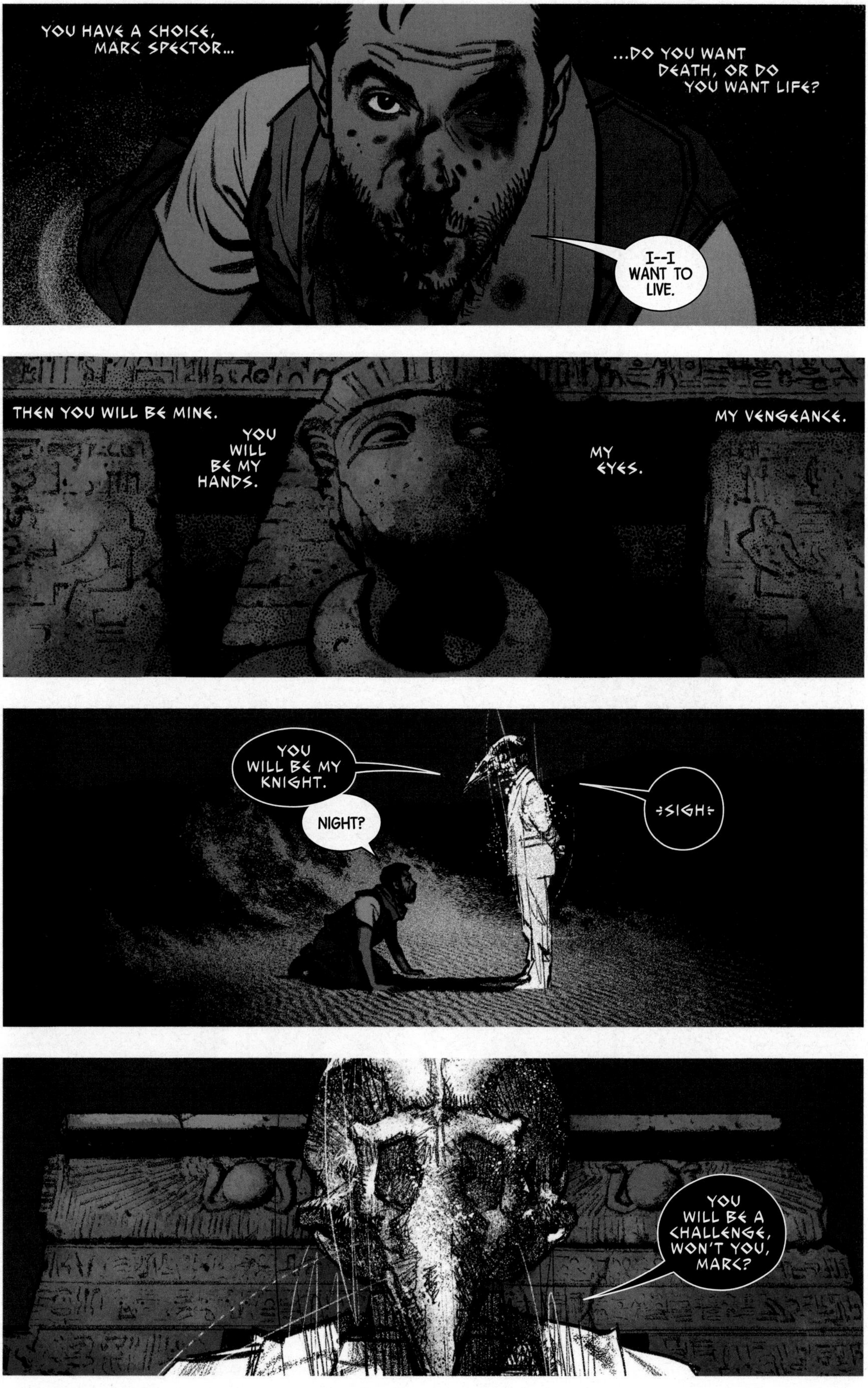
YOU HAVE A CHOICE, MARC SPECTOR...
...DO YOU WANT DEATH, OR DO YOU WANT LIFE?
I--I WANT TO LIVE.
THEN YOU WILL BE MINE.
YOU WILL BE MY HANDS.
MY EYES.
MY VENGEANCE.
YOU WILL BE MY KNIGHT.
NIGHT?
=SIGH=
YOU WILL BE A CHALLENGE, WON'T YOU, MARC?

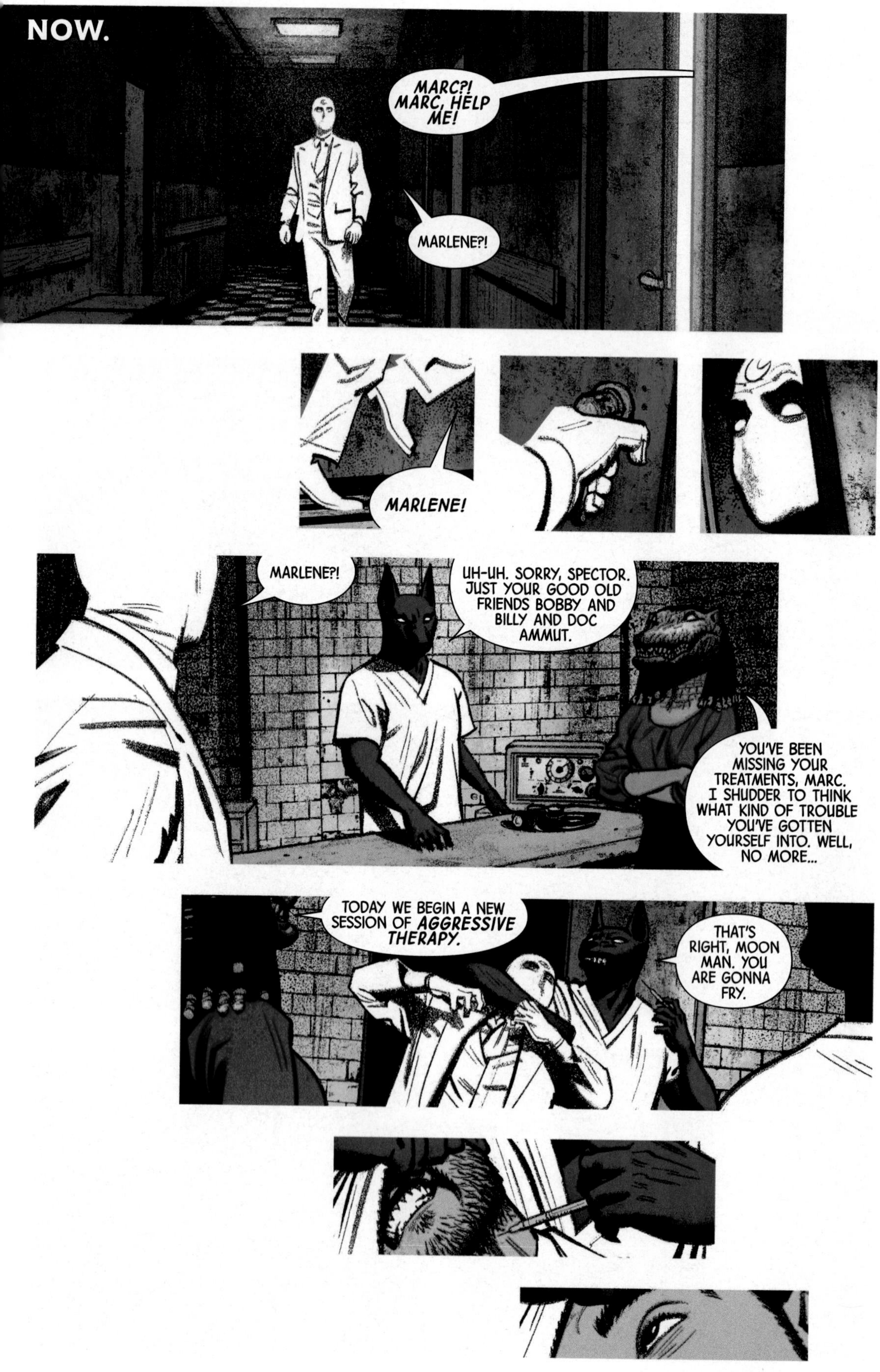
NOW.
MARC?! MARC, HELP ME!
MARLENE?!
MARLENE!
MARLENE?!
UH-UH. SORRY, SPECTOR. JUST YOUR GOOD OLD FRIENDS BOBBY AND BILLY AND DOC AMMUT.
YOU'VE BEEN MISSING YOUR TREATMENTS, MARC. I SHUDDER TO THINK WHAT KIND OF TROUBLE YOU'VE GOTTEN YOURSELF INTO. WELL, NO MORE...
TODAY WE BEGIN A NEW SESSION OF *AGGRESSIVE THERAPY.*
THAT'S RIGHT, MOON MAN. YOU ARE GONNA FRY.

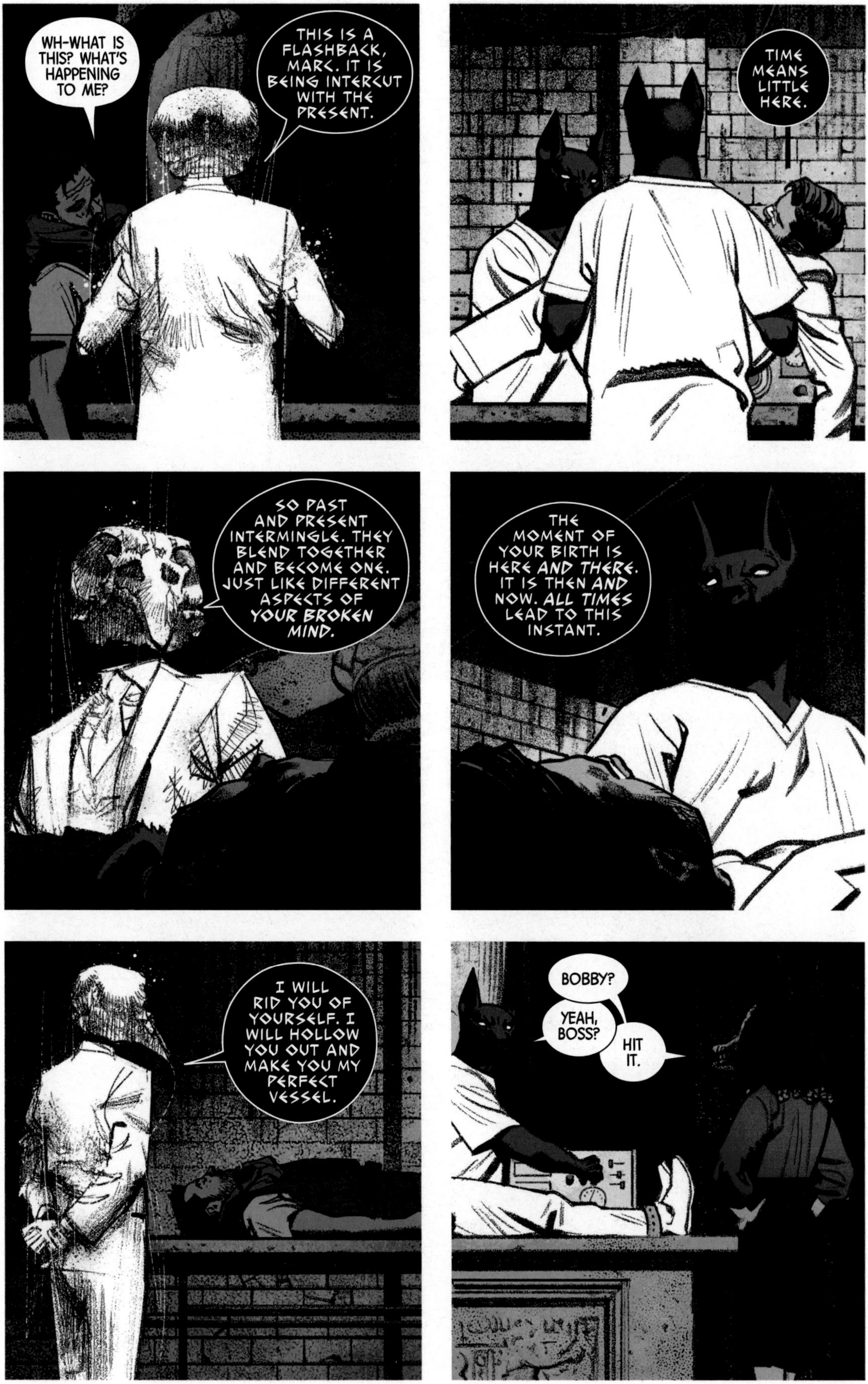
WH-WHAT IS THIS? WHAT'S HAPPENING TO ME?
THIS IS A FLASHBACK, MARC. IT IS BEING INTERCUT WITH THE PRESENT.
TIME MEANS LITTLE HERE.
SO PAST AND PRESENT INTERMINGLE. THEY BLEND TOGETHER AND BECOME ONE. JUST LIKE DIFFERENT ASPECTS OF YOUR BROKEN MIND.
THE MOMENT OF YOUR BIRTH IS HERE AND THERE. IT IS THEN AND NOW. ALL TIMES LEAD TO THIS INSTANT.
I WILL RID YOU OF YOURSELF. I WILL HOLLOW YOU OUT AND MAKE YOU MY PERFECT VESSEL.
BOBBY?
YEAH, BOSS?
HIT IT.

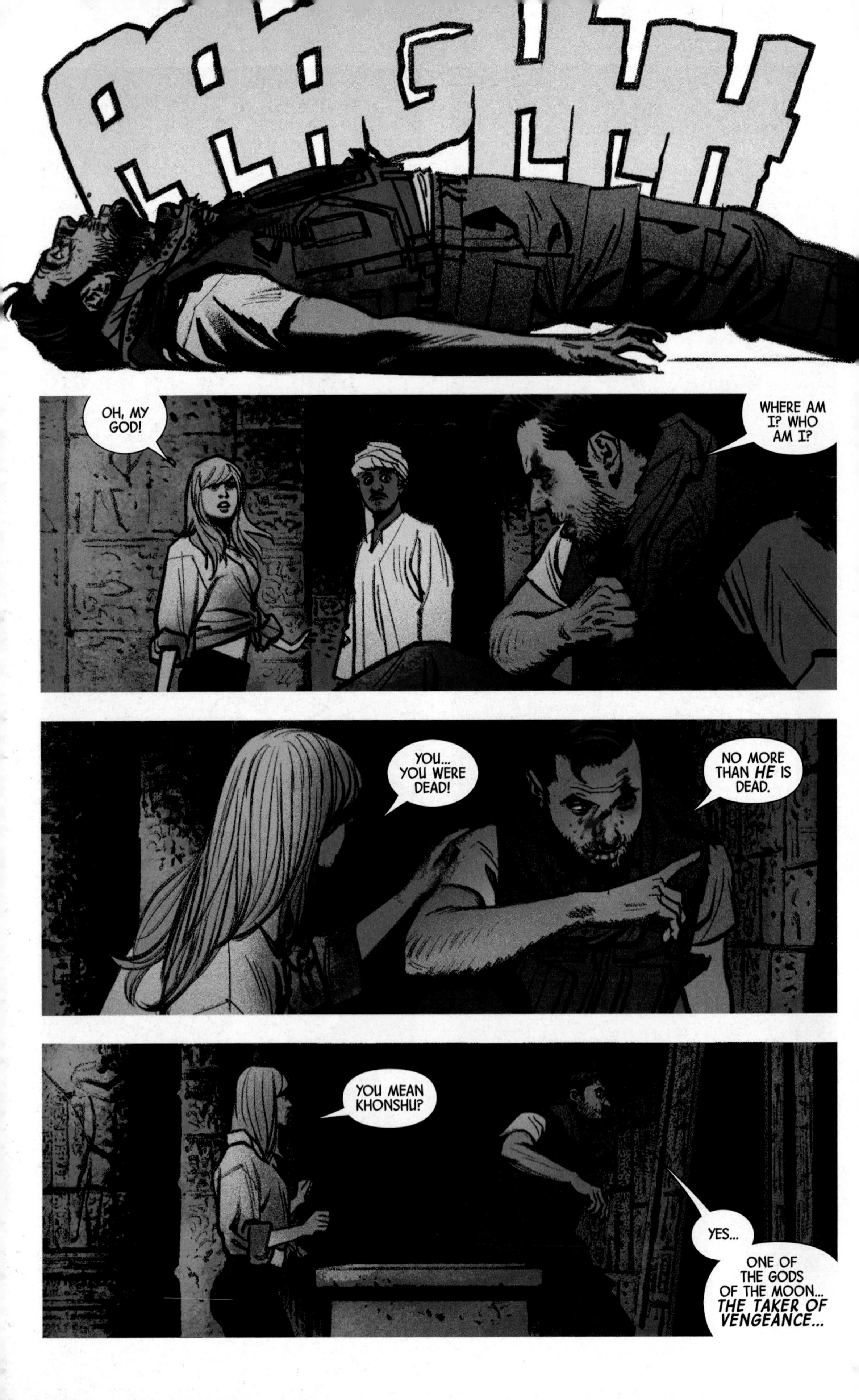

OH, MY GOD!
WHERE AM I? WHO AM I?
YOU... YOU WERE DEAD!
NO MORE THAN *HE* IS DEAD.
YOU MEAN KHONSHU?
YES...
ONE OF THE GODS OF THE MOON... ***THE TAKER OF VENGEANCE...***

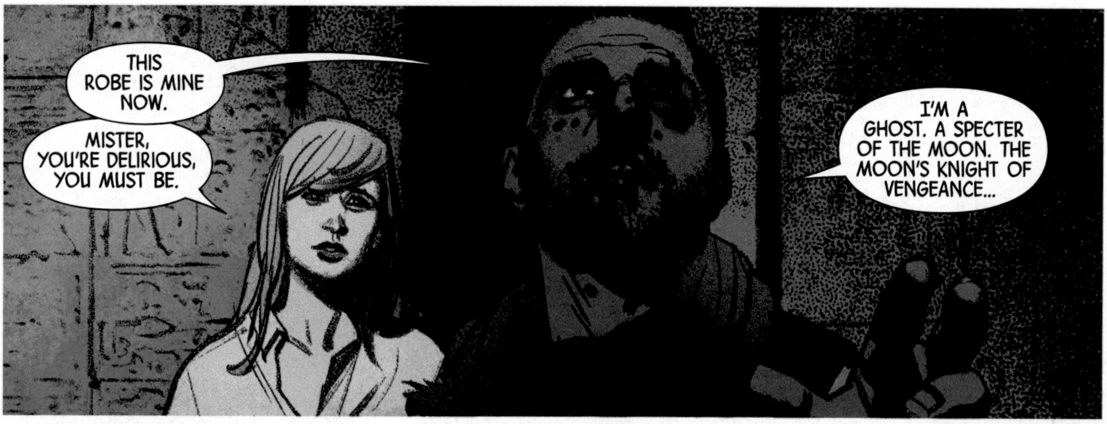
THIS ROBE IS MINE NOW.
MISTER, YOU'RE DELIRIOUS, YOU MUST BE.
I'M A GHOST. A SPECTER OF THE MOON. THE MOON'S KNIGHT OF VENGEANCE...

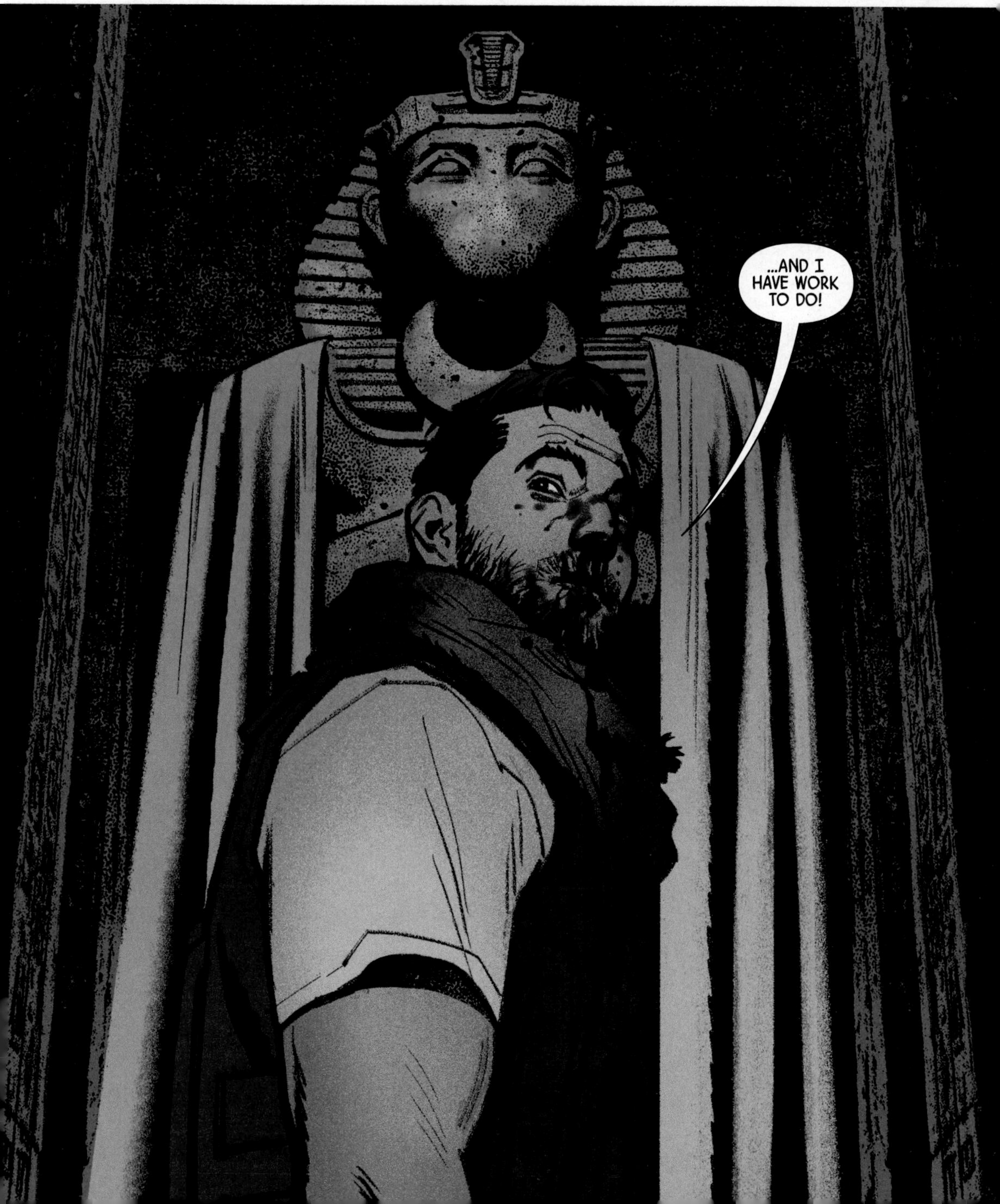
...AND I HAVE WORK TO DO!

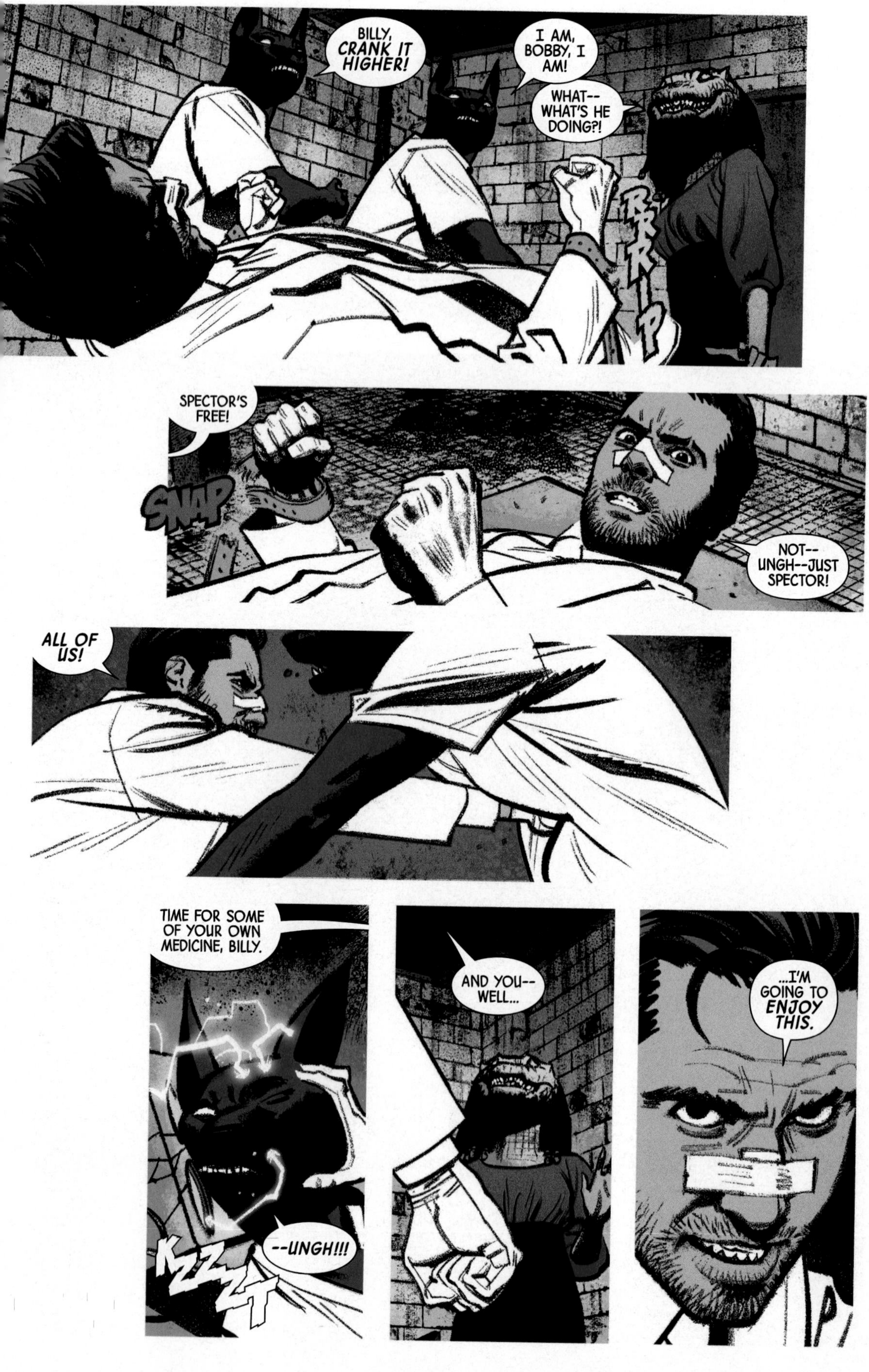
BILLY, CRANK IT HIGHER!
I AM, BOBBY, I AM!
WHAT-- WHAT'S HE DOING?!
RRRIP
SPECTOR'S FREE!
SNAP
NOT-- UNGH--JUST SPECTOR!
ALL OF US!
TIME FOR SOME OF YOUR OWN MEDICINE, BILLY.
KZZZT
--UNGH!!!
AND YOU-- WELL...
...I'M GOING TO ENJOY THIS.

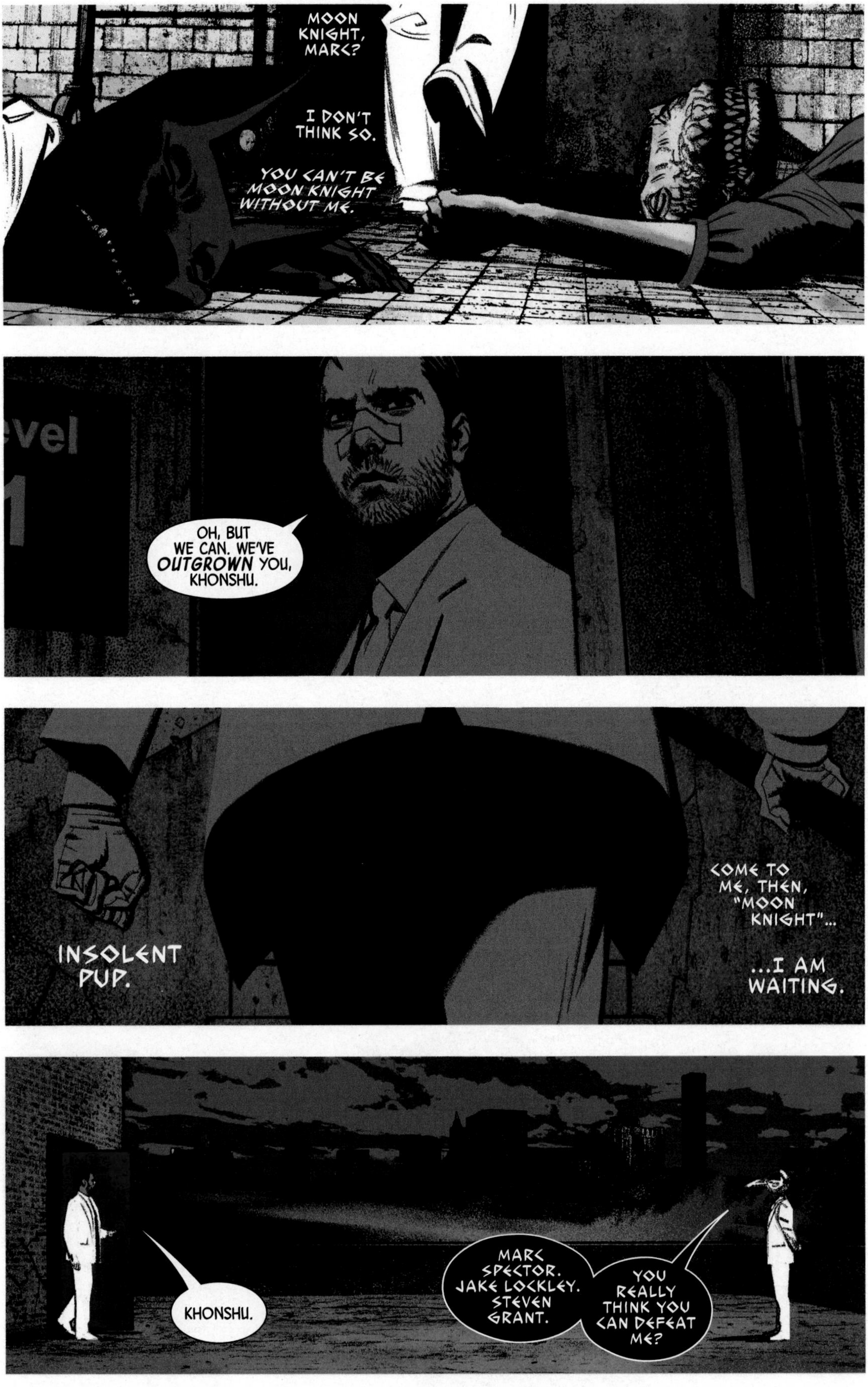
MOON KNIGHT, MARC?
I DON'T THINK SO.
YOU CAN'T BE MOON KNIGHT WITHOUT ME.
OH, BUT WE CAN. WE'VE OUTGROWN YOU, KHONSHU.
INSOLENT PUP.
COME TO ME, THEN, "MOON KNIGHT"...
...I AM WAITING.
KHONSHU.
MARC SPECTOR. JAKE LOCKLEY. STEVEN GRANT.
YOU REALLY THINK YOU CAN DEFEAT ME?

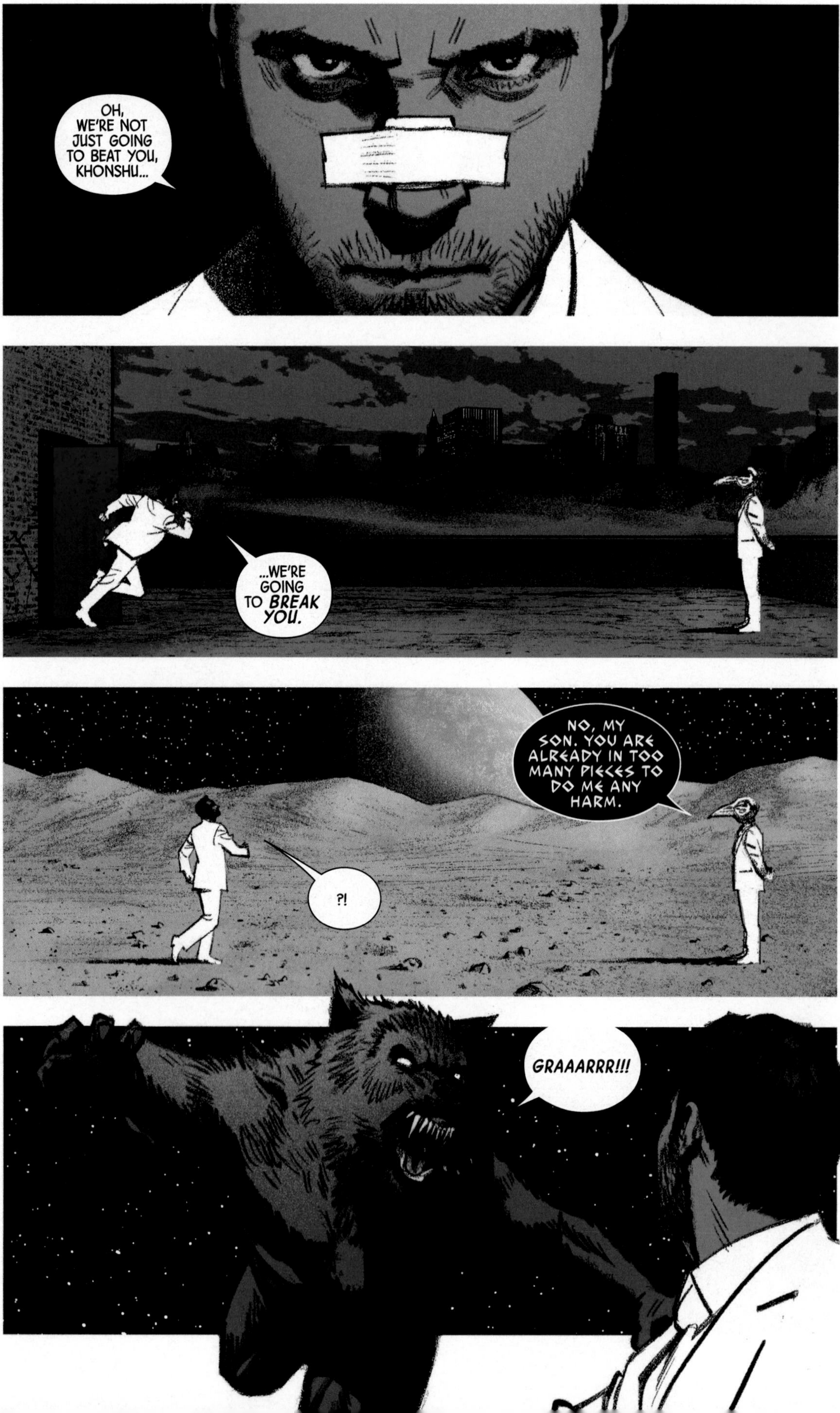
OH, WE'RE NOT JUST GOING TO BEAT YOU, KHONSHU...
...WE'RE GOING TO BREAK YOU.
NO, MY SON. YOU ARE ALREADY IN TOO MANY PIECES TO DO ME ANY HARM.
?!
GRAAARRR!!!

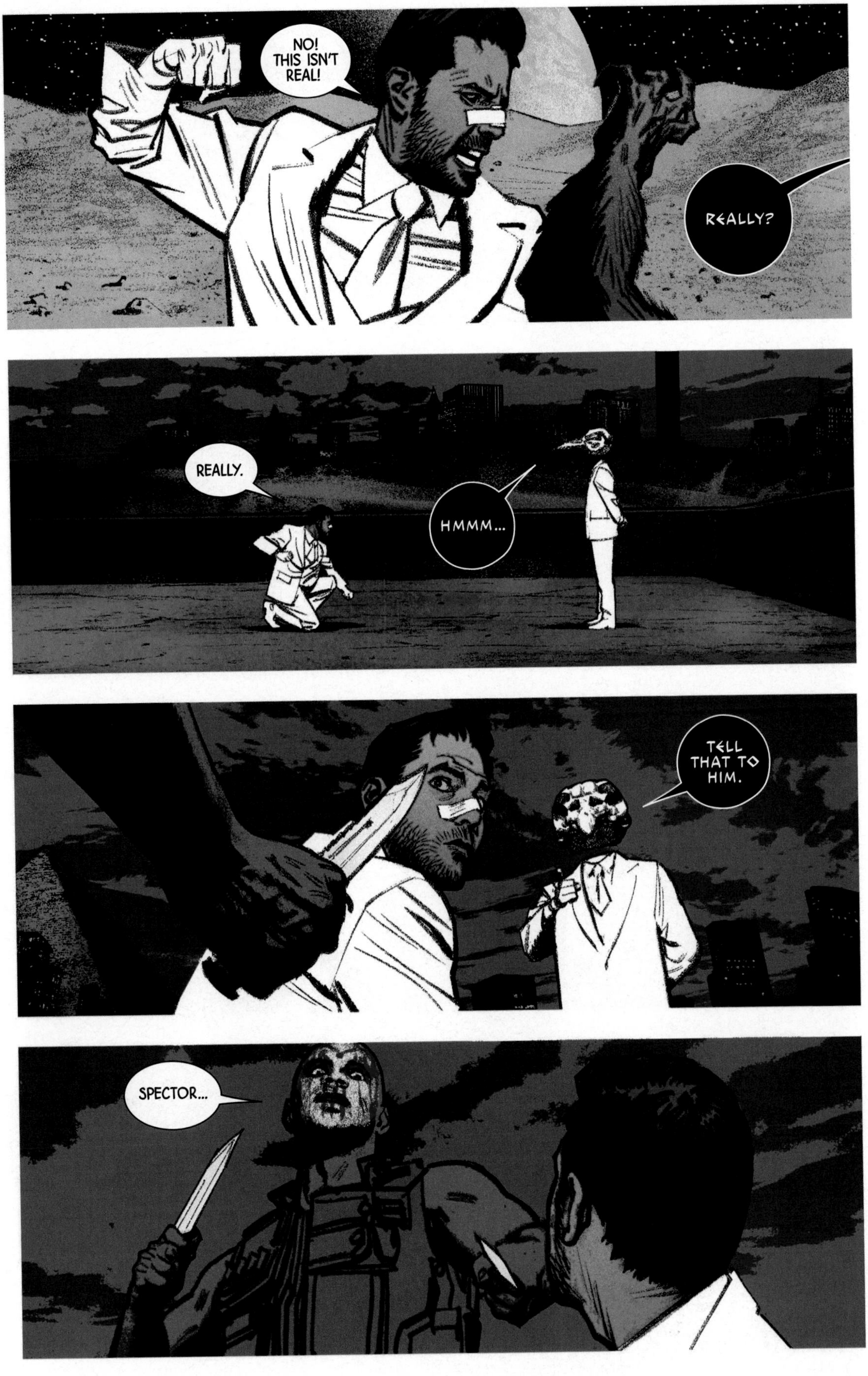
NO! THIS ISN'T REAL!
REALLY?
REALLY.
HMMM...
TELL THAT TO HIM.
SPECTOR...

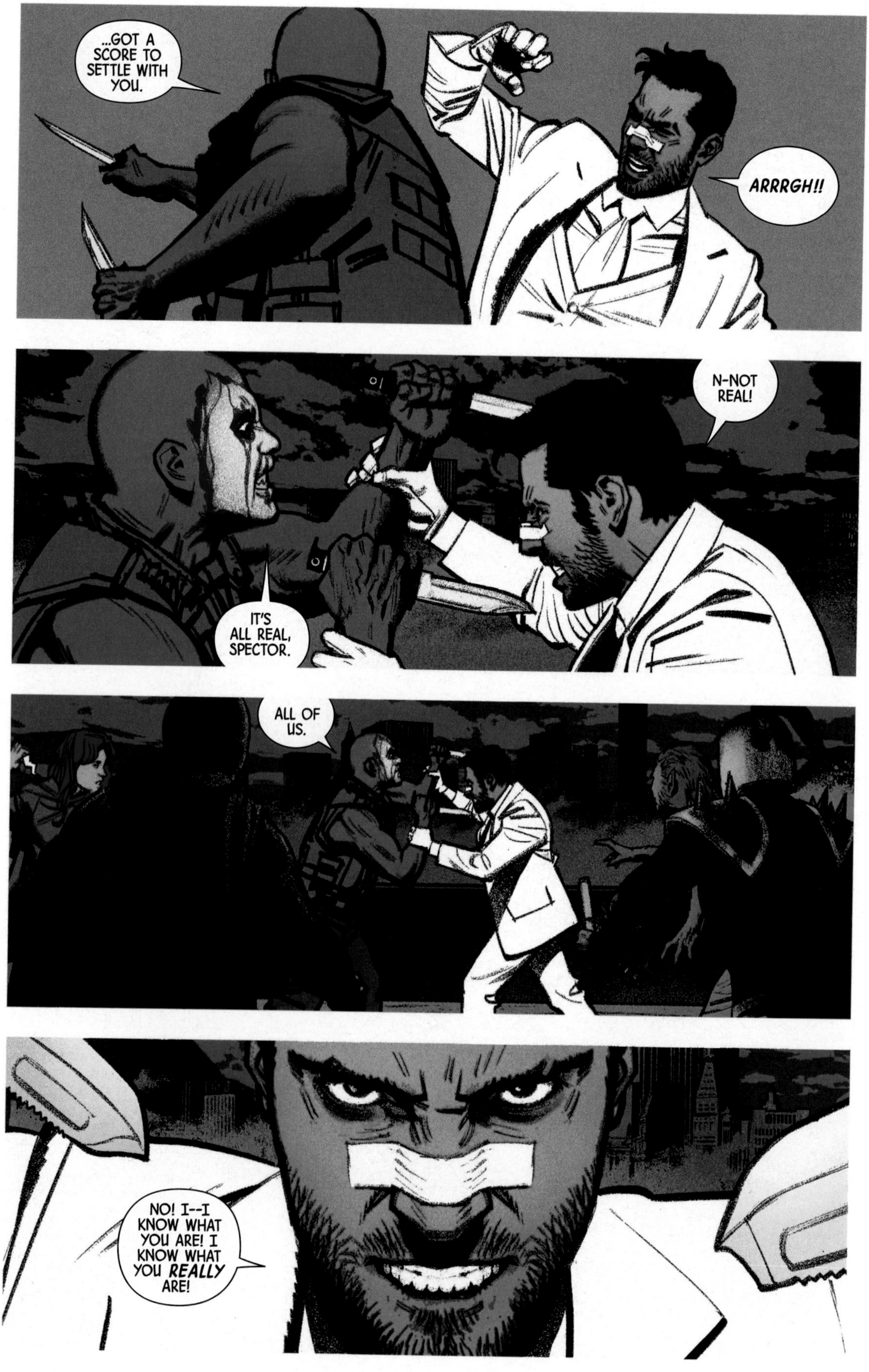
...GOT A SCORE TO SETTLE WITH YOU.
ARRRGH!!
N-NOT REAL!
IT'S ALL REAL, SPECTOR.
ALL OF US.
NO! I--I KNOW WHAT YOU ARE! I KNOW WHAT YOU *REALLY* ARE!

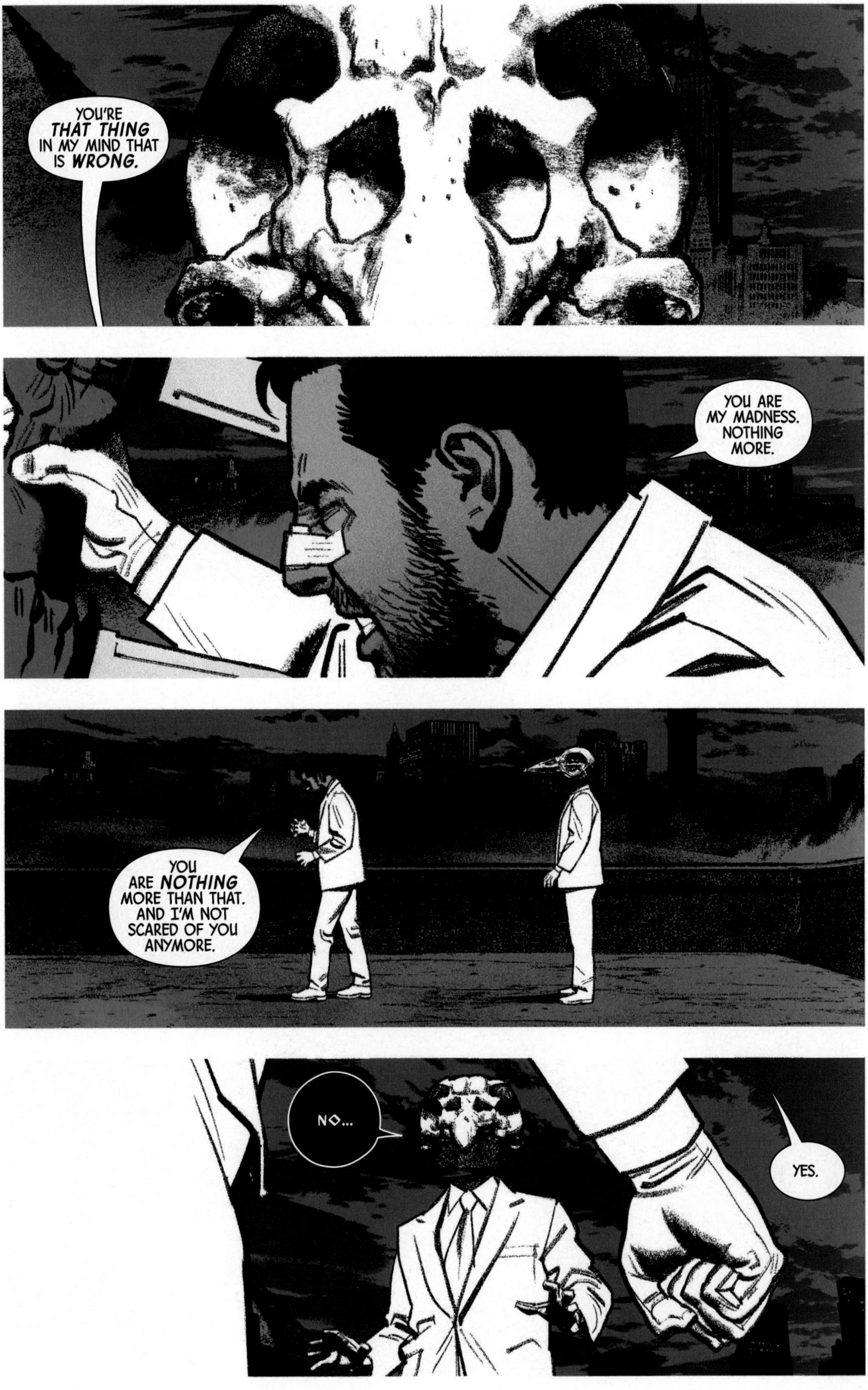
YOU'RE *THAT THING* IN MY MIND THAT IS *WRONG.*
YOU ARE MY MADNESS. NOTHING MORE.
YOU ARE *NOTHING* MORE THAN THAT. AND I'M NOT SCARED OF YOU ANYMORE.
NO...
YES.

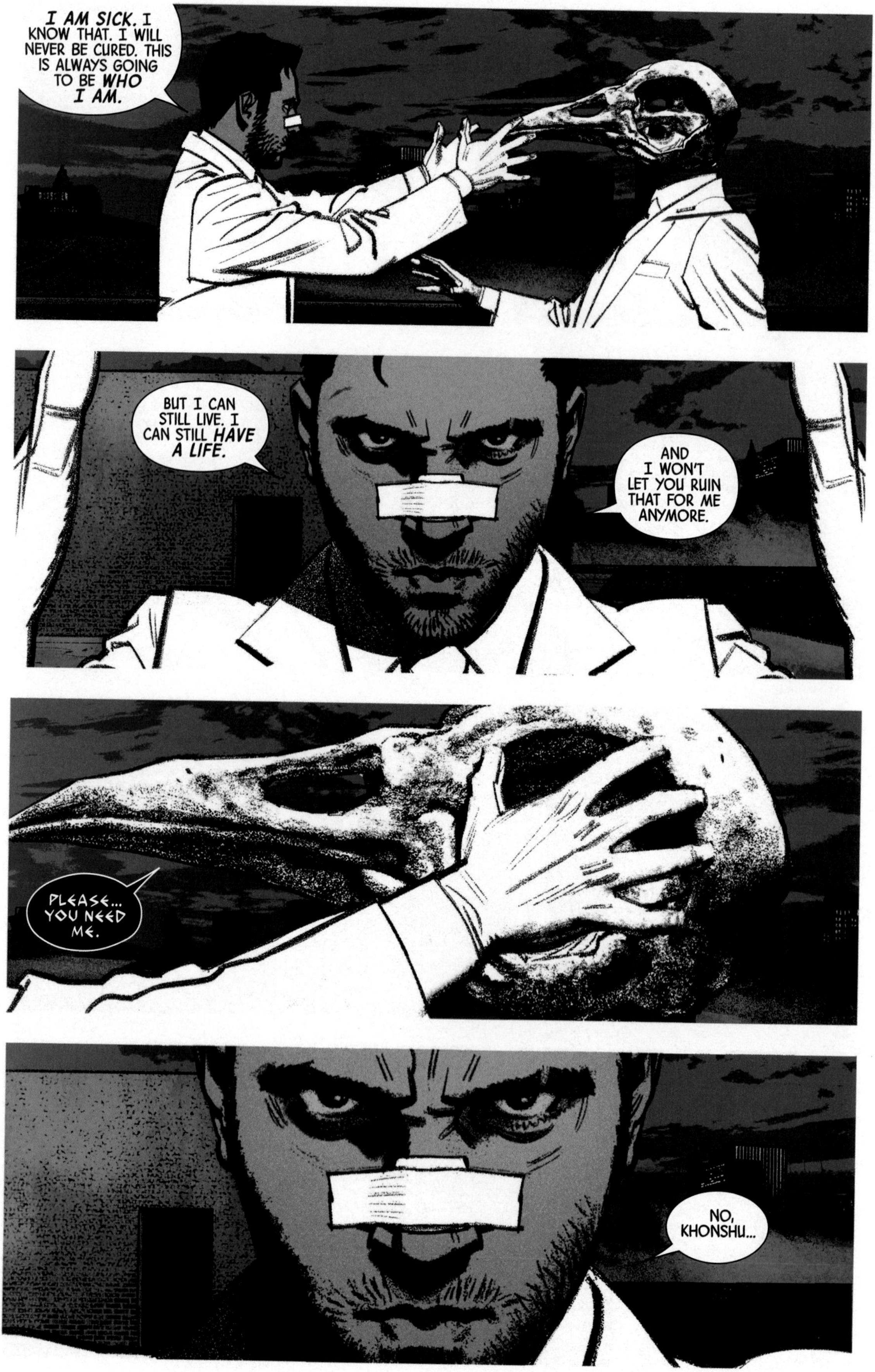
I AM SICK. I KNOW THAT. I WILL NEVER BE CURED. THIS IS ALWAYS GOING TO BE WHO I AM.
BUT I CAN STILL LIVE. I CAN STILL HAVE A LIFE.
AND I WON'T LET YOU RUIN THAT FOR ME ANYMORE.
PLEASE... YOU NEED ME.
NO, KHONSHU...

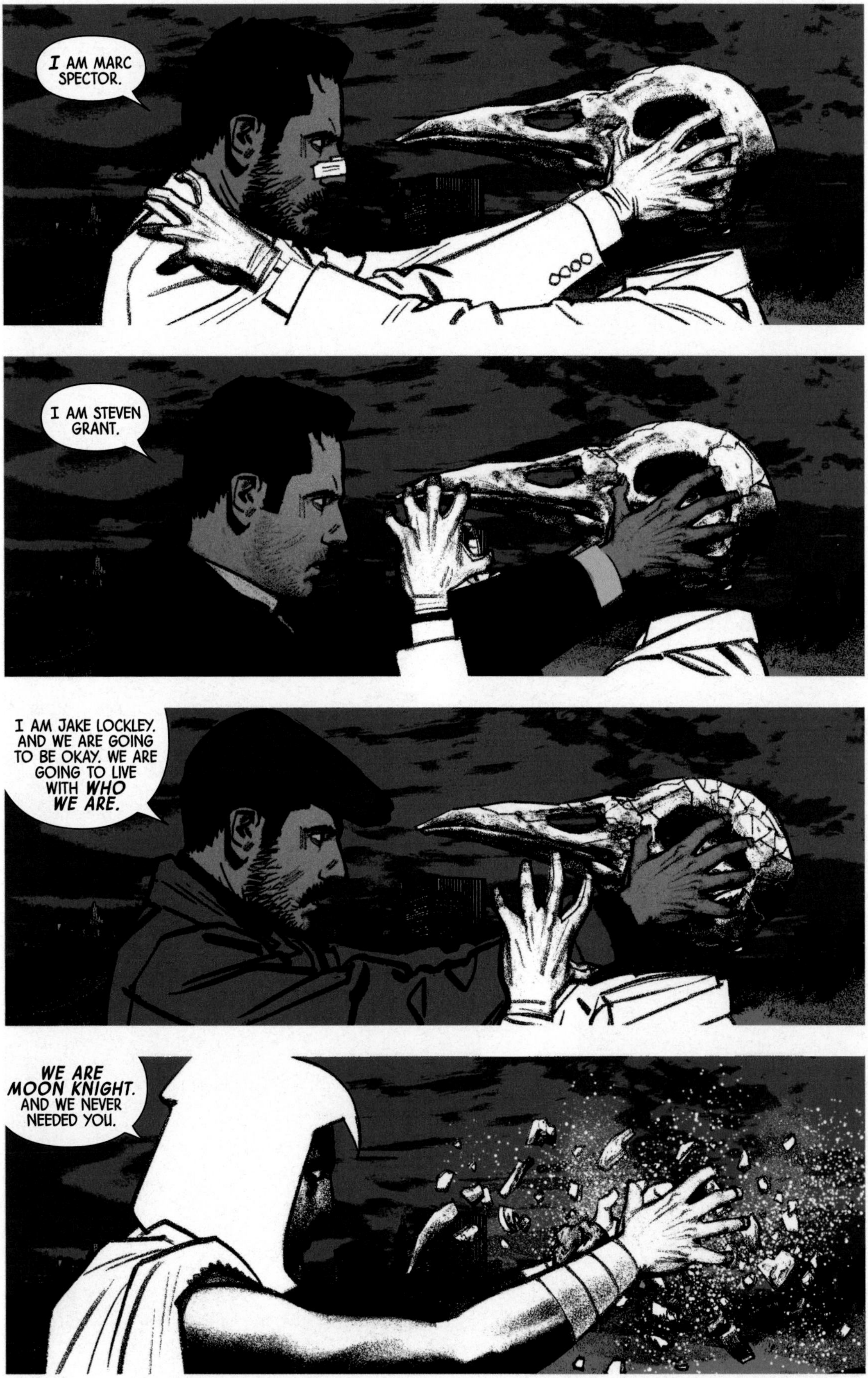
I AM MARC SPECTOR.
I AM STEVEN GRANT.
I AM JAKE LOCKLEY. AND WE ARE GOING TO BE OKAY. WE ARE GOING TO LIVE WITH WHO WE ARE.
WE ARE MOON KNIGHT. AND WE NEVER NEEDED YOU.

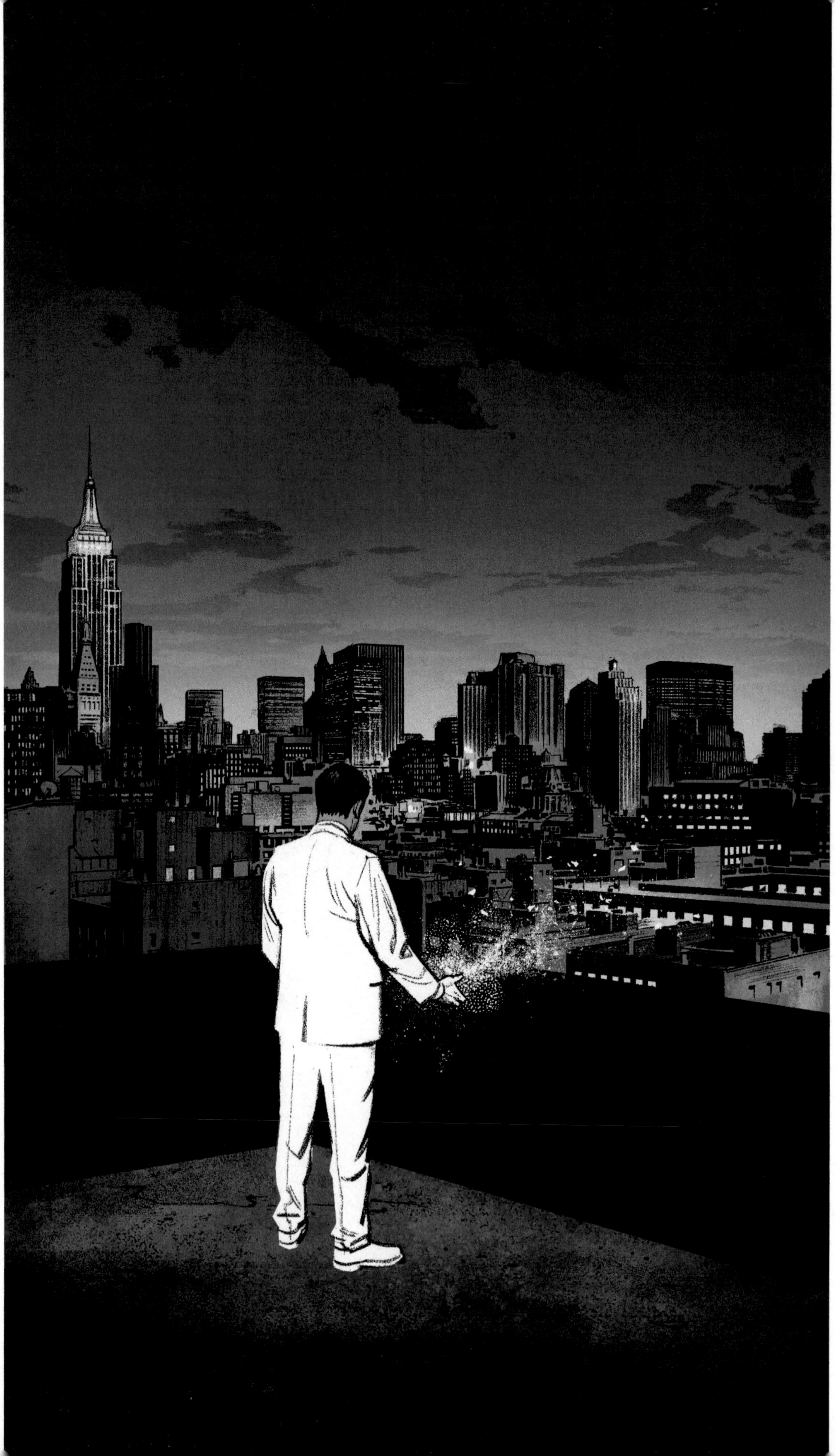

QUIET.

FOR THE FIRST TIME IN A LONG, *LONG* TIME, OUR MIND IS QUIET.

AND I...I JUST LET IT WASH OVER ME. I LET IT BE QUIET.

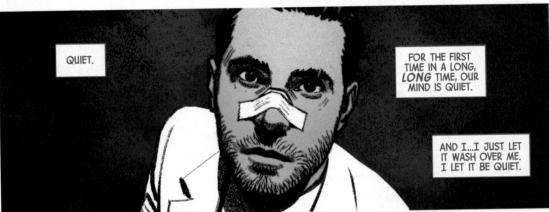

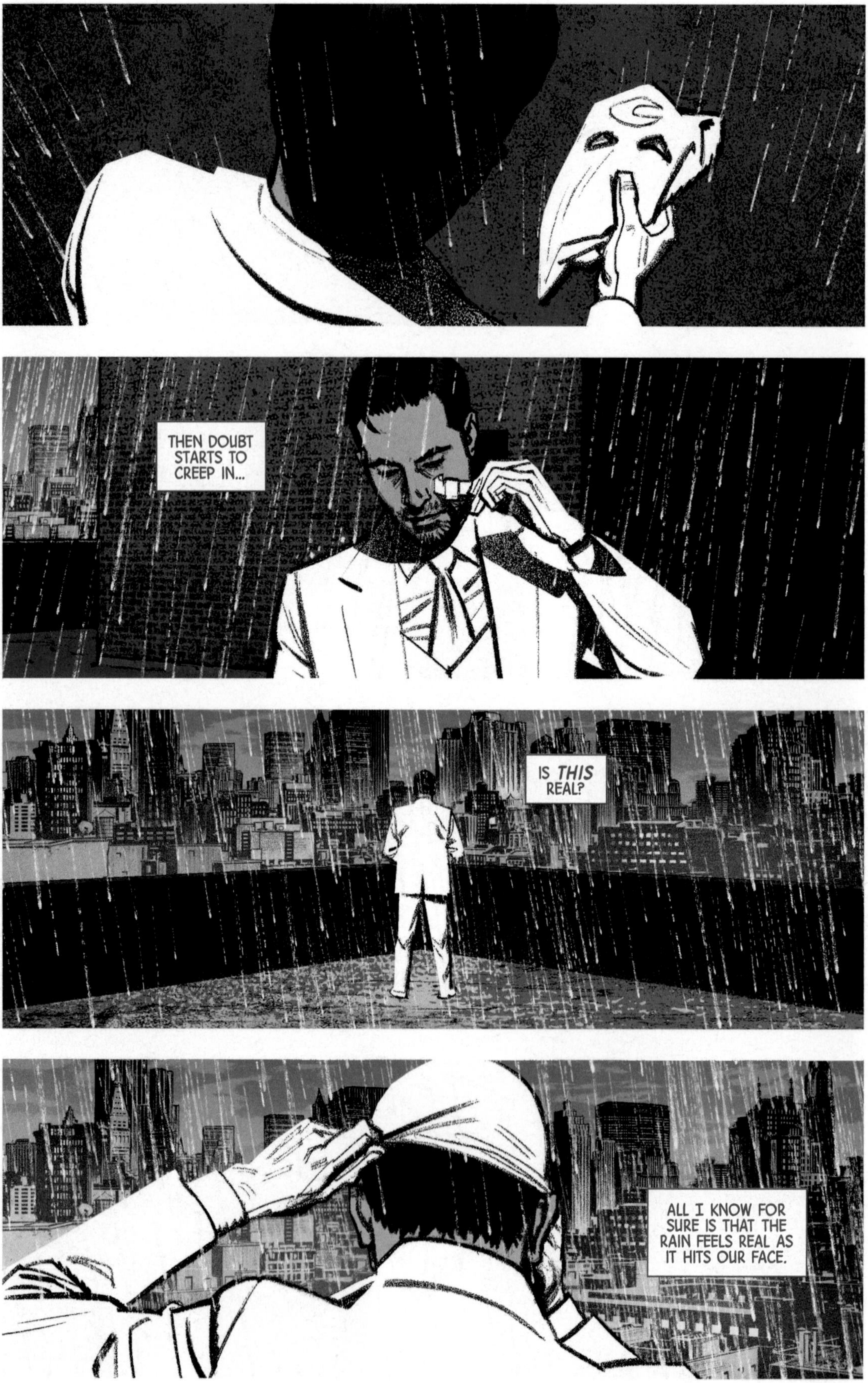
THEN DOUBT STARTS TO CREEP IN...
IS *THIS* REAL?
ALL I KNOW FOR SURE IS THAT THE RAIN FEELS REAL AS IT HITS OUR FACE.

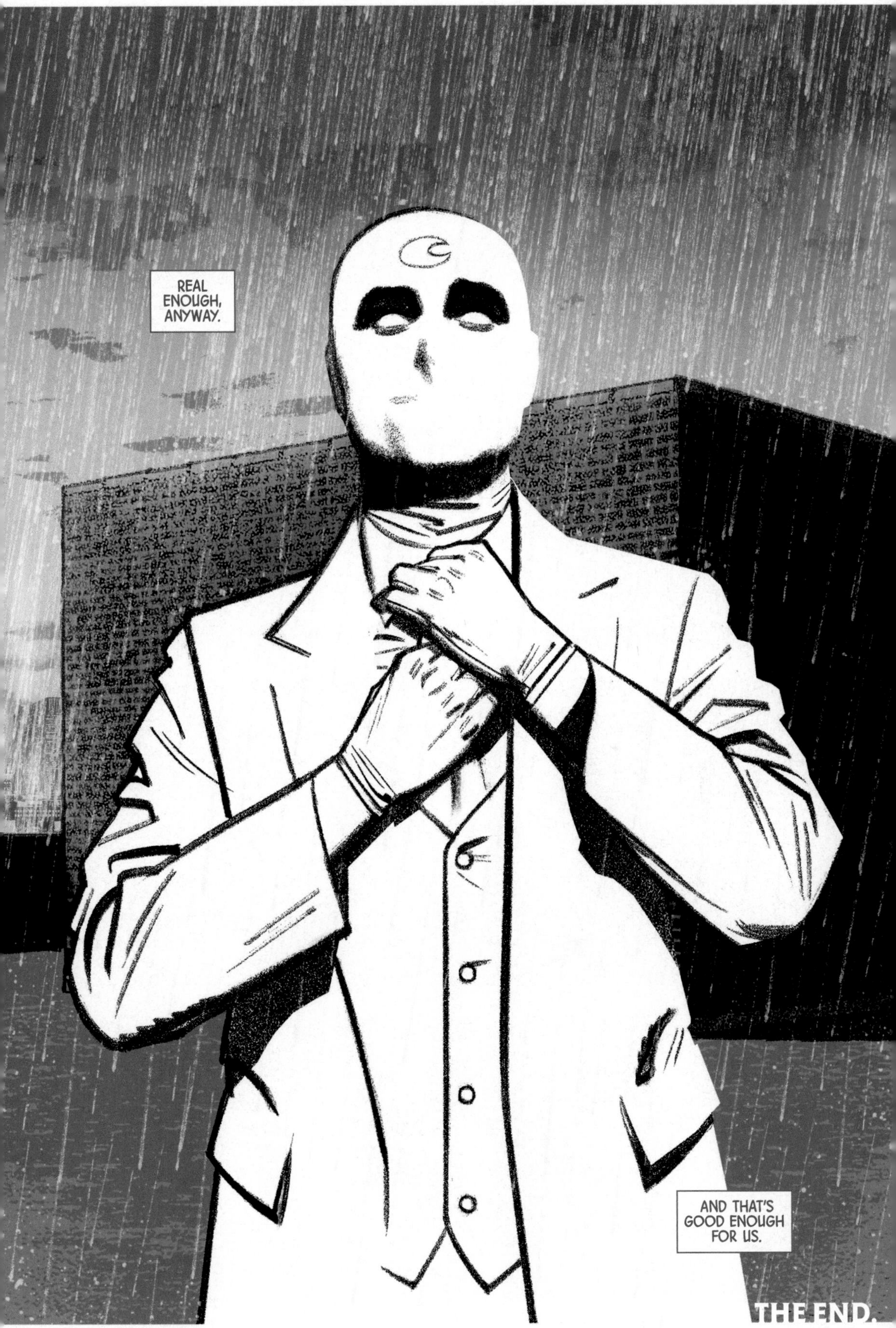
REAL ENOUGH, ANYWAY.
AND THAT'S GOOD ENOUGH FOR US.
THE END.

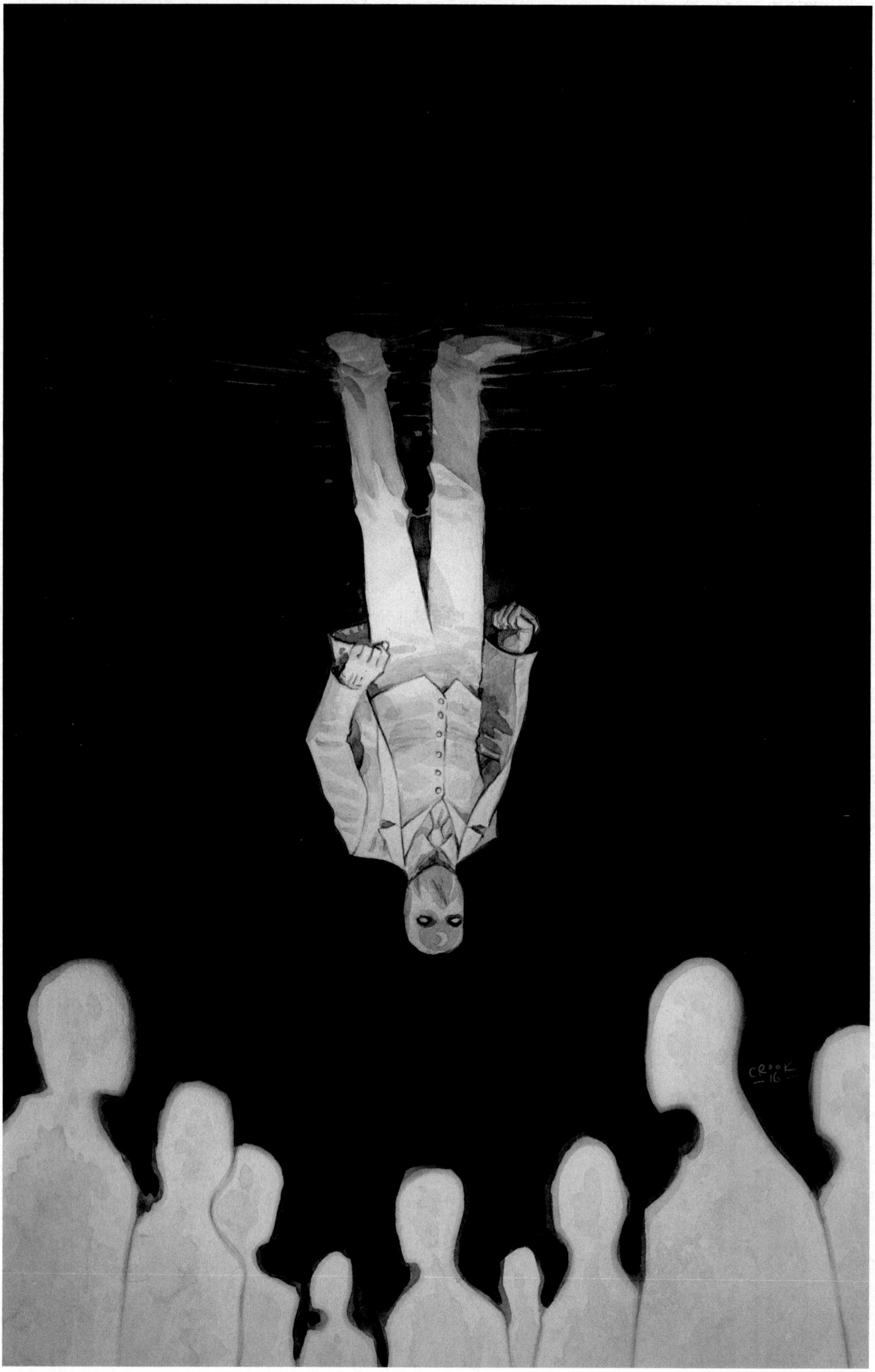
CROOK
16

#10 VARIANT BY TYLER CROOK

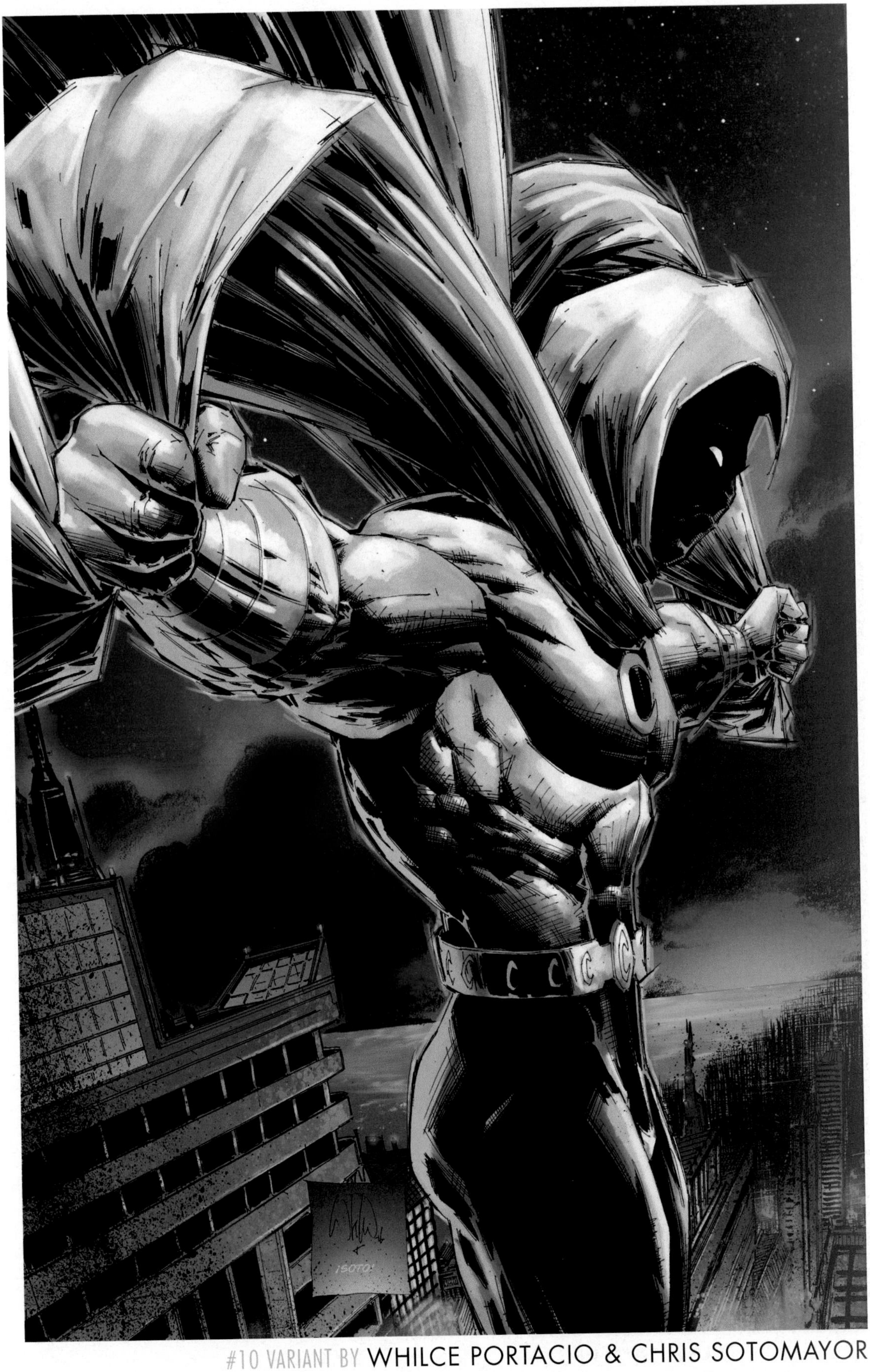
¡SOTO!
#10 VARIANT BY WHILCE PORTACIO & CHRIS SOTOMAYOR

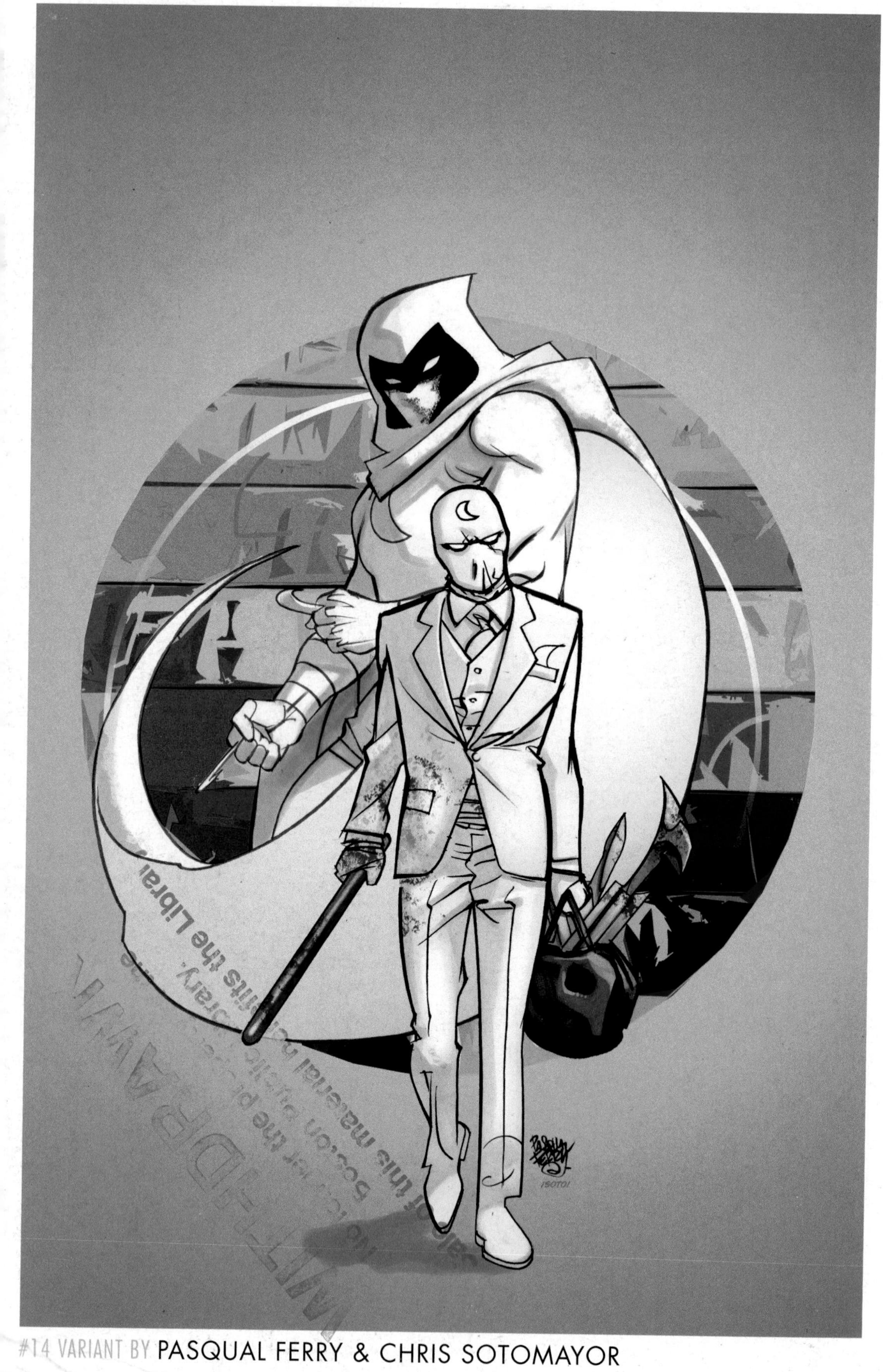

#14 VARIANT BY PASQUAL FERRY & CHRIS SOTOMAYOR